AFRICANS IN EUROPE

STUDIES OF
WORLD MIGRATIONS

Donna R. Gabaccia and
Leslie Page Moch, editors

A list of books in the series appears at the end of the book.

AFRICANS IN EUROPE

The Culture of Exile and Emigration from Equatorial Guinea to Spain

MICHAEL UGARTE

UNIVERSITY OF ILLINOIS PRESS
Urbana, Chicago, and Springfield

∞ This book is printed on acid-free paper.

The Library of Congress cataloged the cloth edition as follows:
Ugarte, Michael, 1949–
Africans in Europe : the culture of exile and emigration from Equatorial Guinea to Spain / Michael Ugarte.
p. cm. — (Studies of world migrations)
Includes bibliographical references and index.
ISBN 978-0-252-03503-6 (cloth : alk. paper)
1. Equatorial Guineans—Spain—History—20th century. 2. Equatorial Guineans—Spain—Social conditions—20th century. 3. Equatorial Guinea—Emigration and immigration—History—20th century. 4. Spain—Emigration and immigration—History—20th century. 5. Exiles—Equatorial Guinea—History—20th century. 6. Exiles—Spain—History—20th century. 7. Ndongo-Bidyogo, Donato, 1950–
I. Title.
DP53.E7U337 2010
305.896'718046—dc22 2009027104
Paperback ISBN 978-0-252-07923-8

Printed and bound in Great Britain by
Marston Book Services Limited, Oxfordshire

CONTENTS

ACKNOWLEDGMENTS

I would like to thank two friends and associates in the growing field of Afro-Spanish studies. First is Equatorial Guinean novelist, historian, journalist, poet, and educator Donato Ndongo-Bidyogo, whom I consider my mentor in virtually all things African: literature, art, religion, customs, history, and contemporary politics. Whenever I needed information—a date, a book, the details of a conflictive relationship—he was there to provide it for me. Also thanks is in order to Professor Marvin Lewis, formerly my colleague at the University of Missouri–Columbia, whose pioneering work on the language and history of Equatorial Guinea brought me (at first grudgingly) into this field. His book *An Introduction to the Literature of Equatorial Guinea: Between Colonialism and Dictatorship* is the first book-length monograph on this topic. Although this study appeared during the ending stages of my own, it has served me well as a confirmation that I have been on a felicitous path: the cultural figures he studies as well as the texts (with some exceptions) coincide with mine. I hope the reader will find Lewis's study an inroad into mine, from an introduction dealing with a body of cultural production from Equatorial Guinea, to an inspection of that body of work from a specific, albeit widely encompassing, angle: exile/emigration or what I'm calling *emixile*.

I would also like to thank the University of Missouri–Columbia Research Council for the time and funds absolutely crucial to the completion of this book. Also, I want to acknowledge the librarians at my university's Ellis Library Inter-Library Loan Department for all their help.

Thanks are also due to Professors Silvia Bermúdez and Leslie Page Moch for their careful readings. My friends, colleagues, and comrades in the growing movement among Hispanists to focus on Africa in the light (or lack thereof) of Spanish colonialism, Benita Sampedro and Susan Martin Marquez, have offered many, many insights that have shaped my understanding of Equatorial Guinean culture.

The same goes to all the contributors of the special issue of *Arizona Journal of Hispanic Cultural Studies* dedicated to Equatorial Guinea and edited by Mbaré Ngom and yours truly: Montserrat Alás-Brun, Igor Cusack, Dosinda García-Alvite, John Lipski, Kathleen McNerney, Clerence Mengue, Gabriel Quirós Alpera, Elisa Rizo, and Benita Sampedro, and to the colleagues who participated in the roundtable discussion: Juanamaría Cordones Cook, Gabriela Díaz Cortez, Rangira Bea Gallimore, Chris Okonkwo, Margaret Olsen, Cristina Rodríguez Cabral, and Flore Zephir. I am indebted as well to the editors of the University of Illinois Press, Rebecca McNulty, Angela Burton, and especially freelance copy editor Mary Lou Kowaleski, for their help in the polishing of the manuscript. Thanks as well to Derek Gottlieb for the index.

Also, for their encouragement I want to thank other Missouri colleagues, Professors Joseph Otabela Mewolo, Monica Marcos-Llinas, and Deborah Cohen.

To Kathleen McNerney, a special thank you a thousand times and more.

Thank you also to *Journal of Spanish Cultural Studies, Arizona Journal of Hispanic Cultural Studies,* and *Studies in Twentieth and Twenty-first Century Literature* for allowing me to reprint portions of articles I published in these journals.

All translations of Spanish are mine unless indicated otherwise.

INTRODUCTION

> Remember that you and I made this journey, that we went together to a place where there was nowhere left to go.
> —Jhumpa Lahiri, *The Namesake*

As a first-generation North American whose parents were born and raised in Spain, I have been interested in the cultural exchanges arising as a result of repatriation, exile, or emigration. Lives that move through time according to departures and arrivals make for transformations of all kinds—psychological, political, social, linguistic. They determine how an individual will read the world and his or her place in it. In many ways, the immigrant experience is the North American experience par excellence, and in my case, it serves as a constant, albeit changing, factor in virtually all my daily activity.

In 1954 when I was five, I went to Spain for the first time, the first meeting of the family in eight years. I remember vividly the encounter: tears, shrieks, hugs, kisses, many of them over and over again, all in that perfect symmetry between jubilation and sadness. There was much touching. My brother and I were groped and squeezed in ways we never would have imagined by people who to us were perfect strangers. I remember one kiss more than any of the others: my cousin Marina kissed me good-night on the forehead and put me to bed. I had never experienced anything like that, for it was the kiss of someone other than my mother, a face, a voice, a manner of speaking and comportment, a tenderness that were all new to me. As I look back on that kiss, I don't think there was any Freudian transference: Marina was not my mother. She was a few years older than I, the third child of my mother's sister who was also named Marina, after my maternal grandmother. Everywhere I looked I saw Marinas, but this Marina was at that moment closer, more tangible, palpable.

In 1985 at New York's Kennedy Airport, as I sat with my own family waiting to board a plane that would eventually take us (back) to Spain, I noticed another family, far different from my own. They were also waiting but for another plane whose destination I do not recall. I did not know their nationality; they were South Asian, I believe, perhaps Indian or Pakistani, Sri Lankan, or Bengali. As to many non–east Asian people, this family's circumstances were out of grasp to me, let alone that they spoke in a language unintelligible to me. What I was able to understand, however, was that they were not happy. It was not that they were unhappy, for I could certainly have imagined gaiety and laughter in the father, mother, and relatives in another situation. They sat there, very somber, along with the children, what looked like grandparents, and a few members of the father and mother's generation—aunts? or uncles? or cousins? or brothers? or sisters? The family permutations were no doubt endless. Someone was leaving, I thought. And sure enough, when they got up to move to another waiting area after a flight was announced, I saw that a little girl (perhaps eight years old) was sobbing. It was the sadness of a youngster about to lose something precious. She was clinging to her mother as she sobbed. The rest of the family paid the child little attention; they must have considered it a natural reaction, nothing to fret about. It was expected, and there was nothing that could have been done about it. As they walked off, I sensed it was the mother who was leaving—there was relatively little hand luggage. The mother had an air about her, a stoical seriousness of purpose that set her apart from the other members of the family as she kept her arm around her sniveling daughter and walked down the hall in what looked to me like a procession. Was she going? Was it a permanent departure? Or was it simply the beginning of a short trip home, a home from which she would depart once again? Immigration and emigration tend to make for a long string of departures.

On a June morning in 2006 on the number 21 bus I was on, from El Campello to Alicante, Spain, I saw a black man standing alongside his large plastic bag, probably filled with items he would sell without a merchant's permit on the streets of Alicante, perhaps on the Esplanada or the promenade that runs parallel to the Postiguet Beach, along with other black men who looked very much like this man on the bus: a faded T-shirt, a cap, blue jeans. His expression was blank as were those of the other passengers, who by that year had become accustomed to sharing public transportation with men such as this one. He was the only black person on the bus. Yet, he was by no means the only person of color to have made that trip from who knows where to downtown Alicante. To everyone on the bus, including me, he was the incarnation of a new Spain, that is, a Spain that began to change in a significant way with the first massive wave of immigration into that country around the mid-1980s. Yet, as I tried not to stare, I thought of what his day's activity would consist of. No doubt—at least no doubt for me since it was difficult to look at him as anything other than the symbol of a sociological phenomenon—he would join his companions at the Postiguet Beach, spread out his blanket, organize his items for sale (pirated CDs, sun glasses, T-shirts, ivory or false ivory, figurines, scarves, dresses, chewing gum and other packaged sweets), and stand behind his articles for sale ready to enter into a haggling contest with anyone showing even a mild interest. But I also wondered where he came from. Senegal? Cameroon? Nigeria? Ivory Coast? Mali? How did he get here? Was he one of the thousands of Africans who had crossed the hundred-kilometer (about sixty miles) body of water between Western Sahara and the Canary Islands, a waterway that separates Africa from Europe? In other words, did his photograph appear on the front-page or middle pages of *El País,* shivering, half dead, with that expression typical of all the "illegally" arrived Africans, as if to ask the viewers of the photograph, "OK, now what are you going to do with me?" But this man, I thought, has a history, a family, a life before the departure. What was that life?

I recount these situations because they manifest the multifarious intentions of this book, which have as much to do with the revelation and exploration of issues and cultural artifacts that have not been studied enough—the intention of virtually all academic studies—as with an attempt to bridge that daunting gap between the personal and the intellectual. Not only am I the son of immigrants/emigrants/exiles, but I also began to think about racial, class, and gender injustice at a relatively early age—although awareness of gender inequities came a bit later. As such, the relations between Africa and Europe, Equatorial Guinea and Spain, the colonized and the colonizers, blacks and whites, the marginal and the privileged are all of intense interest to me at a level that transcends the purely intellectual and/or professional. And when all of these issues are inspected through both the microscopic and telescopic lenses of migrations, they become even more complex, compelling, and urgent, particularly today in the age of disappearing national borders. Thus, I hope the reader will not only discover new texts, ideas, and artifacts in these pages but also perspectives on those phenomena that challenge his or her way of thinking.

The first two chapters of the current volume provide a foundation in that the first, "Emixile," covers the theoretical underpinnings for understanding emigration and immigration in the age of postcolonialism through the perspective of exile. Exile and emigration are interwoven, not identical. The writings of philosopher Emmanuel Levinas especially influenced the concern here with the ethical dimensions of the phenomena of exile and emigration. Chapter 2, "Out of Equatorial Guinea," covers the specifics of that nation's history. Due to the lack of familiarity with Equatorial Guinea on the part of the critical establishment, it is important to place the issues of exile and emigration from that country in a historical context and is done so here using the phenomenon of slavery, an exile experience in and of itself, as the unifying thread.

Chapter 3, "The First Wave," treats exile and emigration in the colonial period and immediately after. The beginnings of literature from Equatorial Guinea, as critics point out, have much to do with the Spanish colonial presence. As a result, Guineans have been in constant contact with that world. Argued here is that in the colonial literature of Equatorial Guinea, despite an apparent acceptance of the colonial power structure embodied by the Spanish, there is marked ambivalence about it, especially as it relates to black subjectivities. Thus, the chapter explores the cultural production of those who left the native land (not always definitively) to study and live in Spain. These cases show a constant process of negotiation between two worlds, a cultural hybrid. While some of these writers are favorably disposed to Spanish colonial culture, there is a pervasive ambivalence, a double consciousness, as W. E. B. Du Bois and others have called it, that comes to the fore. One of the first Guinean novelists, Daniel Jones Mathama, in his autobiographical *Una lanza por el boabí* (A spear for the chief) is a revealing example of this ambivalence and a major work that has not been given much attention other than cursory descriptions.

Chapter 4, "Donato Ndongo: Model of Emixile," discusses Ndongo's case as an incarnation of virtually all the issues arising from previous chapters' discussions. Born in the colonial period, he left Spanish Guinea to study in Spain in 1965, three years prior to his native country's independence. He lived the life of a young African immigrant in Spain (a country in which very few blacks resided at that time), with a sense of loss of his home as well as anxiety arising from the deplorable postcolonial political conditions in the form of a brutal dictatorship. His entire career as a creative writer, historian, and journalist has consisted of an exploration of that very exilic-migratory nostalgia and anxiety. *Tinieblas de tu memoria negra* (*Shadows of Your Black Memory*) and *Los poderes de la tempestad* (Powers of the tempest) are his most important creative works, as they pinpoint both an exilic and a migratory African Spanish experience. (I have translated *Tinieblas de tu memoria negra* into English, published in 2007).

Ndongo's novel *El metro* (The Subway) (2007), an exploration of the epic journey from Africa to Spain by a Cameroonian man, is the topic of chapter 5. The journey of Lambert Obama (no relation to the U.S. president) may be seen as that of the present-day African everyman. Burdened and embittered with life at home, he sets out for the north after a plethora of experiences in various African countries as he works to amass the funds needed for the trip. One of the chapters reads like a testimony of the perilous crossing of the body of water separating western coastal Africa from the Canary Islands of Spain. I read this novel as an epic narration of emixile.

Chapter 6, "Between Life and Death: The Macías Generation," deals with the culture that arose as a result of the regime of Francisco Macías, the first Guinean leader (dictator) of the country following independence. Thousands of Guineans were forced to leave or left of their own will. The chapter explores the writing of the members of this generation—Francisco Zamora, Joaquín Mbomío, and Justo Bolekia, among others—as expressions of political dissidence as well as introspections of their own otherness not only in Spain but also in relation to a political system they abhor. Dissidence and protest are related here to a search for a very evasive Afro-Spanish identity. Poetry becomes an important outlet for the expression of this identity ambivalence, especially in the texts of Zamora and Bolekia, whose enigmatic, if not hermetic, verses fuse the Spanish and African subjectivities.

Chapter 7, "Exiles Stay at Home," deals with "inner exile." The experience of exile and emigration is often compared to that of those who stay, as has been the case in the Spain of Francisco Franco. This chapter discusses the tribulations and dangers of writing against the dictatorial regime while living within that regime and a sense of estrangement from within. The most representative of this group is Juan Tomás Ávila Laurel, arguably the most prolific Equatorial Guinean writer. While Ávila Laurel's voice is that of a dissident, one hears as well a constant ambiguity about his homeland and its relation to Spain. Also discussed in this chapter are two younger writers who presently reside in Equatorial Guinea—José Siale and Maximiliano Nkogo. It is clear that Siale is motivated by the words of writers who left as he carries on an open dialogue with them in his texts. Nkogo's case witnesses a vividly narrated account of a typical day in squalid Malabo (the capital) in which two policemen devise various schemes of survival. In virtually all the writing of the inner exiles, emigration is both a theme and a possibility.

Chapter 8, "Gendering Emixile: The Mythic Return," is an attempt to understand exile from a feminine perspective. Women writers from Equatorial Guinea exist, but they are few. In an attempt to interrogate the issues surrounding emixile from the perspective of gender, I concentrate on the figure of return embodied in the trope of "Mother Africa." While I include male writers here, beginning with a discussion of Léopold Senghor's famous poem "Femme noir" ("Black Woman"), the bulk of this chapter consists of a reading of María Nsue Angüe's gripping novel *Ekomo,* which has been discussed by several critics. None, however, reads this novel from the point of view of a return to Africa. I believe this reading not only adds a new perspective to Nsue's work but enhances understanding of what exile and emigration mean to Africans, particularly women.

The conclusion, chapter 9, "Ending with a Beginning," summarizes the main arguments of this book by addressing an issue rarely covered by cultural critics: the lack of visibility and dissemination of the cultural expressions of exiles and emigrants from Equatorial Guinea. This is not a new phenomenon in the history of diasporic cultures. Cut off from a nation or a home in which to carry on a dialogue with members of a community, Guinean writers are obligated to create new communities. Yet, the receiving culture is often unfamiliar (if not utterly oblivious) to the home culture of these exiles and emigrants, and that lack of acknowledgement of the existence of the migrant or exilic other produces yet more anxiety. I describe this lack of visibility as an "out-of-body-ness," a liminal stage between life and death not uncommon among the characters who populate the creative expressions of Equatorial Guinean exiles and emigrants.

A word to the skeptical: Why, one might ask, study the literature of a tiny country whose population is between about a million if we include those who left and a little over half a million if we only count the present inhabitants? And why study works of literature very few have read, texts that, as the final chapter describes, suffer from neglect (at times benign, at others not so benign) by those in charge of cultural dissemination, that is, publishing outlets and communications industries? While my answers to those questions are contained in all the pages that follow, suffice to say here that the cultural and historical issues emerging from tiny Equatorial Guinea serve as a window to an understanding of the realities that will define the cultural, economic, and political currents of the twenty-first century. I don't think I would be overstating my case if I submitted that the literature and culture of Equatorial Guinea provides an inroad to "the consciousness of an age," as T. S. Eliot said of the so-called classical work of literature. After years of studying the area, I am convinced that Equatorial Guinea should be of interest to people other than the personnel of petroleum conglomerates and their political subalterns such as the heirs of George W. Bush and Tony Blair.

AFRICANS IN EUROPE

CHAPTER ONE

EMIXILE

Yo vengo de todas partes,
Y hacia todas partes voy.

(I come from everywhere,
And to everywhere I go.)
—José Martí

What is it to be an exile? What is it to be an emigrant? an immigrant? a seeker of a new geography? an escapee from an imprisoning, impoverishing social system? a stranger in a new land? a woman stranger in a new land? an other? a postcolonial other? an individual member of a diasporic community? What does it mean to have a divided self as a result of a departure? And what is it to represent those experiences? In short, what are the confluences of exile and emigration?

All these questions presuppose not only an experience but also a condition: in all of them there is an implied preposition *in,* as "in exile" or "in search of a new setting, a new life," although "to be *in* emigration," or "*in* immigration," or "*in* other" sounds awkward in English. Yet, a writer might get around the grammatical restriction by referring to "the state of," or "the process of" emigration or escape. Similarly, *otherness* does not work grammatically—not in most languages—if one wishes to put an *in* before the word, and it would be equally awkward to speak of a "process" of otherness (although as pointed out later, postcolonial critics have used "othering," which is not yet an accepted word in most dictionaries). In all cases (exile, migration, wandering, moving to a new land, and otherness), what works well both linguistically (Germanic and Romance languages) and conceptually is the noun that refers to a human being: an exile, a migrant, wanderer, a seeker, an other. As I said in *Shifting Ground,* which is about Spanish exile literature, what stands out above the condition of losing one's land is the specific person who loses (and wins) in the departure. Thus, exile-emigration, or what I am calling *emixile,* is the primary subject of exploration in this book. These pages are at once about a phenomena, a concept, and also about the people who suffer and enjoy the experience of the concept: the exiles and migrants of flesh and bone who will serve as the raw material. This book deals with human beings and how they represent themselves and others as they move through a process of shifting grounds.

In the last years of the twentieth century and the beginning ones of the twenty-first, one cannot help being aware of the countless numbers of people arriving into Spain, the "gateway to Europe"—from Africa, Eastern Europe, Asia, and Latin America. One also notes that most of these people left (and continue to leave) their homelands in the direst of political circumstances; they are escapees from not only material want but also in many cases from persecution, censorship, and oppression. What separates the two groups, emigrants and exiles? Where does exile end—if it ever ends—and where does emigration begin—if it is ever possible to designate a precise point of departure? Is the difference a semantic one, terms that might be used interchangeably according to the circumstances? Clearly, the definitions in most languages denote two different experiences. Exiles—the Latin root is *exsilium,* banishment, and *exsul,* banished person—are either forced to leave or choose to do so as a last resort due to harmful political circumstances, while emigrants, from *emigrare* (to depart) leave their land willingly for a perceived gain, usually a material one. So goes the conventional wisdom.

But, of course, those definitions and that conventional wisdom, that is, that exile is involuntary, and emigration is voluntary, do not tell us the whole story. Particularly in the age of disputed, at times disappearing, political borders, exile is becoming a global phenomenon related to issues that transcend a series of circumstances specific to a single nation. And when one delves into those specific circumstances, not only for the purposes of literary/cultural understanding but also to resolve a legal or diplomatic conflict, such as those of an exile, expatriate, or political dissident fleeing from oppression, one must deal with the relationship between the condition of exile, on the one hand, and emigration/immigration, on the other. The argument contained in my neologism *emixile* is not that exile and emigration are synonymous. Rather, as overlapping concepts, they are symbiotic, mutually beneficial to one another because in tandem they allow us to understand all kinds of geographic departures of the modern and postmodern periods. Ultimately, *emixile* lays bare our omnipresent and difficult relationship with the other. In the words of Nikos Papastergiadis in a book about the changing nature of movements of populations in the age of blurred national borderlines

(*The Turbulence of Migration*), "Displacement [in today's debates about multiculturalism] is not only more common but also a more complex experience" (20; also qtd. in Calavita 18).

In need of specificity, as any student of exile must be, my point of departure is a land unfamiliar to most inhabitants of the so-called first world, or global north: Equatorial Guinea. It is a tiny country in central west Africa with a population of a little over half a million inhabitants—although that figure nearly doubles if we include the many Equatorial Guineans, exiles and emigrants, now living outside the country's geographical boundaries.[1] Its importance, nevertheless, has little to do with numbers and much to do with symbols; it is a model for what some have called the postcolonial condition with all its problems, uncertainties, and ambivalences. As detailed in the second part of this chapter, Equatorial Guinea used to be a Spanish colony, the only one in Sub-Saharan Africa; its official language is still Spanish, but the majority of its citizens speak at least one indigenous language as well (Bubi, Fang, Ndowe, Anobonese, Pichin, or pidgin English); it went from colony to brutal dictatorship after independence in 1968; many have been forced to leave either for political or economic reasons or both; its geographic boundaries have to do with European land negotiations and treaties rather than with internal ethnic or even geographic unity, thereby questioning the very idea of nationhood. Equatorial Guinea's history tells much about the self-conceptions of its former colonizers and the nation-state of Spain—or what some might call the postnation of Spain—along with the postcolony of Equatorial Guinea. And the country is turning full circle when we consider that once again as the twenty-first century commences, its land and waters are coveted for their natural resources—this time oil. In fact, a journalist called Equatorial Guinea along with the waters off its coasts "the Kuwait of Africa."[2] Both unique and representative, Equatorial Guinea explains a great deal not only about Spain as a formerly powerful empire with all the complexes of past splendor but also about what we have come to call our "global village." Most of all, Equatorial Guinea reveals much about modern migrations, global material inequalities, personal stories of people forced to leave and those who leave of their own accord, collective shifts of human beings from the native land of colonization to other lands, often the land of the former colonizers and all the physical, psychological, and intellectual exchanges that emerge as a result.

But the story of Equatorial Guinea is also the story of the country that colonized it. Not so long ago, Spain was the land out of which its citizens set forth, migrations of the nineteenth century (mainly from the south and from Galicia to various arrivals in the Americas), exiles from the Spanish Civil War of the 1930s and emigrants of the postwar in search of livelihoods, jobs, or better working conditions from the 1940s through the 1960s. Ironically, in the last years of the twentieth century and the beginning years of the twenty-first, Spain is the receptacle of those very two categories of people: exiles and emigrants. Yet, in the case of the Spanish Civil War, whose exiles have been much discussed and are crucial to the understanding of Spanish history, those leaving might very well have been considered emigrants. Conversely, in the subsequent decades of material deprivation due to the aftermath of the war, many exited the country for explicitly political reasons. These were the years when Spaniards were, in many ways, the Blacks of Europe.

Indeed, the Blacks of Europe is how Ramón Gómez de la Serna, not known for his anguished discourse on the tragedy of exile, might have characterized certain immigrants. In his two-volume autobiography with the tongue-in-cheek title *Automoribundia* (loosely translated as Self-dying), he playfully discusses the difference between immigrant and emigrant by asserting that the former is something of a persona non grata not for a noble act of resistance in the previous residence but because the immigrant is viewed as someone who snuck in: "Quizás sea más señor, más residencial, más de puertas adentro lo de immigrante, pero lo romántico es ser emigrante, que quiere decir el que se vino porque se fue y no como inmigrante que parece ser que se metió dentro y parece que no vino" (Perhaps *immigrant* sounds more lordly, more residential, more doors-open-to-the-inside, but *emigrant* is romantic; it's about the one who came because he left, not like immigrant, who looks as though he snuck in without coming) (614).[3]

One notes, of course, the literary levity of these words, self-deprecating in the specific case of "Ramón," as he was called by those familiar with his humor, a man who left Spain for Argentina before the Civil War and decided to stay there until his death in 1962. Yet, the levity belies a glaring reality that many years later has become a crucial issue. "Meterse dentro" (to sneak or slip in), as he says, is what immigrants do from the point of view of those living in the country of arrival; it seems as though they have no experience of "coming," which is another way of saying they have no history. To speak of immigrants as exiles appears inappropriate or imprecise because the salient features of an immigrant have to do with sociology, not history: exile is a phenomenon of political history and literature, while immigration and emigration are relegated to the synchronic, that is, today's politics, statistics, changing demographics, societal processes, and the like. The country or area of origin does not exist in the eyes of those concerned with immigration, as the citizenry of the new land asks, "OK, now what do we do with them?"

Unfettered immigration from Africa is seen as one of the scourges of a plethora of European nations, not the least of which is Spain—for many the port of entry to Europe—whose government finds itself having to decipher ways of curbing the numbers of Africans who risk their lives trying to reach Spanish soil. In the summer of 2006, agreements were made between the European Union (with Spain heading the negotiations) and Senegal in an effort to intercept the many boats and rafts on their way to the Canary Islands.[4] Some might see this relatively new gesture toward an agreement with the countries of origin of immigration as a recognition of internal African issues that lie at the center of the immigration "problem," but in reality it does little to acknowledge historical circumstances. A related ploy to enlist the assistance of African countries in curbing immigration has been to offer aid for projects that develop infrastructure in the countries out of which the immigrants come. According to Spain's premiere news daily, *El País*, in a July 2006 article, one of many on immigration, these projects focused on transportation, communication, energy, and water. The article also reports that Spain would provide economic and humanitarian aid such as debt relief, immunization programs, and other health-related benefits.[5]

While these measures represent a liberal or social-democratic "first-world" response to rising immigration—Jürgen Habermas, it seems, would be in favor[6]—they are also typical of an overriding dismissal or neglect, at times benign, at others not so benign, of the immigrant "other" as an entity with a sui generis set of circumstances and traits thereby turning that recent arrival into a reflection of first-world concerns. In a thought-provoking study of visual media in contemporary Spanish life (filmic, photographic as well as linguistically pictorial images in written texts), Yeon-Soo Kim (*Family Album*) discusses the ethics and politics of a "new" Spain coping with ethnic diversity and the perceptions of African immigrants as they reach Spanish soil. As the eyes of the global north—again with Spain as the entrance to Europe—gaze at the global south through depictions of African immigrants (photographs, a story based on a photo, and paintings), Kim notes the void or the "silence" of these images as they erase the histories of the people washed up on the shores of southern Spain and the Canary Islands. A case in point is Kim's analysis of "Cailcedrat," a story by Nieves García Benito in which the maternal protagonist fills in that photographic void by telling the story of her son, an African man found dead on the beach of Tarifa, a tourist attraction on the southernmost tip of the Iberian Peninsula approximately twenty miles from the Moroccan coast. Thus, "Cailcedrat" represents not so much the norm of first-world perceptions but a counterpoint to them. I might add that in its attempt to fill this void, it becomes as much a story of exile as immigration.

In another cultural artifact, similarly pathetic in its depiction of a lamentable situation, Joakim Demmer offers a documentary rendition of the very arrival at the gate of Europe—in this case Tarifa. Indeed, this documentary film, titled *Tarifa Traffic,* narrates something of an epic instant. If we could make an ahistorical comparison, it would be akin to the depiction of the last or penultimate stage of the middle passage in which African slaves (those who survived the journey—of the estimated fifteen million forced into the "middle passage," three million did not survive[7]—reached their destination at the new world of bondage. In Demmer's film, Tarifa's "traffic" represents a conversion of the waters of leisure with the city's propitious conditions for wind surfing into the waters that provide a vehicle out of want. The color contrast between those who use the first waters (clear) and those who use the second (dark) are pointed out in the film with poignant clarity. The Spanish "characters" represent various institutions: the press, the police, the death bureaucracy, and the benevolent nongovernmental organizations (NGO) genuinely concerned about the health and well-being of the new arrivals. The film moves from interviews with various spokespersons from these institutions, to a harrowing scene filmed first-hand of the arrival of one of the "pateras" (vessels of African immigration to Europe), and ends with a segment that focuses on a specific case of two Moroccan brothers who come to Tarifa legally to recover the body of a family member who is one of the victims of Tarifa's "traffic accidents." The representatives of the Spanish immigration establishment are portrayed in all their exasperation. They are seen by both camera eye and viewer eye as benevolent players in a horrendously unjust situation that has both domestic and global implications. The viewer cannot help but sympathize, not only with the Africans but also with the people who must cope with them.

Demmer, a young filmmaker, has achieved his unstated (albeit transparent) goal: to foment sentiments of compassion that might—one hopes—lead to policies that would lessen the burdens of immigration for everyone. An aesthetic tour de force—dim lights amidst the darkness, the cemetery attendant with his dog, and eerie sounds—the final scene covers the ironically triumphant departure of the corpse from Tarifa accompanied by the family members back to Morocco. The journey home, by contrast to the arrival, is on a regularly scheduled ferry that is seen off by a member of the death-bureaucracy personnel who has helped them through the entire ordeal. Documentary pathos notwithstanding, the final words coming from the elderly caretaker of the cemetery from which the body was exhumed might lead to a call to action, or if not, certainly a denunciation: "Alguien tiene la culpa" (Someone is to blame).[8] Indeed, this statement encapsulates the entire film for it contains a hidden question: Are we to exculpate all the players in this dreadful narration and place the blame on an amorphous "alguien" (someone)? It is a crucial issue, not only in this documentary but also in the entire gamut of circumstances surrounding emigration and immigration. What is the responsibility of those who sympathize (even empathize) with the plight of the immigrant? The implied interrogation of first-world complicity (in the form of those who come to Tarifa for the wind surfing) represents also the beginnings of an understanding of the exilic circumstances surrounding immigration.

Similarly, Juan Goytisolo's many words on Spanish immigration come to mind not only in terms of the first-world's complicity but also in the relation between the concepts of exile and emigration. Corroborating with Sami Naïr, an Algerian-born member of the European Union Parliament and prominent writer on African migration to Europe, Goytisolo takes the opportunity afforded to him by the press headlines sensationalizing the Africans' harrowing entrance into Spain to point out (once again) the disparities and pathologies of his ex-land. In *El peaje de la vida: Integración o rechazo de la emigración en España* (The toll of life: Integration or rejection of emigration in Spain), both writers tackle the problems from their unique perspectives, Naïr as a professor of political science at the University of Paris and Goytisolo as the dissident novelist-intellectual. Predictably, Naïr's discourse is far more within the realm of policy, statistics, and the changing demographics of Europe—the sociology of immigration—while the novelist's is filled with anecdotes, remembrances, and rhetorical condemnations of the agents of Spanish history, not the least of whom are the once poverty-stricken natives of Almería in southeastern Spain, people with whom Goytisolo sympathized decades ago, prior to his own self-imposed exile. At the turn of the millennium, the former peasants of Almería have become *nouveau riche* due to the very economic policies and realities that contribute to the rise in immigration. Naïr attempts to answer the pressing questions: Where do the immigrants go and why? What are the policies, both global and specific to the receiving countries, that explain the rapid rise in immigration? What are the problems and desires of the people who yearn to reach Europe? The professor of social science even proposes new policy initiatives that might be taken as coping measures—since solutions are far between if not impossible, while Goytisolo, dissident, postexistentialist, postmodern, postnational writer that he is, leaves us with a justifiable sense of indignation, always in harmony with his voice of exile from Francisco Franco's Spain. At one point, he recalls Spanish Civil War exile and Spanish emigrants of the 1950s and 1960s: "Like their grandfathers and fathers, economic emigrants and political exiles living in Argentina, Venezuela or Mexico, Spaniards were received with open arms. The Republicans, forced like cattle behind by wire fences of Argelés, Saint Cyprien, and other concentration camps in the south of France in February of 1939, evoked with bitter irony a very different fate: 'They are welcomed while no one knows about the treatment we are getting.' History was moving forward, however, no one foresaw what would happen afterward" (182).

It is significant and understandable that the self-exiled novelist is more inclined to acknowledge the overlapping relations between exile and emigration than the political scientist, yet even in the latter's essays, at times one finds an implicit understanding of the connection: "To emigrate is to disappear in order to be reborn again later. To immigrate is to be reborn never to disappear again" (19). This is the aphorism of a creative writer, an exile. While he does not say it explicitly, all the (birthing) pains, losses, gains, ambivalences, uncertain identities of exile—the very stuff of exile writing—also constitute the experience of emigration and immigration.

In all the above cases, the representations of emigration and immigration in the form of pictures, narratives, or essays are manifestations of an exilic condition. While it may be uncommon for those who study immigration to conceive the departure as a form of exile, I suggest that to do so deepens the understanding of the journey. Too often in studies of immigration (including Naïr's and Goytisolo's), we have portraits without history, pictures, or renditions of the lives of people who are trying to "sneak in," as Gómez de la Serna would playfully say. "Parece que no vino" (It looks as though he never came) is a revealing sentence when we think of the ways in which we structure the experience of immigration as distinct from exile. Undeniably, the renditions of the act of coming in these portraits are well worth consideration if we seek to understand the experience. Yet somehow, the history that led to this act of coming or arrival is nowhere to be found. Rather, the focus (a no less noble one, and deeply ethical) is on the witnessing, the gaze, the story with an interest in and of itself, a story without a prestory: hence the indignation.

It seems, and this is perhaps the most salient argument of this current book, that the postcolonial world at the turn of the twentieth century to the twenty-first obligates us to rethink the distinction between migration and exile. Admittedly, it is not as though the similarities or the overlapping nature of the two concepts have never been pointed out as aspects of specific geographies and histories within the time frame of the modern period. There are many examples in world history in which exile and immigration/emigration go hand in hand. Kerby Miller's exploration of Irish immigration to the United States, *Emigrants and Exiles: Ireland and the Irish Exodus to North America,* is a telling example among many accounts of a long historical departure. In his lengthy study, Miller makes virtually no conceptual distinction, arguing that the hardships a great majority of the Irish population endured have had all the trappings of politics, specific policies devised by British elites that forced a good portion of the citizenry to leave. And in Spanish history there is the case of Galicia, an area of the Spanish nation-state, some would say a nation in itself, which has suffered the experiences of mass migrations since the nineteenth century, migrations very much akin to the experiences of exile and other forms of forced departure. The Galician intelligentsia have been obsessed with the reality of emigration for well over a century.

A case in point is Adolfo Rodríguez Castelao, who, in his famous essay on the history, culture, and suffering of the people from his native Galicia, *Sempre en Galiza* (Always in Galicia), makes little or no distinction between emigration and exile. Founder of the Galician Nationalist Party in 1931, Castelao went into exile after the Spanish Civil War. He was also a novelist and short-story writer—virtually all his works are in Galician—as well as a plastic artist who depicted the "disasters" of the Civil War, clear invocations of Francisco de Goya's *Desastres de la guerra* (Disasters of war). Yet, while Castelao was an exile artist in every sense, he insisted on emigration as the mainstay of the history of his homeland. *Sempre en Galiza* is above all a political-historical exploration of the political and social factors that have served as the prime movers of emigration. As Galician intellectual and Castelao expert Ana Carballal asserts, "Emigration and exile are very similar realities, because Galicians, due to their poverty or to political retaliation have to abandon their land in large numbers in order to make it in life. Galicians are and see themselves as victims; victims of a political system that oppresses them or victims of socioeconomic dispositions that work against the idiosyncratic characteristics of their region. . . . For Castelao, emigration is an opportunity to give testimony, to voice the conflict among the social classes, to mourn the sentiment of loss and abandonment, and most importantly, to reaffirm Galicia's identity" (Carballal 3).[9]

Indeed, "idiosyncratic," says Carballal, a designation that perhaps extends to any subnationality given the present-day ambivalences of the nation-state itself. Exile is also "idiosyncratic" in that it comes from ostracism, an attempt by the "normal" society to separate an individual from the mainstream.

And when we call an entire geography "idiosyncratic," we add a collective dimension, a dimension more part of emigration than exile. Exile connotes individuality and the private sphere of life, while emigration suggests collectivity in the public realm. For the Galician, intellectual and dissident-politician exile and immigration are by no means passive acts. In fact, Carballal says, they serve to counter the Spanish stereotype that Galicians are by nature fearful of power and prefer silence to open resistance:

> There is a force that pushes us into the world and another that attracts us to the native land; this is why paths leading outward tempt us, because the light is left on in the home in which we were born, waiting for us until the end of our lives. . . . Emigrants represent the only expansive desire left in Spain. . . . The time has come for our sacrifices to be acknowledged, or at least we should be allowed to consider as slanderous the loyal Spaniards' lack of understanding, Spaniards with whom we share the pains of war and, now [circa 1944], we share the pains of exile. (qtd. in Miguez, *El pensamiento político de Castelao* 68–70)

This notion of exile and emigration as a collective political act is as much true for Castelao as for other historians and writers dealing with similar experiences in relation to nationality.

Otherness of Exile and Emigration/Immigration

By definition, the concepts of exile, emigration, and immigration, as well as the person who corresponds to those ideas, presuppose the experience of separation. As has been said on numerous occasions and in a variety of contexts, exile has to do with a divided self: split identities, competing senses of belonging, a heightened awareness of justice and the ethical, and ostracism (Gurr, Said, Eagleton, Siedel, Guillén, Ugarte). The same is true for immigration and emigration even though theorists along with cultural and social critics tend not to focus on this division perhaps due (again) to differences in disciplinary discourses: the realm of exile is literary as well as political while that of immigration tends to be social or sociological. Yet, there is no denying, no matter the focus, that any discussion of a departure from a homeland and the subsequent arrival and reception in a new one has much to do with the relationship between self and other. The effect of treating exile and immigration/emigration within the same frame, however, shifts the focus from an individual self (the turmoil, inner ambivalences, in some cases the joys of displacement) to that same self with all her/his difficulties and particularities in relation to (an)other self. It is not that exile excludes the consideration of others—indeed, the other always intrudes hauntingly into an exile's changing self-definition in the new land. It is that exile, in conjunction with immigration/emigration, forces the consideration of a "face-to-face" relationship between self and other.

Perhaps no modern philosopher has focused as much attention on the relationship between self and other as has Emmanuel Levinas (1906–96), a Lithuanian-born Jew whose work figures among that of his fellow post-Heideggerrians (Sartre, Derrida, Lacan, Lyotard, Foucault, and others).[10] From the point of view of cultural and postcolonial studies, what distinguishes Levinas from other thinkers dealing with the issue of self-other is that the former frames much of his discussion on power. Whereas most previous discussions of the self-other relationship depend on reciprocity and reflection, it seems that Levinas speaks more of an exchange—a deeply ethical one—between two separate and unequal entities. He states, for example, that we cannot know physically the other's suffering; we cannot experience it (qtd. in Hutchens 90–93). We can only know of it, and that knowledge leads to responsibility, which is another highly charged term in his writing. In effect, the responsibility to the other that we all share as human beings defines our existence. In *Alterity and Transcendence,* when Levinas asks himself about the relationship between philosophy and ethics in reference to his previous work *Totality and Infinity,* he asserts that the mere act of addressing another person "expresses an ethical disturbance . . . a going outside oneself that is addressed to the other, the stranger" (97). In the same chapter, "The Proximity of the Other," he states that the "proximity" of the other is the "origin of putting all into question of self" (99). This assertion leads to further exploration of that supposedly reciprocal relationship that Martin Buber conceives of as an I-You. Yet, Levinas is troubled by the notion of reciprocity:

> My interrogation consisted in questioning that initial reciprocity [Buber's I-You]. The other whom I address—is he not initially the one with whom I stand in the relationship one has with the one who is weaker? For example, I am generous [another of Levine's loaded terms] toward the other without generosity being immediately claimed as reciprocal. . . . This concept of reciprocity bothered me, because the moment one is generous in hopes of reciprocity, that relation no longer involves generosity but the commercial relation, the exchange of good behavior. In the relation to the other, the other appears to me as one to whom I owe something, toward whom I have a responsibility. Hence the asymmetry of the I-You relation and the radical inequality between the I and the you, for all relation to the other is a relation to a being toward whom I have obligations. (100–101)

One hears echoes of Immanuel Kant's categorical ethical imperative, yet what distinguishes Levinas from previous moral philosophers is his rejection of any attempt to prescribe or proscribe behavior. The other is present before we enter into relationships, and this again leads to this notion of responsibility, a "'primordial' state of interhuman relations" (Hutchens 19). There is no "ought" in Levinas's ethical discourse. In my reading, for Levinas, human existence is made up of challenges, unsettling encounters between self and other. It is no wonder that postcolonial critics have seized upon these notions as they attempt to unravel relations between colonized and colonizer. *Other* has even become a verb in postcolonial studies, as in *othering*: "Othering describes the various ways in which colonial discourse produces its subjects, . . . [this is] a dialectical process because the colonizing *Other* is established at the same time as its colonized *others* are produced as subjects" (Ashcroft, Griffiths, and Tiffins, *Post-Colonial Studies* 171). In keeping with Levinas's seemingly conceptual contradictions, these words are imbued with a moral indictment, and at the same time there is no specific judgment. That is, an ethics of the other seems to be omnipresent in postcolonial criticism, while the inequalities of power are described de facto. Thus, the discussion of exile as a persistent postcolonial phenomenon is marked, explicitly and implicitly, by separation and otherness as in all the following situations and categories: racial distinctions that lead to separation (apartheid), differences between colonizers and colonized along with their respective cosmologies, conflicts between native-born colonizers—likewise displaced from their homeland—and those who remain in the land of the colonizers, discrepancies between the residents of the colonizing land and the colonized subjects who choose to leave the native land for the land that colonized them, and, of course, those more traditionally defined exiles who are expelled from their native land both at the time of colonization as well as the time of postcolonization, as is later described in the case of Equatorial Guinea, most of whose exiles are escaping a "native" power structure. All this, as the following chapters show, constitute what has come to be known in African diaspora studies as "double-consciousness."

But what about immigration and otherness? That is, what of that otherness as it is viewed and assimilated in the first world? The discourse of and on the other is crucial to understand the vicissitudes of a nation that becomes subjected to rapid influx of immigrant others escaping poverty. It is telling to once again consider Spain as a new model nation of incoming arrivals from the south. Clearly, for Spain and Spanish consciousness, the issues surrounding immigration point to an ethical quandary surrounding the crossing, as the diaspora is set into motion and proceeds in a plethora of directions. Mikel Azurmendi deals with immigration his work *Estampas del Ejido* (Vignettes of El Ejido) (2001), which offers a series of vignettes of life in Almería, where, just one year prior to the publication of the book, there had been racially motivated riots against immigrant Moroccan agricultural workers, the same riots that provided the impetus for Goytisolo and Naïr to write as well. Azurmendi's intention, however, as a vocal and highly visible Spanish member of the European Union's Forum for the Social Integration of Immigrants—he is also a former repentant member of the Basque armed independence group ETA—is to explain the causes of the riots and to offer ideas on how societies might begin to deal with the reality of immigration.[11]

Azurmendi is a public intellectual, and as such he grounds his commentaries on today's Spain in certain philosophical hypotheses. Of crucial importance in his views on violence arising from African immigration is his articulation of the concept of the other. Azurmendi's *Estampas* makes frequent references to "un otro" (19) from the second chapter on, and with this word as well as with the social/political arguments for remedies to the problem of immigration, one finds a notion borrowed from the renowned thinker Jürgen Habermas in his *Inclusion of the Other.* In a presentation delivered in Madrid at a conference on immigration and the labor market, "Is Multiculturalism Helping or Hindering Integration in Spain?" Azurmendi answers the question with a definitive "hindering" and states that the key to integration must be the law and the political agreement to uphold it. In his reading and affirmation of Habermas, Azurmendi calls for the necessity of counterbalancing the notion of "minorities" by redefining the word in terms of every citizen's obligation to enter into and accept the decisions of the body politic. Indeed, for Azurmendi, immigration threatens to unravel that very body politic, and the very last way of solving the problem is through multiculturalism:

> "[M]ulticulturalism, which is not integration, rather a juxtaposition, a segmentation into societies, into micro-societies, into mono-cultures, cannot lead to any kind of democratic future. Moreover, this is a great illness." I called it gangrene and I continue to think of it as such.
>
> On the plus side, however, there is now a capacity to respond to the challenges we face. Our society is 25 years old. . . . [A]fter Franco died, the inclusion of Spaniards into one society became possible, precisely because we all forsook something in order to accept a common future, of tolerating each other, respecting the same laws and being equal before the laws but with guarantees that each human being is different from the next. . . .
>
> [A]s Jürgen Habermas says in his great book *The Inclusion of the Other,* we need to counterbalance what are called "minorities." ("Is Multi-Culturalism" 2–3)

Thus, Azurmendi, in alliance with Habermas, calls on the democratic state's ability to absorb ("include") the other as the test of its viability: in the final analysis we are all "others," and, as such, it is our obligation to accept differences, live together ("convivencia"), and reach consensus. Yet, he does not consider the most glaring reality lying at the heart of an issue that goes well beyond the specifics of Spain in the twenty-first (post-9/11) century: the crossing of the real/symbolic space that separates Africa from Europe, with Spain playing the role of gatekeeper, which is in many ways an exilic crossing as well as a migratory one. The act of crossing is a reality so obvious, so manifestly present (or "always already" as the poststructuralists would say) that he fails to offer a rendering of the other that would achieve what Levinas calls for, a primordial call for responsibility. In a word, Azurmendi is oblivious to the overlapping nature of immigration and exile.

Also in question in the consideration of the crossing is a concept of the "other" that lies not as much in opposition to Azurmendi and Habermas but as an interrogation of the entire enlightenment project which "includes"—and of necessity inserts—the other into the social fabric, particularly the postcolonial or immigrant other. In the preface to one of Michel de Certeau's major books, *Heterologies: Discourse on the Other,* Wlad Godzich succinctly elucidates a series of philosophical discrepancies on the notion of the other by positing the twentieth-century dissatisfaction with the enlightenment notion that the other is always within our reach, apprehensible through reason, and a vehicle to self-understanding, that is, the goal of the understanding of the other is the understanding of the self. But with notions of fragmentation of the self, modernist divisions of labor and knowledge, alienation, existential anxiety, the other, that which is not-self, not-same, becomes less apprehensible. Indeed, the very act of apprehension of the other may be seen as an act of power, reductive, subjugating. The ideology of enlightenment universalism can lead down the path to enslavement of that very "other" (Habermas notwithstanding), an enslavement that in its own way calls for an exodus.

Indeed, it seems that postcolonial realities call for a new or different approach to exile. George Lamming, a renowned West Indian novelist and essayist, a canonical figure in English Caribbean literature, writes often about his own case as an immigrant-exile as he explores the special or specific complications involving postcolonial writers not in direct contact with their home and difficultly inserted in the so-called mother land:

> When the exile is a man of colonial orientation, and his chosen residence is the country which colonized his own history, then there are certain complications. For each exile has not only got to prove his worth to the other, he has to win the approval of Headquarters, meaning in the case of West Indian writer, England. . . .

> In England he does not feel the need to try to understand an Englishman, since all relationships begin with an assumption of previous knowledge, a knowledge acquired in the absence of the people known. This relationship with the English is only another aspect of the West Indian's relation to the *idea* of England. (24)

The "approval of Headquarters" is a particular restriction, perhaps even a call for self-censorship, with which postcolonial exile and immigrant writers must contend. Lamming continues by asserting that even James Baldwin, another canonical writer whose U.S. roots are without question despite his dissidence and his years of self-exile in France, shows a certain ambivalence about "headquarters." Baldwin, too, writes as an "interloper," a man in search of a tradition. The tradition of the "West," however, "'did not contain my history. . . . At the same time,'" Baldwin writes, "'I had no other heritage which I could possibly hope to use. I had certainly been unfitted for the jungle or the tribe'" (qtd. in Lamming 14). Baldwin's case is an excellent model not only for what Lamming wishes to explore but also for the separateness and special alienation of postcolonial exile and emigration. For Baldwin, a stranger in a variety of ways, including his avowed homosexuality, otherness is at the crux of everything he wrote. While he found himself "Equal in Paris," it is anything but equality or oneness or cultural harmony that this famous essay from *Notes of a Native Son* evokes.

While Baldwin may be seen as a special case—his homosexuality, his criticism of certain tendencies in the African American community of his day, including anti-intellectualism—the importance of his otherness cannot be overlooked.[12] He is in many ways the incarnation of what W. E. B. Du Bois famously characterized as the "double-consciousness" of the "Negro . . . in this American world." Yet, what both Baldwin and Du Bois epitomize both in their writing and in their role as intellectual leaders is the manifestation of otherness as an essential dimension of humanity. Moreover, as in many instances the writing of Guinean exiles and emigrants in Spain will show, that otherness makes for an awareness of a divided self and a double-consciousness that provides a major impetus for writing and other forms of cultural expression. The following oft-quoted words from Du Bois's *Souls of Black Folk* transcend the condition of African Americans and reach into all the members of the African diaspora, including those who left Equatorial Guinea: "It is a peculiar sensation this double-consciousness, this sense of always looking at one's self through the eyes of others, of measuring one's soul by the tape of a world that looks on in amused contempt and pity. One ever feels his twoness,—an American, a Negro; two souls, two thoughts, two reconciled strivings; two warring ideals in one dark body, whose dogged strength alone keeps it from being torn asunder" (7). From the "twoness" of Du Bois, these "reconciled strivings" and "warring ideals," it is possible to move to the "pleasures of exile": pleasure in the sense of a double consciousness as a heightened consciousness, a perspective that allows for at least two conflicting subjectivities in one "body." While one also notes the plaintive tone—"contempt and pity"—of the above passage (as well as in the entire work), it is also clear that experience in two (or more) worlds at once provides inroads to the understanding of otherness as all too human.

It is arguable that exile is a primordial condition in postcolonial writers, (Ashcroft, Griffiths, and Tiffin, *Post-Colonial Studies* 92–94), and when it is related to or fused with a collective experience of immigration, the permutations seem endless. In "Waiting," a gripping short story from a collection titled *The Joys of Exile* by a displaced African writer of a more recent generation, these permutations manifest themselves even before the protagonist-narrator's birth. The author, Paul Tiyambe Zeleza, a native of Zimbabwe, who left at an early age with his parents to Malawi, is obsessed with exilic departures from and within Africa. But in this first story in the collection, exile is such an all-encompassing force that it is conceived before birth, that is, conceived before conception. In a macabre, magical-real narrative, the protagonist finds himself in the "spirit-world" *waiting* to be born. Life for him is exile by definition: "If we were really given a choice, none of us [he and his spirit friends] would have wanted to be born, to go into the terrifying exile of human life" (3). Curiously, the protagonist is given three choices of parents, but if he rejects the first two pairs, he is required to choose the third. In an at-once epic and allegorical rendition of the entire gamut of African history, we witness the narrator's descriptions of the ordeals of his possible parents-to-be at pivotal stages of the continent's history. The first couple would have been ideal were it not for the sudden disappearance of the father, whom we learn "was not dead, but he was gone forever. In a sense, then, he had died. He had been taken to the coast to be packed on a ship for a journey to the end of the world across the vast, furious oceans" (5). The fate of the second pair is equally tragic as they fall victims to an invasion of the "pink people" who had overrun the coast on their way to conquering the entire land as they destroyed many villages along the way (8). In the sixth month after conception, the mother refuses to flee from her village and seek protection from the invaders. Thus in a noble act of preservation of the shrine of Chauta—who was "everything," "the Creator" and "overseer of their past and future" (9)—she refuses exile and is raped as a consequence. As a further outcome, the protagonist decides against being born losing, as he says, "interest in birth and living" (10) and must now cast his fate on his third choice of parents.

In this third stage of the story, a reference to the postcolonial stage of African history, the convergences of the "terrifying exile of human life" and the pitfalls of immigration come to the fore. The final set of parents-to-be of the protagonist are independence fighters. While the struggle for self-determination is successful, renewed problems emerge: those who won independence abuse their power, drifting "aimlessly unemployed" or decaying in low-paying work (13). These parents, however, are fortunate; they win scholarships to study overseas. Life in the new land, however, is no panacea. While they wait for things to improve in the homeland, news of more slaughters by those in power impedes both their desire and ability to return. Moreover, new problems emerge in the new land of modernity: marital infidelity and separation, the suggestion being that the private disjuncture of a love relationship is one more permutation of the public notion of exile in its larger sense. The story ends tragically, devastatingly. The mother attempts suicide as she goes into labor, a labor whose end result is the inauspicious birth of the protagonist, his exile, the beginning of what promises to be an ordeal in keeping with all the hardships, trials, and tragedies of African history.

I relate the details of this story for its nearly perfect manifestations of emixile, that is, exile in all its senses including especially emigration and immigration, a category of displacement both specific and universal, a conception of exile that makes a theoretical gesture by its direct connection to an experience of human life, all life, however "terrifying." Yet, at the same time, the title of the story collection is *The Joys of Exile,* and Lamming's collection of essays on the subject is *The Pleasures of Exile.* I read these words—*joys* and *pleasures*—not only as an acknowledgment of gains along with the losses but also as an affirmation of life by way of separations and journeys, at times voluntary at others forced, with all the face-to-face encounters with others (as Levinas would say) along the way. I ground my exploration of these encounters in the postcolonial renditions of these displacements in the uneasy relationship between Spain and Equatorial Guinea.

CHAPTER TWO

Out of Equatorial Guinea

According to historian of Africa James Ferguson (*Global Shadows*), the age of global markets and free flow of capital regardless of national borders has brought back slavery.[1] Indeed, postcolonial migration begins with slavery. How could it be otherwise? And how can we not see slavery as exile—diaspora, uprooting, loss of home, loss of identity, new identity, new nationality, questioning of the very concept of nationality. The tiny nation-state of Equatorial Guinea is no exception in its historical migratory patterns. It has been known throughout its history as a land into which and out of which people flow due to many factors, not the least of which is slavery. We academics, like entrepreneurs, are becoming more familiar with these movements as the twenty-first century presses on, due largely to the country's recent status as an oil-producing nation, a development that leads to even further movement in and out, despite the present government's strict control of its borders. In any case, the considerations of the historical circumstances of these movements, migrations, and exiles—both the phenomenon and the people—are paramount.

A Sub-Saharan country in the Bight of Biafra on the central west coast, Equatorial Guinea today constitutes the islands of Bioko (formerly Fernando Poo), Annobon, Corisco, and Elobey, as well as the continental area known as Río Muni. The first encounters between the inhabitants of what is today Spanish-speaking Equatorial Guinea and the European explorers and conquerors took place in the late fifteenth century. It was the Portuguese who first established control of the islands in 1472. Notwithstanding its proximity to the Portuguese-speaking islands, Sao Tomé and Principe, Equatorial Guinea has a very different history. Unlike the former Portuguese colonies, the colonial plantation system and the slave trade did not take hold in Fernando Poo until the early nineteenth century. This does not mean that slavery was a minor factor in its historical development. The many European explorers and conquerors were Portuguese, Spanish (who took control of the islands in 1778), and the British, and they were all involved in trafficking of forced laborers to varying degrees and in different ways.

In an eye-opening historical exploration—eye-opening not only in its exposition of the area's crucial importance to African colonial history but also in terms of the ubiquitous presence of the postcolonial other—Ibrahim K. Sundiata deals with the slave trade among the islands in the Bight of Biafra, with a particular focus on what the former competing empires once called Fernando Poo (Spanish orthography). A full consideration of the information offered by Sundiata reveals that the colonial slave trade had virtually everything to do with Equatorial Guinea's history, even though there was significant resistance to the entire enterprise of colonization (see also Bolekia Boleká, *Aproximación* 29–30). In the early years after that first encounter with Europe, not only were indigenous populations taken out of the homeland—although this would become a greater factor later on, both in the islands and in the mainland area of Río Muni—but also slaves and forced laborers were taken in.[2] So much so, that a good percentage of the population of these islands were of nonnative extraction, that is, many ancestors of those whom we call Equatorial Guineans today came from elsewhere. In at least one way, the country is a land of exiles comparable to Australia in its inauspicious beginnings as a penal colony. According to Sundiata, there were many misfits in Equatorial Guinea as well: "Over the years [referring mainly to the sixteenth century] Portuguese convicts, designated *degredados,* and Jewish exiles were transported to the Bight of Biafra. More importantly for future developments, the holders of land grants were authorized to trade in slaves with the [African] mainland. The majority of the captives brought to the island came from the kingdom of Kongo. Female slaves were imported for the specific purpose of creating an island population" (12).

In these early years of European dominance, it is clear from the historical accounts in Sundiata's study that cultural influences on the people of these areas were more British than Spanish. The British were known as antislavers, although the interests of the British crown had more to do with competition with Spain for international markets than competition for the moral high ground. As the period of colonization proceeded in the late nineteenth and early twentieth centuries, of important consequence for the population is the constant influx of nonnative peoples into the area due at once to the sparse indigenous population as well as the resistance of the island's main tribe, the Bubis. Another important ethnic group, the Fernandinos, by contrast, had no indigenous claims: their exile was that of freed slaves from Sierra Leone and Liberia brought in to work the plantations. Their language was pidgin English, and their religion was Protestant.

Exilic lamentations from this period are hard to come by for obvious reasons. Historians and cultural critics are forced to rely on the written documentation of the colonizing and slave-trading forces, and even when the "authentic" voice seems to cry out amidst economic reports, judicial agreements, and missionary accounts, that authenticity comes under scrutiny given the circumstances of the transcription.[3] Be that as it may, Sundiata, perhaps unwittingly, comes across a few examples of what we might think of as an exile's testimonial, in this case a demand for justice. The situation has to do with an early-twentieth-century land conflict between the Spanish administrative overseers and a burgeoning cocoa economy often in the hands of small farmers, most of whom were African British subjects (Fernandinos). As reported in Sundiata's study, someone named Joseph Emmanuel Taylor, a cocoa farmer, takes his case to a British consul:

> Permit me approaching you with this my humble cry. I am a native of New Calabar, Southern Nigeria. I came to this land in the year of 1880, and I have several children here, who are all educated under the British Flag. And I have properties here which are taking [*sic*] from me by force by the Judge of Fernando Poo, and give [*sic*] to his countryman for which reason I cannot tell.
>
> And the Judge stated to me that I being an English Subject I am not worthy of having such properties. . . . So I am begging your Majesty's help and assistance to assist me in a strange land being an English subject. (qtd. in Sundiata 97)

Reading these words for their rhetorical strategies, Mr. Taylor sounds as if he were evoking Psalm 137, the psalm of exile: "How shall we sing the Lord's song in a *strange land*" (chapter 5 discusses this psalm). Apparently, his case had to do with an unpaid mortgage, at least on the surface. But more important for the permutations of exile and immigration—because after all Mr. Taylor had immigrant status in Fernando Poo—his protest highlights not only the varieties of movements in and out of Equatorial Guinea throughout its history but also the difficult hybridity that comes about as a result of these movements. His appeal to the "British Flag," that is, his assertion that his children were educated by the British, is also of note in terms of his native land and culture, that of Calabar (what is today Nigeria). His complaint, unlike that of the typical story of exile, which bestows a primordial (almost mystical) quality on one's land of origin, as in the psalm cited above or in Ovid's *Tristia,* arises from his allegiance to a foreign, dominating power in which he is an other, despite his suggestion to the contrary. Yet, at the same time, we cannot take his appeal to the consul's sense of British nationalism at face value. It may be a strategy. Clearly, he is turning himself into an ally of the British against the Spanish. Moreover, he is speaking, as George Lamming would say, to "headquarters," in this case quite literally.

By the next decades of the twentieth century with rising nationalism in Spain, which made for greater attention to its African colonies, cocoa had replaced palm oil as a lucrative export, a significant factor in the Guinean-Spanish economy, along with lumber and coffee. But here again the plantation system necessitated a labor force that neither the island nor the mainland areas of Equatorial Guinea could fully supply. Thus, with the abolition of slavery becoming more and more the norm, some form of labor compulsion was necessary. Laborers were recruited from Cuba and other parts of Africa, including Río Muni, which by 1900 had become part of the colony after conflicting claims to it were settled by stipulations drawn in the Treaty of Paris, the very agreement that had brought an end to the Spanish-American War two years prior. Enticements were used for recruiting purposes, but the promises to potential African laborers were rarely realized, and some were absolutely false, as in the following account in 1912 by a worker from the Gold Coast (today Ghana) quoted in Sundiata's study:

> I am a native of Amanfru, in Secondee. About 9 months ago, Benjamin, came to Amanfru and asked one, Kwakun, to get him some men to take to Calabar. . . . Benjamin asked us to accompany him to Elmina [on the Ghanaian coast]. We did so. After a week at Elmina the steam ship "Bakana" arrived at Fernando Poo. The Lagos man took us ashore and handed us to one Bikitana [Vigatana?, asks Sundiata], a Spaniard. Bikitana took us to his cocoa farm and gave us machets and set us to work at the farm. He gave us two cups of rice weekly, and some salted fish. We worked for four months, but no pay was given. He used to flog us every day. (135)

Recorded well after slavery had been legally abolished, this man's story is not only indicative of the ambiguous semantics of slavery—where does slavery end and voluntary labor begin?—it stands as a precursor to the modern and postmodern age of the globalization of labor. According to Sundiata, it is typical of the plight of many Africans who were brought into Equatorial Guinea in the early twentieth century, yet it also gives a further example of the strikingly divergent cultures that come into play with migration. As the reader will soon be aware, the words of this man from the Gold Coast are prophetic. Contemporary Guinean writers are intent on recasting them, as has been accomplished in a major literary work by Donato Ndongo-Bidyogo.[4]

Despite Sundiata's assertion that the island's culture and economy were predominantly British and its religion Protestant, there is no denying that Spanish encroachment into the area in the twentieth century has had a lasting effect. We see this not only with the new acquisition of the mainland area of Río Muni, four hundred miles southeast of Fernando Poo, but also with the renewed spirit of the "white man's [Catholic] burden" in relation to economic gain. So much so that Spain became Equatorial Guinea's principal modern force of colonization and postcolonization. Prior to the twentieth century, the Spanish territorial islands in the Bight of Biafra (Sao Tome and Principe remained Portuguese) were victims of Spanish administrative neglect. After the so-called disaster of 1898, however, and the definitive end of Spanish colonial control of Latin America, Spain turned to Africa to establish a renewed interest in the continuation of its colonizing past with the "Patronato de Indígenas." This governmental body devised a policy toward Africa with a 1904 statute on local administration that called for "the fomenting of culture, morals, and well-being of the indigenous peoples and to assure their adhesion to Spain; to protect non-emancipated blacks; to facilitate the emancipation of those indigenous peoples who were incapable of ruling themselves; to exercise at all times the high functions of the Tutelary Counsel responsible for the guardianship of the blacks; . . . to intervene in the normalization of work and to act as advisory body of the governor general in relation to policy [in regard to Equatorial Guinea]" (qtd. in Ndongo-Bidyogo, Castro, and Martínez, 116).[5]

The Spanish policy and general attitude toward their neglected (other) colony manifested in the above description encapsulates a burgeoning Spanish nationalism that leads to the dictatorship of Primo de Rivera (1923–30), the Civil War, and eventually to the dictatorship of 1939–75 headed by Francisco Franco. The colonial wars in Morocco beginning in the mid-nineteenth century and most intense during the rule of Primo de Rivera might be seen as one of the most crucial factors in the development of the Spanish nation-state in the mid-twentieth century. As anthropologist Gustau Nerín has insisted, Spanish Africanist ultranationalist discourse was characterized by an aggressive expansionism that laid claim on territories south of the Sahara in addition to the more obvious ones in the north. Yet, he also discusses the tensions of that discourse between paternalism and economic gain and the central importance of the evangelizing Catholic church in the expression of those tensions, reminiscent of Spanish colonial relations with Latin America.[6] Indeed race and sex—as Nerín well notes—are as crucial factors in the Spanish domination of Equatorial Guinea as are the economic ones. With more than a touch of irony, Nerín calls the Spanish presence in Africa "colonialismo light," which is the title of his chapter 1.

Of importance in the understanding of Equatorial Guinean exile and emigration vis-à-vis the Spanish presence there, especially in the twentieth century, is that Spain, unlike Britain, creates a sense of home, however false.

It is not that the Spanish administrators, bureaucrats, clergy, and plantation entrepreneurs had any sense of equality in relation to the colonized subjects. On the contrary, Spanish views of indigenous peoples and their justifications for their presence in what they saw for the most part as a godforsaken land were anything but democratic—clearly in keeping with postcolonial studies' notion of the other. Yet, language and Catholicism—in many instances a syncretic Catholicism—were not only tools of domination, they provided cohesion, however artificial. Indeed, they made for an "imagined community" (Anderson), a critical sense of belonging that any area calling itself a nation must revert to, especially when its citizens are forced out or leave of their own accord for extenuating reasons. The Spanish nationalist poem "¡¡León de África!!" (Lion of Africa) written during the Franco regime by Spanish Guinean Juan Chema Mijero (b. 1924 in Musola, a town in then Fernando Poo) is not atypical of a significant element in Guinean consciousness:

> Despierta Rey de tu cuna
> orgullo de África
>
> (Awake, King, from your bed
> pride of Africa)
> (qtd. in Ndongo and Ngom 61)

Chema Mijero intones, sounding something like a Spanish Guinean rendering of Walt Whitman's celebration of America. What is different in this poet, along with other Guineans writing during Spanish colonization such as Constantino Ocha'a, is that the colonizing power is evoked positively as part of the poet's identity:

> España . . . la noble nación
> que te rige prudente y
> ofrece su gran corazón
>
> (Spain . . . the noble nation
> that rules you prudently and
> offers her great heart)
> (62)

The poem ends with a resounding,

> ¡¡Viva España!!
> ¡¡Viva Guinea!!
>
> (Long live Spain!!
> Long live [Spanish] Guinea!!)
> (63)

While Mijero's ode to the African lion, at once a tribute to his native land and to "civilizing" Spain, will later be rejected by writers more interested in self-determination, there is no denying that Equatorial Guinean resistance to colonialism and postcolonialism, expressed both in real political activity as well as in writing, falls within the confines of Spanish hypernationalism. This tendency is comparable to that of Lusophone Africa, as the very independence of Angola, Mozambique, and Guinea Bissau becomes interwoven with the political discourse of the Portuguese dictatorship of 1926 to 1974 (see Chabal). Yet, as the poem demonstrates, Spanish nationalism provided a force of belonging, in essence a home that later will become a place out of which to go into exile or emigrate.

In the 1940s and 1950s, Franco extended the African policy with the expansion of the Bureau of Moroccan and Colonial Affairs. It is difficult to deny that due to Franco's paternalistic policies, there was an economic amelioration: an increased health budget, Catholic education, and agricultural initiatives that bolstered Guinean exportation of coffee, cocoa, and lumber. Responding to indigenous anticolonialist pressures, Equatorial Guinea was granted autonomous status in 1965. Anticolonialism notwithstanding, it has been acknowledged that as a result of the later years of Spanish domination, especially the politics and economics of autonomous federalism in the late 1960s, Equatorial Guinea had a high per-capita income in comparison to other African areas, along with one of the continent's highest literacy rates.

During this time, mass emigrations or exiles out of the country did not take place on a large scale. On the contrary, Africans from Nigeria and Cameroon were immigrating into Spanish Guinea. Those moving out of Equatorial Guinea were going to the land that provided the cohesion—"headquarters." These tended to be the fortunate ones, chosen by their tribes or by priests as people who would benefit from further education in the land of advancement and "civilization"—Mijero himself now resides in Spain (Ndongo and Ngom 453). These professionals, including those studying to become members of the clergy, were emigrants out of Equatorial Guinea and immigrants in Spain with all the accompanying traits of those categories. And in the case of those who would become disaffected by the culture of "headquarters," as many did, their relationship with Spain tended to be ambivalent, part of a process of formation of an always-changing identity. Moreover, it is deeply ironic that the Spanish language will provide at once cohesion and an outlet for resistance, a language of multicultural exile. A number of the writers with whom this book deals, in all their double consciousness, think of Spanish as the language of home and not-home.

But the home/not-home in the consciousness of Guineans will be thrown grotesquely out of kilter in the years following independence in an all-too-typical pattern of postcolonial Africa. Autonomy and independence were followed by the brutal dictatorship of Francisco Macías Nguema (1970–79), which might be described as a twentieth-century African holocaust in keeping with that of other countries on the continent, the kind perpetrated by Africans such as Mobutu Sese Seko, Idi Amin, Ahmadou Ahidjo, Sani Abacha, Gnassingbé Eyadéma, Mengustu Haile Mariam, and others, a phenomenon that Max Liniger-Goumaz calls "Afro-fascism" (*De la Guinée Ecuatorial*).[7] Almost as if he were imitating the early patterns of the Franco regime, by 1972 Macías had taken complete control of the government, outlawed all political parties except one (PUNT—Partido Unico Nacional de Trabajadores), and assumed the title of president for life, imitating, and in many ways going beyond the Generalísimo in his obsession with power. The Macías government was responsible for state-sponsored terror: mass executions, the exit of up to one-third of the entire population, imprisonment of thousands of citizens, pilferage, ignorance, and neglect of rising malnutrition and infirmity that many citizens were forced to endure. The country's infrastructure—electrical power, water distribution, road construction and maintenance, transportation, and health care—what there was of it during Spanish colonization, fell into ruin. Even Catholicism came under attack, thus putting an end to formal education. The economy collapsed; skilled citizens and foreigners left for relatively less draconian places such as Cameroon, Gabon, and Nigeria (Bolekia, *Aproximación;* Ngom, introducción; Liniger-Goumaz, all three works; Klitgaard; Ndongo, *Historia y tragedia;* "Equatorial Guinea," Wikipedia).

The Macías dictatorship has been called "the years of silence" (Ngom, introducción 20–25), and while Mbaré Ngom's designation refers predominantly to the forced silence of writers and intellectuals, it was a period of such potent repression that virtually no one living in Equatorial Guinea—the islands as well as Río Muni—was able to escape it. It produced a collective exile, sweeping in its reach, for it applied to all groups: the Fang of Río Muni, the Bubi, the Ndowe (island dwellers of Corsisco and Elobey), the Kriós (Fernandinos), the Spaniards fearing reprisals intent on recovering their losses; Nigerians working in Equatorial Guinea left en masse. According to Justo Bolekia (exiled writer and poet who witnessed the beginning years of the Macías regime firsthand), twenty-five thousand Nigerians fled, thereby seriously hampering the economy, an economy already in ruins due to the run on the banks initiated by Spanish plantation owners (*Aproximación* 126–31). All this was happening in the midst of what has come to be known as a "discurso Nguemista," that is, a populist national exaltation with pseudo-Marxist-Leninist-Maoist overtones by means of vitriolic anti-colonial pronouncements. Macías's speeches were also imbued with racial references designed to stir up his audiences and to show his strength in the face of the white colonizer: "It was common to hear words like 'I'll put the whites in jail and I'll force them to work with the machete,' or like these 'You are free. The whites no longer rule, there is no more slavery,' 'When have you seen a white man in jail during the colonial period? Only blacks were put in jail. Well, now I'm going to throw the whites in, and I'll force them to work if they go against my Government'" (*Aproximación* 118–19).

Bolekia's depiction above is quoted because it is highly representative of a contemporary Guinean exilic voice in essays as well as poetry, a voice featured in these pages. Bolekia's words are filled with historical conviction and indignation, yet, at the same time, they suggest certain ambivalences characteristic of exile and emigration. His exilic history of Equatorial Guinea, *Aproximación a la historia de Guinea Ecuatorial* (An approximation of the history of Equatorial Guinea), while highly critical of Macías's years of brutal rule—on this there is much agreement, ironically even on the part of the dictator who follows him, his nephew Teodoro Obiang—Bolekia by no means perceives the Spanish as harmless observers of the carnage or as victims, nor does he wish to defend them. In 1968, he asserts, the run on the Spanish banks operating in Guinea was part of a concerted effort to "impede development of the new country and to strangle the new government economically" (117). And he names names: "Macías counted on a high official of the Spanish government. It was a man, Antonio-García-Trevijano y Forte, who would not vacillate in redacting all the laws he needed to legitimate his functions and barbarities" (115). The situation described by Bolekia is confirmed by another Guinean exile writer, Donato Ndongo-Bidyogo in *Historia y tragedia de Guinea Ecuatorial* (History and tragedy of Equatorial Guinea), who, along with Bolekia, decries Spanish complicity with the Macías regime by means of the infamous Spanish policy of "Materia Reservada" (classified information) that made it illegal in Spain to report any of the atrocities that were being committed in the area. Indeed, even discussion of the issue was prohibited, a censorship that made for a language of exilic ambivalence. Thus, political criticism, denouncement, or indignation at the abuse of human rights was not allowed public access, which does not mean it was nonexistent. Indeed, the consciousness of the slaughter of Equatorial Guineans in the 1970s was double: it took the form of an inner repulsion, an unwritten text yearning to take shape in a written text. Even after the so-called years of silence regarding the Macías regime, discussions of Guinean postindependence history are tempered, as they should be, by explanations of ethnicity and by national identities. It is telling, for example, that Bolekia's unique history of the area is grounded in a conception of the island and continental areas as a land of various (albeit converging) ethnic groups, thereby making it clear to his readers that Guineans do not all speak with one voice or one language, as he fosters a certain unity of resistance to dictatorship in conjunction with ethnic pluralism.

Macías's bloody dictatorship (some might call it a holocaust) gave rise to a coup plotted by his nephew Teodoro Obiang, who had been a high-ranking official in the former regime. He claimed he wanted democracy, yet a more credible reason for the coup was that he himself was put on Macías's list of disloyal citizens in need of punishment. Admittedly, the new regime made for significant changes: diplomatic relations with Spain were renewed in the form of cooperation programs directed from of the new Spanish embassy in the capital, Malabo (formerly Santa Isabel), some political prisoners were freed, the churches were allowed to function once again, and the monetary unit was changed to the "franco-cefa" or African franc, thereby shifting the country's economic dependence with France (Bolekia, *Aproximación* 140), another ex-empire with significant interests in all of west Africa. However, Obiang's rule (1979–present) provided little or no relief from Macías's oppression: critics of the new "Nguemista" regime were, and continue to be, imprisoned, tortured, or executed, and while the Guinean economy opened its doors to Europe and the "West," the profits for renewed exports were destined not for needed domestic advancement and infrastructure but for the new ruling class made up of a small cadre of Obiang's supporters and family members. The list of Obiang's victims are many, as Bolekia and others have shown (see Bolekia's list of Obiang's victims, *Aproximación* 147–48). One among many examples is that of Plácido Micó, who was imprisoned and tortured in 1993 and has been detained periodically since then (Silverstein). Due to international pressure, however, Micó has managed to organize a very weak opposition party, Convergencia Para la Democracia Social (CPDS). Indeed, Micó is a good example of an "interior exile" (see chapter 7).

While some Guineans returned from exile after Obiang's coup, the continuation of the second phase of the Nguemista dictatorship caused further exile and emigration; as described in these pages, some of the returning exiles were expelled again after their return (see Benita Sampedro, "African Poetry" 205–8). Economic decline, little or no attempt to rebuild infrastructure, and increased poverty brings us to the discovery of oil in the 1980s and its exploitation in the 1990s, making way for the new arrival of the first world at the beginning of the twenty-first century—this time in the form of CEOs and personnel of energy conglomerates such as ExxonMobil,

Triton Oil, and other Texas-based companies. Spain and France are also highly interested in Guinean oil profits and tend to turn the other way in the face of human-rights abuses. Today, Equatorial Guinea is among the poorest countries in Africa despite the oil boom: the infant-mortality rate is ninety-five per every thousand births, running water is scarce, and in Río Muni, electricity is sparse. While some Guineans and Spaniards continue to address these issues, the pattern of jailing or exiling dissidents remains intact (Silverstein; Liniger-Goumaz, *De la Guinée Ecuatorial, Small*; Klitgaard; Nerín; Ndongo-Bidyogo, *Historia y tragedia*).[8]

Bolekia's 2003 exilic history of his country is a telling indication not only of the problems plaguing his country but also of the frustration with the former colonizing power. In his *Aproximación,* he includes the colonial period not as a beginning of the area's history, thereby perpetuating a myth of origins, as do many histories of African countries. Rather, Bolekia sees Spanish dominance as one of many impediments to the creation of self-determination and authenticity. He insists not only on a "pre-history" of the area but also on a historical development acknowledging ethnic/tribal specificities that helps readers understand this land. The Spanish are seen as perhaps one more group among the Bubi, Fang, Ndowe, Kriós, and Annobonese with a stake in the benefits of the area. Moreover, as he decries the atrocities of the latter twentieth century and the beginnings of the twenty-first, he is careful to point out not only Macías's intimate relation with certain elements of the Franco regime but that of Obiang as well. The latter, educated at the military academy in Zaragoza, Spain, was the director of the prison of Santa Isabel under Macías. He presided over torture sessions in the infamous Black Beach prison, which was a penal complex established during colonial Spanish rule (130), still functioning despite protests by exiled Guineans and human-rights activists.[9] Bolekia is by no means the only one to indicate the Spanish government's complicity in both Nguema dictatorships. Another opposition leader in exile, now living in Spain since 1992, is Severo Moto, who was sentenced to Black Beach prison by Obiang. In 2004, he is said to have been part of an attempted coup organized by a group of oil entrepreneurs, mainly from Britain, including Margaret Thatcher's son Mark. Moto disappeared for several weeks, and when he reemerged, he told Spanish media that he had been kidnapped by Obiang's agents working with the cooperation of the Spanish government, and that in his view, Miguel Ángel Moratinos, the foreign-affairs minister, and his friendly relations with Obiang, is far more interested in Guinea's oil that in its violation of human rights. Moto was unable to provide evidence that his kidnapping had taken place (Roberts 270–71).

As Equatorial Guinean exilic discourse continues in the early twenty-first century in much the same tone as that of the late twentieth, it is undeniable that the language of that discourse is Spanish. This is yet another salient feature of Equatorial Guinean exile and emigration, a feature that makes for a great deal of tension. Indeed, for virtually all of the writers and historical agents I speak of in this book, Spanish is both the tool of liberation as well as an outlet, a process of exploration of double consciousness. Of importance also is that the Spanish language will give rise to certain ambivalences among the Guineans who use it, an issue discussed later on. The racial dimensions of Spanish and the entire gamut of this exilic discourse, especially in the light of the recent awakening of many Spanish citizens to their own racist inclinations with the advent of African immigration, are yet two more complicating threads of the discussion.

Moreover, what makes the present discourse different than previous exilic models is the dominance of globalism and all that comes and goes with it. We witness not only the international importance of oil as an economic factor but also rising immigration into Spain, as Guineans are both linked and differentiated from their African cohorts coming into Spain. Here again the issue of language and comprehension is paramount. Shifting identities will always be part of a diasporic discourse, but as we trudge further into the twenty-first century, the age of the "postnation," it seems that exile is more and more blatantly a human condition. In the age of globalization, can one suffer a geographically specific exile when the existence of the nation out of which the emigrant-exile emerges is under so much scrutiny that it seems to disappear? Exile from what or where? Emigration from which "nation"? As Paul Gilroy eloquently submits in his pioneering book *The Black Atlantic,* "The specificity of the modern political and cultural formation I want to call the Black Atlantic can be defined, on one level, through desire to transcend both the structures of the nation-state and the constraints of ethnicity and national particularity. These desires are relevant to understanding political organizing and cultural criticism. They have always sat uneasily alongside the strategic choices forced on black movements and individuals embedded in national and political cultures and nation-states in America, the Caribbean, and Europe" (19). Although these words refer most directly to the history of the slave trade in the Atlantic Ocean, they may refer as well to Equatorial Guinea in "the strategic choices forced on black movements and individuals."

CHAPTER THREE

The First Wave

> Pena me da llamarte así:
> Indeterminado, sin rumbo
> ni nombre; sin objetivos,
> ni lugar fijo de residencia.
>
> (It pains me to call you this:
> Indeterminate, without direction
> or a name; without purpose,
> or a fixed place of residence.)
> —Ciriaco Bokesa

In the colonial literature of Equatorial Guinea, despite an apparent acceptance of the colonial power structure embodied by the Spanish, there is marked ambivalence about that very power, especially as it relates to black subjectivities. As Paul Gilroy suggests in sweeping terms, the culture of the entire "Black Atlantic" is based on a desire to transcend (i.e., cross) national boundaries, and it is this yearning that leads us to modernity. I read that "desire" as something at once voluntary and conditioned by the diaspora. Indeed, migrations of any sort, almost by definition, question borders, and the departures from Equatorial Guinea are no exception. Even in the nationalist poem by Juan Chema Mijero quoted in the previous chapter, there is a desire, however unwitting, to tread beyond the nation-state. While the "civilizing" force of Spain will awaken this "lion of Africa," it is clear that neither Spain nor Africa will be the same as a result; there will be a transformation. The entire poem has to do with change, an awakening that comes from the contact of civilizations. The consequence, however unintended, is the questioning and transcendence of borders.

The debate concerning *negritude* in Equatorial Guinean writing may be seen in precisely these terms: transcendence of boundaries as a result of cultural contact and migrations. Unlike the majority of African nations, however, Equatorial Guinean cultural history is not bursting with expressions of black or African pride nor with a corpus of writers and/or political activists who were forced out of the colony as a result of their dissent. According to Mbaré Ngom, due to Spain's isolation from post–World War II European trends as a result of its support of fascism in the 1930s, there was an absence of Castilian translations of European texts of the mid-twentieth century—I might add a scarcity of the texts in the original as well—and a lack of cultural contact between Equatorial Guinea and other African colonies, some of which were in the process of becoming independent (introducción, Ndongo and Ngom 19).[1]

In Donato Ndongo-Bidyogo's essay, "El marco de la literatur de Guinea Ecuatorial" (The frame of Equatorial Guinean literature), there is an attempt to differentiate the development of Guinean literature with that of other African nations. *Negritude,* he argues—as have other African intellectuals of the mid- and late twentieth century, Franz Fanon included—operates according to hierarchical precepts of "Western civilization," notwithstanding *negritude*'s empowering attempts to rid the culture of Africa and the African diaspora of the low esteem or neglect in which it has been held by that very "West."[2] Its unstated raison d'être is to replace an internal or self-contained hierarchy, values, and cosmology all its own, with an external one. It is grounded on a notion of authenticity in keeping with certain European existentialist ideas of identity—note Camus' and Sartre's concern with French colonialism in Algeria—that unwittingly expose a series of "complexes" ("liberarse de complejos") (37)—and that belie the very quest for authentic identity. I read Ndongo's key word *complexes* here as a notion that goes beyond the cliché of "inferiority complex," referring instead to a series of psychosocial ambivalences leading to crises of identity.

For Ndongo and other contemporary African intellectuals, the proponents of *negritude* either accept or go through contortions to reject their own limitations vis-à-vis Western culture, perhaps the most important one being the apparent nonexistence of a written language. African literature's *real* authenticity—notwithstanding the redundancy—is thus found in the oral tradition: stories, legends, beliefs, figures of ancestors, animism, all of which are elucidated by Ndongo in his essay and with anthropological and linguistic evidence. His conclusion about negritude, then, is that its followers are intent on countering the dialectical deception on which Western racism is grounded, that is, that their struggles against alienation engendered by their "complexes" lead to the "discovery"—he emphasizes this word in order to debunk it—that the African is as human an anyone else on Earth ("El marco" 37). That said, the exiled author proposes something of a compromise or extension of the negritude project: "the *construction* of a national culture directly rooted in universal culture, without having to compensate for the harsh consequences of having awakened from alienation" ("El marco" 37; my emphasis). Previously in the essay, Ndongo had suggested (satirically) that the proponents of *negritude* were engaged in the discovery and fascination of their own navels (33), hence my parenthetical suggestion that Ndongo mocks the proponents of *negritude* as having been asleep ("awakened") or having escaped from more urgent realities.[3]

Still, there are underlying tensions, if not contradictions, in these post or counter*negritude* positions and the search for a "real authenticity" free of (Léopold Senghor–inspired) crises of identity: Just how does one define this supposedly authentic identity? How do we transcend the very notions of identity and the essentialism that underlie the term? Where do we draw the limits that separate "national cultures"? And what are the languages of that national culture? The *construction* of a national culture by, for, and about indigenous African peoples, as Ndongo calls for in relation to Equatorial Guinea, must consist, almost by definition, of a piecing together of a variety of differing elements constantly in movement: migrations, historical circumstances, ethnic encounters, changing boundaries. The very term *indigenous* is shaky in the light of migrations that occurred before the European arrivals. In the last analysis, the post*negritude* position is both illuminated and thrown out of kilter by the departures and arrivals of exiles and emigrants. Indeed, the construction of that national culture is the task of intellectuals and interpreters often, if not without exception, working outside the homeland in the libraries of the colonizing power, or "headquarters," as George Lamming calls it.

There is a certain irony, for example, in the fact that the first black bishop of Equatorial Guinea, Rafael María Nzé (1924–91), wrote most of his anthropological and linguistic studies of the Fang of Río Muni from exile in Madrid. The case of Daniel Jones Mathama (1908–83) is similar. In the same way that we cannot apprehend an "authentic" voice of the indigenous victims of the Spanish conquest of the Indies despite all the recent and not-so-recent attempts to recover it, the transcriptions of the oral African tradition or the compiling and anthologizing of stories both written and told by Equatorial Guineans (which is another a shaky category, given the information in the previous chapter) are based on a mediation between what someone was saying, writing, praying, or singing at a given point in history and the other someone who is recording it and interpreting it. Here, as in any historical document, we must rely on the "other someone." It is not that these considerations are unique to African culture; indeed, the very recovery of the past, as critics as dissimilar as Hayden Whyte and Stewart Hall have conveyed, is based on previously codified linguistic structures and narratological devices as much as on the attempt to recover the empirical truth of what happened. What strikes us in the case of Equatorial Guinea as both a model and an exception in African culture is that in these mediations, particularly in the writings of the exiles or immigrants, the condition of the compiler is often foregrounded, as the ambivalent subject position consciously intrudes into the texts of the compilations and descriptions.

Thus, the writing of the first waves of Guineans out of their country in the early and mid-twentieth century, when the area was still a Spanish colony, was both dependent upon and ambivalent about the colonizing power. In terms of "negritude," while there are very few elaborations of the reality or beauty of blackness, they do reveal certain "complexes" or alienation in relation to race in subtle, at times unstated, ways. Indeed, the ones who leave written records of experiences, customs, and commentaries about the area—Juan Chema Mijero, Rafael Mariá Nzé Abuy, Jones Mathama, Constantino Ocha'a, Trinidad Morgades Besari, Eugenio Nkogo—often do so from outside the native land, thereby consciously following the structures and thought patterns of the new land; that is, the land that at the moment of writing is providing a window through which to re-view their own culture. As we inspect their texts carefully, there is something about the writing of the exiles and emigrants that makes their ambivalent condition, their otherness, all the more apparent. Often there is a conscious understanding that their subject position is itself mediated, as they in turn mediate their supposedly first-hand experiences.

In this light, it is important to trace the beginnings of Guinean writing as a result of that initial contact with the Spanish. In the publishing outlets that served as a means of dissemination of information concerning Equatorial Guinea, most, if not all, of the essays and reports describing its communities and customs were sponsored by Spanish colonial authorities, mainly the Catholic Church. The Clarentians, a religious order of missionaries founded by a Catalan priest, Antonio María Claret, were central players in the colonization, indeed perhaps the most important factor in the creation of what is known now as a written Equatorial Guinean culture.[4] The journal *La Guinea Española* (founded as early as 1903) was pivotal, as both Ngom and Ndongo point out. Not only was it the principal source of information about Equatorial Guinea for the rest of the world—mainly for Spain and Spanish interests—but it also later provided the first vehicles by which Guinean writers could express and describe themselves. At first, the native Guineans were used (in all senses of that word) as what linguists have called "native informants," much as did the anthropologists of the nineteenth through the mid-twentieth centuries who recorded and interpreted stories and customs for publication. In some instances, native Guineans rendered these stories in their own words in Spanish. According to Ngom, in 1947, *La Guinea Española* initiated a new section "devoted exclusively to the culture of the Guineans," titled "Historias y cuentos" (Histories and stories). The new section was announced in the following way: "[This new section of the journal will be] an exponent of the thought of our [*sic*] indigenous peoples, compiled in the traditional way in stories, histories, narrations, proverbs and songs, for the purpose of contributing to their *perpetuation and distribution.* In addition to our personal effort and the collaboration of the missionaries, we rely on our students in the Seminary, teachers, students in the mission, the Indigenous Secondary School, and catechumens of our settlements who will send us as many 'histories' as possible on whatever topic" (qtd. in introducción 17; emphasis in original).[5]

While it would be imprecise to call this initiative the beginning of Guinean literature, it is undeniable that it marks an important moment in the history of consciousness in this part of the world. The missionaries might have regretted having invited the submissions of these stories, for, as it turned out, as *La Guinea Española* and other Guinean publishing outlets began to emerge, these "native informants" became more and more adept at telling their own stories, which were at times critical of the Spanish, notwithstanding the necessarily Spanish frame of reference and thought.

The content of Guinean writing from the late 1940s, however, reveals relatively few conscious elements of racial awareness and even less, if any, knowledge of the precepts of *negritude.* Few at that time read Senghor or Aimé Césaire. Their formation in the homeland had consisted for the most part of what the Spanish missionaries had provided. And even in Spain, where many, if not all, Guineans continued writing as a result of the intellectual talent they had shown the missionaries in the native land, the Francoist intellectual atmosphere did not provide a basis for criticism of the social realities of race. Similarly, as Ndongo asserts, anticolonialist tendencies or writings critical of Spanish power were few and far between. On the contrary, Spanish nationalism in all its spiritual fervor was more prevalent.

While the cries of Mijero's poem "Long Live Spain" (see previous chapter) are not as visceral those in the contributions of Guinean émigré and exile Constantino Ocha'a (1943–91), there is much evidence of the absorption of Spanish nationalist consciousness, with something of a tropical twist. Ocha'a is representative of this tendency in his contributions to *La Guinea Española* (reproduced in Ndongo and Ngom) in the early 1960s with stories such as "Las aventuras de Biom" (Biom's adventures) (118–19), "Biom se dirige hacia un pueblo extraño" (Biom addresses himself to a strange village) (120–22), and "Biom se convierte en su suegra" (Biom turns himself into his mother-in-law) (122–24). In 1967, just one year prior to independence, Ocha'a set forth for Madrid's Universidad Complutense to study history and did not return to his country until after the end of Macías's rule in 1979.

In an important work cited by many Guinean intellectuals titled *Semblanzas de la hispanidad* (Semblances of hispanicity) (1985), Ocha'a synthesizes African and Spanish history in relation to that of his country in a discourse resembling that of many Spanish and Latin American essayists who explore both the uniqueness and universality of their own cultures. Echoes of José Vasconcelos, Miguel de Unamuno, Angel Ganivet, and Ramiro de Maeztu, even Octavio Paz, are heard throughout his essay; Ocha'a seems almost literally to write for the approval of "headquarters." *Semblanzas* reveals an all too conventional wisdom among Spaniards writing on the so-called Spanish national character (Unamuno's "intrahistoria," for example) that the imperial Spanish project of colonization was put into action as part of a moral-religious impulse that went sour with the advent of capitalism. The uniqueness of this Equatorial Guinean's contribution to the many essays written in this vein from the early twentieth century through the Franco dictatorship (and beyond) is the intense interest in Africa. So much so, that one might call *Semblanzas de la hispanidad* the first, if not the only, Afro-centric work of Spanish intellectual history, albeit a nationalistic one. This nationalism, however, is not anticolonial; rather its gesture is universal, a concept of "Hispanicity" in keeping with the one put forth by Ramiro de Maeztu in his well-known *Defensa de la hispanidad* (Defense of hispanicity)—the similarity of the titles is significant. In this view, the civilizing and evangelizing impetus of imperial Spain in the early modern period is akin to virtue itself with the righteous gaze of the Almighty smiling at the conquerors of the uncivilized world. Taking his cue from Maeztu, Ocha'a writes, for example, that Philip II was "fired by the moral and spiritual stimuli that inspired the Christian kings during the reconquest" (57), and at another point, he asserts, "The presence of Spain in the five continents of the Earth created the Spanish soul in the entire world" (77).

However, don Ramiro would never have thought to devote attention to Africa with as much detail as did Ocha'a. Indeed, Africa is what saves Ocha'a from a crude imitation of his precursor or mentor. While Maeztu does include Africa in his assertions on the high-mindedness of "hispanidad," it is done almost in passing, as a mere assumption that Spain has historical claims on northern Morocco and Sub-Saharan Spanish Africa, all for the good of Africa. Ocha'a, on the other hand, (unwittingly) seeks to transcend boundaries as he traces the monarchies of Morocco and elucidates with empirical precision all the international treaties in the early part of the twentieth century in which Spain played a role in the partition of Morocco. And as he arrives at his final section on "El africanismo español," one senses that as a Guinean, these culminating pages are what he has been driving at all along: the assertion of what he calls "la guineidad" (the national essence of Equatorial Guinea) as a subcategory of "hispanidad." Here he defines the concept of "guineidad" as

> the conjunction of the permanent values of the Hispanic world with the Negroid Bantu reality, the latter of which is a mosaic of ethnic groups, a human pluralism. Guineaness is a cultural symbiosis that arises from the past century under the sign of providence [and] that guides history as a constant in its becoming. In this sense Guineaness emerges from the African world bursting with universality, a transcendent cosmopolitanism; similarly, it is born yearning to learn, open to the beneficial developing influences of a world of strong technological advances and stimuli, in keeping with its humanistic historical legacy, a lover of liberty and progress scaling the pinnacle of real happiness. . . . From here the Hispanic world acquires a wider dimension, more profound, more human and integrating. (162)

Thus, in the same way as Latin American culture forms part of "Hispanicity," "Guineaness" is an outgrowth of the moralizing and unifying Spanish spirit. The difference, however, is that Ocha'a, as a diasporic writer, transcends borders literally. The absorption of his land into the spiritual grandiosity of Spain is immediate; it has to do with his own experience of migration.[6]

The tension in the essay, especially when Ocha'a deals with the Spanish presence in Africa, is in the incoherence (an unwitting one, at least on the surface) between this a priori notion of "Spanishness" and the social and economic realities that serve as the raw material for his discourse: the lucrative coffee, cocoa, and lumber production and exportation. It is not that Ocha'a does not mention slavery, forced labor, economic gain on the part of Spanish merchants and plantation owners, much in keeping with the more recent historical account of the area offered by Ibrahim K. Sundiata in the work discussed in the previous chapter. Indeed, these two renderings of Guinean history complement one another. The point of deviation manifests itself in the discussion in *Semblanzas* of a higher notion of Guinean unity under Spain, higher, that is, in moral terms—far more true to Spanish-Guinean-universal identity than any facts or figures. Indeed, unity seems Ocha'a's guiding principle, perhaps understandable given the intensely diverse nature of the Guinean people. Note that both the historical logic and the incongruity in the following description of what was in colonial times Santa Isabel (today Malabo): "The cosmopolitanism of Santa Isabel is rooted in the heterogeneity that the historical capital of the Spanish colony saw pass before it in America, or in African immigration to Guinea. These are people from the most diverse tribes in equatorial Africa, above all from Nigeria (the Ibos and the Calabars). As the colonial possessions are consolidated in the exchange among the three converging forces—the Portuguese, Spanish, and British—the presence of these tribes on the island becomes more and more unified" (175).

The absorption of ultranationalist discourse within an African voice seems today more than incongruous. Even in a subsequent book exclusively on Equatorial Guinean politics in the aftermath of the Macías dictatorship, *Guinea Ecuatorial: Polémica y realidad,* the vestiges of his and Maeztu's idea of "Hispanicity" still prevail. Yet, given the specificities of Spanish history in relation to Africa, that is, that Spain sought to reengender its imperial past with renewed activity in Morocco and Equatorial Guinea, this seemingly glaring incongruity might be understood. The ensuing cultural exchange that came from emigration and immigration was precisely what brought on the incongruity.

Again, part of the explanation for the apparent absence of anticolonialist texts from the mid-twentieth century to the 1980s revolves around the importance of ethnic cohesion, a language-based unity that the Spanish, more than any other colonizing power—for better or for worse—were able to provide. Indeed, as part of this legacy, the Spanish authorities facilitated migration to the "mother country" in special cases having to do with three main categories: potential clerics who intended to return to the native land to continue the project of Catholicization, students who showed intellectual talent, and people who were in acute need of medical care and were able to travel to Spain usually because of a family connection. Ocha'a was in the second category, and it is clear that, as Ngom and others have argued, the prevailing atmosphere in Spain at the time of his residence there (1967–79) was heavily influenced by Francoist culture, a culture in which the idea of Hispanic unity through language is paramount.

Daniel Jones Mathama: A Fernandino in Spain

Ocha'a is by no means the only example. A revealing, indeed fascinating, case study of colonialist double consciousness arising from migration is that of Daniel Jones Mathama. Jones Mathama (1908–83) was a Fernandino;

his life work as a writer and educator is predicated on that circumstance. Descendants of freed slaves, principally from Sierra Leone, Liberia, and Nigeria, Fernandinos were brought to then Fernando Poo by the British and gradually assumed much of the agricultural production of the area, mainly cocoa, by expropriating indigenous Bubi land, usually with the consent of the European powers, both British and Spanish.[7] The language of the Fernandinos is predominantly pidgin English (in Spanish *pichin*), a form of Creole spoken in Equatorial Guinea. The educated Fernandinos often speak three languages, pidgin, English, and Spanish, which was the case of Jones Mathama. Son of Maximiliano Jones, one of the richest men in Equatorial Guinea, black or white, he was sent to study in England in his early adolescent years and obtained a secondary degree at the College of Oxford. In 1931, he moved to Barcelona to study medicine, and there he founded an English-language academy that later in the Franco regime became one of the Catalonia's most prestigious English schools, catering to the well-to-do Catalan bourgeoisie (Ndongo and Ngom 455–56).[8]

Jones Mathama's most important work is undoubtedly *Una lanza por el boabí* (1962) set in what was then San Carlos, today Luba which is the second most important city in the island of Bioko. While it is narrated in the third person, it is nonetheless an autobiographical novel filled with "costumbrismo" (local color) as are many of the Guinean texts of the colonial period. The *boabí* (chief) is surely the author's father, both a character in the novel and a life model for the author's real progenitor, Maximiliano Jones, famous in Equatorial Guinea not only for his fortune but also for his entrepreneurship in the plantation economy. Sundiata traces Jones the father's history in the following way:

> Maximiliano Jones [1871–44] was the Fernandino survivor par excellence. Early in his career he had made himself useful to Emilio Bonelli of the Compañía Transatlántica. In 1902 he solicited a small grant of land at a place called Moba in the San Carlos district. Two years later Jones obtained plantations in San Carlos. . . . By 1907 the Fernandino was in a commanding position in San Carlos; this position enabled him to ingratiate himself with the administration by freely granting lands to the town for its expansion. Jones practically owned the place because the inhabitants were dependent on him for building supplies. In 1928 Jones held 275 hectares in San Carlos and title to another forty. Of his holdings only thirty-three hectares were uncultivated. (114)

Maximiliano Jones's life also indicates the tensions of pluricultural identity in the area. As Sundiata writes further on, Maximiliano "illustrates the ambivalences of and pulls on the Fernandino community" (158). Indeed, Jones was British and Spanish; he depended on both powers, and they on him. While he thought of himself as a British subject, he wrote in his testament, "I only have reason to thank the Spanish Nation" (Sundiata 158).

In *Una lanza,* Jones Mathama's intentions are many, yet perhaps in his role as educator not only of Catalans who want to learn English but also, more important, as a leader among Guineans living in Spain, his clear goal (albeit unstated) is to sing the praises of his father, the tribal chieftain ("reyezuelo," the Spanish way of saying *boabí*), and to create a written record of his existence and good deeds. A typically fictional-nonfictional text from Equatorial Guinea, *Una lanza* draws from the oral tradition and at the same time goes beyond that tradition in the creation of dramatic situations filled with conflict and human interaction. Moreover, that Jones Mathama wrote this work in the Barcelona of the Franco period is not only strikingly incongruous, typical of the exilic contradiction between the time-place before the departure and that of the new surroundings, but it is also a further elucidation of the source of its colonialist discourse. Its language is filled with a rhetorical flare not nearly as passionate about the eternal and universal values of "Hispanicity" as that of Ocha'a but eloquent nonetheless in its didactic commentaries on virtually everything from the customs of the author's land to ethical behavior regardless of the geographical setting. Again, as has been said of exile literature, the text concentrates on ethics and does so with self-conscious subjectivity, a first-person interplay in which the unstated goal is the exploration of morality.

Considering the exilic circumstances of Jones the son's life and his text, one notes that the novel's structure is as incoherent as life itself. It has to do with the coming of age of the protagonist, Gue, youngest son of the *boabí.* Gue's father, in keeping with traditional African ways, is a polygamist—not only an accepted practice, but given the norms of the community, it is expected that he have more than one wife in light of his status as an opulent leader. While polygamy is a practice perhaps akin to noblesse oblige due to the added household expenses of having multiple wives, at times it comes under criticism by the dominant authorial voice, which is understandable, for, after all, the author is not only a Catholic but also a committed one. Still, as the protagonist grows up in his natural surroundings, an environment described with a nostalgia typical of one no longer there, the reader cannot help coming away with the sensation that nature (or Nature) cooperates in the traditional practices of the natives:

> Lamento de veras no poder describir adecuadamente la inconmensurable grandiosidad y exotismo de lo que he visto en aquellas tierras. Pero de lo que no

> debe uno olvidarse es de que la sabia Naturaleza dota a todos los habitantes de la selva de un modus vivendi, desde el más débil e insignificante hasta el más poderoso y fuerte. (11)
>
> (I truly lament not being able to describe adequately the incommensurable grandeur and exoticism that I have seen in those lands. But what one must not forget is that Nature in all its wisdom bestows a *modus vivendi* on all the inhabitants of the jungle, from the most weak and insignificant to the strongest and most powerful.)

As the novel progresses we are told of Gue's childhood mischief, the death of his mother, his multiple sicknesses—at times near death—his relation with his always strong, always wise father, his "puppy" loves, his dealings with British, German, and Spanish residents in the area of San Carlos, and lengthy interpolated tales involving his family members, ending with his departure for Spain. At nearly every step forward into the protagonist's life, the reader is constantly reminded of the author's presence. The work is filled with commentaries: lengthy (textbook-like) explanations of the uniqueness of his land, its flora and fauna, explanations of the beliefs and customs of its inhabitants, the interactions between the British missionaries in Mission Hill and the Spanish priests, as well as moral pronouncements perhaps not in keeping with certain norms of distance and structural/aesthetic unity. Yet, considering the strong subjectivity of the entire text, that is, that Jones Mathama wants to tell the story of his life, the incoherence becomes something of a structural leitmotif, by no means the only instance of such writerly practices in world literature. Indeed, each chapter opens with an edifying statement on the human condition, in the form of an epigraph composed by the author himself, such as the following one that opens chapter 8: "La alegría es un gran sentimiento. Cuando nos invade, nos sentimos transportados por indescriptible placer a ignotas regiones. El autor" (Happiness is a great emotion. When it invades us, we feel transported by pleasure to unknown lands. The author) (114).

Yet, as important as the self-conscious narration is to the exilic-emigrant-immigrant dimensions of the novel, equally vital is the authorial voice's intense awareness of the *other* as a source of virtually all of the text's components—both in terms of the discourse and the history. Jones's internal and external dialogues with the other are framed in the context of a colonial subject living in the land of the colonizers. The very beginning—actually a prebeginning—is a striking indication of the author's status as other. He offers an explanation before the prologue (introducción 7–9) for not including his photograph on the front or back cover of the book.

> No quiseira apartarme de la corriente [poner las fotos del autor en el anverso o en el dorso]; pero tampoco quiero que la gente me juzgue de antemano siguiendo la célebre frase "La cara es el espejo del alma" . . . porque sé positivamente que si me tuviesen que juzgar de acuerdo con la mencionada frase sería condenado sin discusión alguna. (6)
>
> (I don't wish to deviate from the norm [placing the author's photo on the front or back cover]; but neither do I want people to judge me according to that well known adage, "The face is the mirror of the soul" . . . because I know for sure that if I were to be judged by the mentioned saying, I would be condemned without any discussion.)

In this passage, the commentary on race cannot be more striking, however understated. Emmanuel Levinas's face-to-face other comes back to haunt. It is brutally honest statement in all its diplomacy ("no quisiera apartarme de la corriente" [(I don't wish to deviate from the norm]), might be read as a peculiarly Guinean addition to the debate concerning *negritude*. The naive (or uninformed) reader must ask him- or herself why a photo might condemn the author, but clearly there is an answer: he is black. And in those days, race determined acceptance in insidious ways, Maeztu's and Franco's insistence to the contrary notwithstanding (or that of Hernán Cortés, Philip II, or Bartolomé de las Casas; see the discussion of Zamora in chapter 3). Indeed, the racial other and all that accompanies it—ethnicity, African history, African customs, colonialism—inform every page of this book.

Admittedly, *Una lanza por el boabí* is not an angry book in the sense of an indictment of colonial racism. The opposite is true: Jones does not only refrain from criticizing the Spanish (or British) for their deeds in Equatorial Guinea, he assumes as given that the Spanish presence has been good for all involved, thereby echoing his father's statement in his will: 'I only have reason to thank the Spanish Nation.' At times, he resembles Ocha'a when he pauses the narration of Gue's life story to praise Spain for having been one of the first nations to have shown an example of the brotherhood of races (261). Yet, Jones Mathama's critiques of the status quo (along with his commentaries on the human condition) are understated, if stated at all. Like Levinas, he avoids judgment while exposing the face of the other for all of us readers ("querido lector" [dear reader] 50) to contemplate as we enter into a relationship with that ubiquitous self that is not "I."

Moreover, Jones Mathama's other is all-encompassing: it takes the form not only of his poor countrymen living in squalor and having to deal with infirmity virtually every day of their lives (50–52) but also of members of his own family, the Germans recruiting Bubis to fight against the British, the "braceros" (day laborers) working for the Fernandino-controlled plantations, such as those owned by the author's father. In this last case, the Fernandino is the other to the Bubi and vice versa. The author himself becomes an other who is critical of the Guineans educated in Spain returning to their land as if they had learned nothing (250–52). In this section, among the most passionate of these frequent authorial commentaries, despite the element of "constructive criticism," the author implores his countrypeople to engage in the task of the development of the country using the tools they learned to use in the mother country. Yet, reading the passage carefully, one considers that here, as elsewhere, the author has turned into a character in his own life novel, and in this case, he is not only the life model for the young protagonist but also a life model of himself, the author, intellectual and educator offering the wisdom of a man in his fifties writing a book about his life, a clear manifestation of exilic self-consciousness.

Another important dimension of Jones Mathama's novel as a discourse on the other is the representation of women. Unlike the preponderance of texts written by Guinean men (including the most recent), *Una lanza* (en)genders Equatorial Guinean society. Yet, here again, the gendering is incongruous, perhaps even incoherent, in that it takes the form of a lengthy interpolated tale (Cerventine in its complexity) told by a woman protagonist, covering over a full chapter of the novel (144–226). As Gue's life story becomes eclipsed by those around him, what emerges, almost without notice, is the voice of Esther, the victim of a series of incidences of sexual abuse by a hypnotizer ("hipnotizador"). This strange figure uses his powers to render women unconscious while, for a fee, his "clients" have their way with them. Jones Mathama, through his (other) protagonist, creates an unjust situation in which there is not just one instance of abuse but many. The dilemma is a collective one; it is not that one man has succumbed to his base instincts, several are involved including the victim's father, who is benefiting monetarily from the situation. Esther's father is portrayed as the worst culprit because his machinations with the hypnotizer have allowed the situation to go on—he has become a pimp rather than a father. The tale is reminiscent of *Fuenteovejuna* not only for the sexual nature of the oppression but also for the collective nature in which it is cast.

While there are no apparent ties to Gue's life story in this tale, there is a thematic association. Indeed, patriarchy is at the core not only in this interpolated tale of the hypnotizer but in the entire novel as well. As the son of a good father, the *boabí* among the Fernandinos of San Carlos, Jones Mathama takes care to show his readers examples of good and bad fathers, never questioning patriarchy itself. Indeed, the solution to the hypnotizers oppression comes not in an arbitrary act of revenge, as Edwin, Esther's brother, proposes: "así satisfago . . . mi venganza personal" (this is how I will . . . take revenge) (208). Rather, justice arises with the adjudication of the *boabí,* not only a symbol of enlightened justice but also the model of fatherly good will. Punishment is quick and judicious:

> Todos recibieron el consabido trato con la sierra en las posaderas. Además les obligó [el *boabí*] luego a dar una cantidad en metálico a todas las muchachas que sufrieron aquel vil atropello y a las que tuvieron hijos les fueron asignadas unas determinadas cantidades que los culpables tenían que abonar mensualmente hasta que los hijos no hubiesen cumplido los dieciséis años. (225)
>
> (All received their aforementioned treatment with the metal sheet on their buttocks. Also [the chief] obligated them to give a sum of money to all the girls who had suffered such a loathsome violation, and the ones who had children were due certain quantities that the perpetrators would have to pay on a monthly basis until the children reached sixteen years of age.)

What makes this tale both unique, albeit typical of the ethical voice of a person yearning for justice in his land, is that it revolves around the lives of women. It is a woman who tells the story of herself and other women, it is they who interact, it is their indignation, and in the last analysis, while they must rely on a higher fatherly authority (by both definition and by custom), it is they who find the solution, unlike Edwin, who, stereotypically virile, wants to take justice into his own hands. Patriarchy itself is never questioned, rather it is idealized, very much in the sense of the implementation of an enlightened justice.

Equally unique, a further marker of narrative incongruity, is the almost imperceptible metamorphosis of the authorial voice from that of the omniscient didactic narrator to that of a maligned woman. As Gue views himself from both the temporal and geographic distance of Spain several decades after the events in the novel take place, in the interpolated tale, his life novel becomes that of Esther, an other, another member of the community with a story to tell. Indeed, Levinas would find it interesting, because while Gue observes this other person tell her story, his responsibility is put into question not by his becoming the other person but by her position, "face-to-face," in front of him. In many ways the relationship, between Gue and Esther is a mirror of the relationship between reader and character in the entire novel. Jones Mathama makes this abundantly clear in his direct address to the reader at several instances. At one point, his words to the reader become a physical gesture:

> Ahora cuando reconozco mi incapacidad para describir adecuadamente lo que ahora me porpongo, haré lo posible para que tú, querido lector, me puedas comprender. Dame la mano, amigo lector, y adéntrate conmigo en cualquier poblado. Y ahora sigue mirando por una de las diferentes chozas donde viven las familias. (50)

> (Now that I acknowledge my incapacity to describe adequately what I propose now, I will do what I can so that you, dear reader, may understand me. Take my hand, friend and reader, and come in to any village with me. Now keep on looking at each of the huts where the people live one by one.)

The author delivers on his promise. What follows is a guided tour of family life in the dwellings of San Carlos and vicinity (50–52): descriptions of the material out of which the huts are constructed, the people who live in them, food preparation, eating utensils, the floors, holes dug in the ground used as toilets into which children have fallen and died, trees, animals, and a long et cetera. In addition, we find a commentary on polygamy, at once a moral criticism and an anthropological explanation with hints of ethical relativism (albeit contrary to the author's previously stated Catholic beliefs).

While metaliterary might be a peculiar designation to describe a book as seemingly straightforward as *Una lanza,* the circumstances of its writing, in addition to its autobiographical nature, are worthy of consideration. Again the subtle reference to the author's race before the novel begins in earnest is a telling indication of those circumstances. Yet, perhaps even more significant is the projection and recreation of the father, the *boabí,* also black yet not nearly as culturally other as his son as he writes from Barcelona. The *boabí* is a leader of his people, a little king ("reyezuelo") in his own right who in several instances of the novel is said to have had direct contact with his majesty ("s. m."), the then king of Spain, Alfonso XIII. Thus, the little king is another blueblood within the context of Spanish society. The equation of King Alfonso with the *boabí* does not compute, it is a telling social/cultural sign of defamiliarization. Thinking of the *boabí* as king, or at the least a powerful aristocrat, compels the reader to think of the very idea of monarchy and aristocracy: On what is the concept based? How does one become king? or a nobleman? What is the relationship between king and subject? What are the responsibilities of the king and the nobility? And if readers (in this case the Spanish reader, "querido lector") curious about life in Equatorial Guinea, compare this *boabí* with their King Alfonso or members of the Spanish land-owning aristocracy, there is no doubt that the Guinean king appears far more kingly than the king of Spain, who was known at that time as a playboy, indifferent to the needs of his people. Alas, the *boabí* is more kingly than the king himself, an enlightened despot.

In like manner, Jones Mathama is an enlightened intellectual, notwithstanding his stated support of Spanish colonialism and unstated adherence to the political status quo in the Spain of the 1960s. The lengthy discussions of scientific remedies to problems, not the least of which is the infirmity that plagued the islands for many years and continues to do so, attest to the author's role as an educator, a former medical student who seeks to understand the role of traditional, or "tribal," medical practices in conjunction with those of the most recent scientific discoveries. *Una lanza,* above all, is a work of Guinean enlightenment. As Edward Said has insisted in a variety of contexts, the Western conventional wisdom that the Arab world (Africa as well) has never had the historical experience of an enlightenment is based on an Orientalist notion of history, the privileging of a colonialist subject position. Indeed, Jones Mathama's novel serves as an African example of counter-Orientalist discourse, and it does so ironically within an assumption of the benefits of colonialism.

By virtue (perhaps misfortune) of having moved to Europe, the youngest son of the *boabí* is in a privileged cosmopolitan position. He offers a view of his land not only from his standing as a product of that land but also from experiences in several areas of Europe and knowledge of several languages. Thus, his view is both expansive and comparative, and as a consequence, hints of ambivalence and contradiction are in his writing, as in the following example of one of the author's epigraphic notes that precede each chapter: "Surcó raudo los mares de aventura, pero, cuan águila en pleno vuelo, sus ímpetus viéronse frenados en dorada jaula. Al autor" (Swiftly he furrowed the adventurous seas, but, like an eagle in full flight, his surges ended in a golden cage. The author) (277). Clearly, movement, the liberty of the waters, the flight of an eagle all connote a form of freedom, as in the freedom (or fortune) to have emigrated. Ironically, the speaker here finds himself in a cage, despite its "golden" qualifier.

These flights of poetic fancy are not common in a precursor to Jones Mathama's novel *Cuando los combes luchaban* (When the Combes fought) (1953) by Leoncio Evita, who, after the publication of this major novel at age twenty-four, lived his entire life in Bata, Río Muni, and never left Equatorial Guinea for an extended period of time. And as far as we know, he has written nothing since. Evita, by contrast to the Fernandino, is neither exile nor emigrant. His foundational novel deals with contact among several groups: the Combes (a group within the Ndowé tribe of the island of Corisco and the coastal area of Río Muni), Spanish explorers, and American missionaries. Yet, at the same time, the novel's plot stays entirely within the borders of his native land. Comparisons like these are admittedly problematical (if not odious) due to the ethnic diversity of the area as well as to the uncertainty regarding the possible influence of one colonial Guinean author on another. The contrast, however, is revealing. *Cuando los combes luchaban* follows a more coherent plot line, it is more dramatic and far less didactic. Mbaré Ngom, echoing the judgment of Carlos Echegaray González—one of the Spanish critics whose editions of Guinean texts did much to bring them into the critical limelight—submits, "Unlike Evita's text, Jones Mathama's novel treats the colonial situation in a very favorable way, at the same time as the narrator [a facsimile of the author] casts a very critical view over the customs and rituals of the indigenous groups of Fernando Poo" (introducción 20).

Yet, in fact, the ideological content of *Cuando los combes luchaban* is colonialist as well, notwithstanding the drama and tightly knit nature of the narrative. Evita's novel deals with a conflict occurring around the latter part of the nineteenth century, in which two Spanish "hunters," later referred to as "aventureros" (adventurers) (99), are enlisted by a delegation of Combes to help them deal with a renegade sect, the Bueti, who have been disguising themselves as leopards with evil intentions. The Spaniards, eager to make their presence known in the area, are happy to make friends with both the natives (the good ones) and the North American missionaries, John Stephen and his wife, Miss Leona McKiver, who have earned a reputation for performing good deeds among the tribe. Thus, the struggle ("luchaban") in the title is by no means a reference to an indigenous defense of the homeland against the European intruders, as one might assume (or hope). Such conflicts were common in then Fernando Poo among the Bubi but much less so among the Ndowé. Rather, the novel depicts precisely the opposite: the strategic historical alliances the Ndowé fostered as a matter of survival. Justo Bolekia Boleká explains that the area covered in the novel—the islands of Corisco, the two Elobeys, and coastal Río Muni—is known for its frequent contact with Europeans due to its geographical location. Moreover, for the explorers and fortune seekers from the sixteenth through the eighteenth centuries, one of the major interests in Corisco and the Cape of San Juan on the southwest corner of Río Muni involved the slave trade (*Aproximación* 34). And toward the end of the nineteenth century, the presence of missionaries was essential to the colonization of continental Equatorial Guinea. Bolekia writes, "Through contact [with the Spanish, French, and Germans] they had maintained for a long time, the Ndowés of Corisco and the two islands of Elobey suffered a brutal occupation more religious than military. Furthermore, the required affability manifested by these peoples toward the Spanish, made the latter confident of their loyalty, often using them as intermediaries in contacts with other African peoples" (*Aproximación* 65).

Thus, *Cuando los combes luchaban* is the story of a typically colonialist alliance between Europeans and a group of natives, on the one hand, against a rival group of natives, on the other. In the view of Donato Ndongo ("Leoncio Evita" 29), the final words of the novel uttered by Martín Garrido, one of the Spanish "hunters," reflect the colonialist project that Equatorial Guinea has been subjected to throughout its history: "No podemos regocijarnos hasta que todas estas hermosas tierras estén bajo la soberanía de España" (We cannot be content until all these beautiful lands are under Spanish sovereignty) (124). Moreover, the entire novel might be read as an epic rendition of the origin of Spanish control of Río Muni at the turn of the century; references to the Spanish war in Cuba abound. That Evita's text might be read as an indigenous mouthpiece, an affirmative voice for Spanish domination (albeit with good words to say about the members of his own community) is more than a possibility. The juxtaposition of this text with that of Jones Mathama, more an emigrant and immigrant than an exile, is a telling indicator of the cracks within that voice. It is not that Jones Mathama assails Spanish colonialism; on the contrary, he celebrates it. Yet, a careful reading of his work along side that of Evita reveals, in the former, an inner, perhaps ambivalent, absorption of Spanish culture that unwittingly exposes not only its flaws but also the ways in which his own indigenous culture mirrors it.[9]

A Poetic Transition: Bokesa, Ilombé, Balboa

On October 12, 1968, Equatorial Guinea gained independence from Spain. Ironically, this major event in Guinean history led to a contradictory situation: on the one hand, the repatriation of Guineans eager to return to their country with high expectations coupled with a will to create a new homeland, and on the other, an ensuing desire to leave. It took the new leader, Francisco Macías Nguema, several months to move the country from a burgeoning democracy in which self-determination would be the mantra to a dictatorship, the brutality of which was unprecedented in Guinean history. This oppositional reality manifests itself in the poetry of Guineans who had been formed during the colonial period and whose connection to Spain was not only political but also tangible, since they had a direct experience of the geography of that formerly controlling power. Experience in the world of the colonizers conditioned them, and in many cases, if not all, it is a primary motivation for writing. The typically exilic themes of loss, identity in the other land, relativity, and nostalgia, all coupled with the otherness of the colonial subject, are the mainstays of much of Guinean poetry of postindependence.

Among the most compelling cases is that of Ciriaco Bokesa (b. 1938), a former Clarentian priest, educated in Salamanca in the 1960s, who later became, of all things, the personal confessor of the head-of-state, Francisco Macías (Ndongo and Ngom 451). This stage of his life, however, considered in isolation, does not define him. Indeed, Bokesa, as a poet who in the 1980s prided himself on his hermeticism, defies definition or easy categorization. If Bokesa is representative of anything essentially Guinean, it is, ironically, the slipperiness of "guineidad" (Guineaness, Ocha'a earnestness notwithstanding); as a writer, he is nurtured by existential and poetic fluidity. His first published poem is an indication not only of this fluidity but also of the hopeful spirit that independence spawned in the late 1960s. It is titled "Isla verde" (Green island) (Ndongo and Ngom 73–74):

> Me encanta verte así,
> isla mía:
> llorando verdes ríos
> los ojos verdes
> de tus montañas;
> buscando esperanzas,
> dándolas también.
>
> (I love to see you this way,
> my island:
> weeping green rivers
> green eyes
> of your mountains;
> looking for hopes,
> giving them as well.)
>
> (73)

"Cry out, cry out, cry out," he pleads at another point in the poem, and at the same time, he qualifies, it is also important to "swim, toil away to survive" (nadar/bregar para subsistir) (74).

One hears echoes of José Martí, perhaps even Walt Whitman (again), in the celebration of an emerging land, an Equatorial Guinea on the verge of (swimming towards) the creation of a new Africa that sings in harmony, an island of the poet's dreams. The poem refers to something specific—the island—as well as to a greater idea—Africa. While the anticolonialist voice is difficult to find in Guinean writing of the 1960s, certainly celebratory independence poetry is not, as in the case of younger writers such as Julián Bibang Oye, Carlos Nsue Otong, Simplicio Nsue Avoro, and Secundino Oyono.[10] Yet, older poets, Bokesa and Raquel Ilombé—Raquel Del Pozo Epita—are more experientially entrenched in the colonial history that has defined them. That being so, the problem of identity, without the "complexes" of *negritude*, are more visible markers of their writing. Both poets are more immigrants/emigrants than exiles, although there are traces of the latter. Neither were expelled, yet the departure from their land of birth colors virtually all of their writing.

Raquel Ilombé (1932–92) went to Spain with no consciousness of having gone. She was less than a year old when her father, Angel del Pozo, a Spanish cocoa-plantation owner, moved to Spain from Corisco where his daughter was born. Ilombé's mother was a native of that island, a woman who disappeared from the minds of the family members—perhaps with the exception of Angel—as she was left behind: deliberately? a simple matter of colonialist protocol? unthinkable to bring the mistress along with the family? the scandal that would have ensued? unwillingness on the part of Raquel's mother to leave her land? We may never know; it is not even clear that Ilombé herself knew the answers to these questions. I read her poetry, however, as an uncertain yearning for a lost mother, uncertain in that the name of the source for a deeply felt anxiety is never specified, typical of many poets. We do know, however, that Ilombé's father returned to Equatorial Guinea frequently with his family and continued his economic activity in the Bata (Río Muni) area.[11]

With independence in 1968, the family fled from Equatorial Guinea fearing Macías's reprisals against Spaniards. The period immediately following Macías's usurpation of power and creation of the Partido Uníco Nacional (Single National Party) was called the period of "emergencia" (emergency), in which Spanish administrators, clerics, and landowners were literally rescued by the Franco government and brought to Spain. Thus, one senses that exile, in the strict sense of the word, applies to Ilombé (perhaps even more so than to Bokesa as will be shown). There is not a trace, however, of a political voice in her poetry. Rather ones finds a strong sensation of loss and uncertainty embedded in a series of self-interrogations on the poet's identity. In her only complete volume of poetry, appropriately titled *Ceiba* (a tree that grows abundantly throughout Equatorial Guinea), "Quien soy" (Who am I), this interrogation resonates from the first line to the end. That there is no question mark in the title is telling in its implication that the affirmation "who I am" is also a question, "who am I":

El cielo hable por mí
Que yo no sé explicarme.
. . .
Pregunta a la pradera verde,
al potro que en ella retoza y se divierte,
al tallo que se yergue con elegancia inmensa,
blandiendo su flor entreabierta,
pregúntale quién soy,
. . .
Pregunta al mar,
que en constante movimiento
parece un corazón que siente y suena,
pregúntale quién soy.
. . .
Dios, hablando de ti estoy.
Pregúntale a El quién soy.

(Let the sky speak for me
I don't know how to explain myself.
. . .
Ask the green meadows,
the colt who frolics there,
ask the stem that elegantly and flamboyantly rises
waving its flower nearly in full bloom,
ask it who I am.
. . .
Ask the sea,
who, in constant movement, looks like a heart that feels and
makes noise,
ask it who I am.
. . .
God, I'm talking about you.
Ask Him who I am.)

(12–13)[12]

Here, Ilombé enlists nature to help her deal with her *question* of identity, and while the closing reference to God may seem at first reading like a spiritual surrender to the Unmoved Mover of nature, it is also an invitation to dialogue. As if to respond to the unasked question, "who are you," Ilombé announces to all involved (the elements of nature, the meadow, the earth, the flowers, the seas, the mountains), that she seeks to learn who she is. But the answer remains an enigma.

Another strongly felt presence in *Ceiba* are the figures of family members, particularly the mother. Images of mother and motherland strongly depend on a sense of place in virtually all poetry, yet in Ilombé's verses, the evocation of a specific locale is at times difficult to ascertain. What the poet provides, on the other hand, is a signature-like gesture at the end of each poem in which she informs her reader when and where the poem was written. The time frame is from 1966 (one single poem written then) to 1977; over half are penned from Madrid, and the rest from Bata. This information, however, is typically exilic (or migratory) in that the place of the writing is not necessarily the place of evocation. Indeed, from Madrid in 1974, she writes of

ese mar,
lleno de calma y de ira

(that sea,
filled with calm and ire)
(19)

and in "Los ríos hablan" (The rivers speak), written from the capital of Spain in 1975, she speaks of what appears as imagined rivers, probably not Madrid's Manzanares, a mere trickle when compared to the rivers of Equatorial Guinea. Indeed, place, while never specific, is crucial to Ilombé, and when considered with family (particularly the mother figure), the imagined geography seems to be one of the motivating forces of her verses. In a poem dedicated to her mother "Por ti fui" (For you I was/For you I left) from Madrid in 1977, she writes,

Era en ti en quien pensaba
cuando a mi paso,
todo de paz me hablaba.
. . .
Eras tú quién decía,
espera con fervor
la luz de un nuevo día.
. . .
Difícil ganar,
difícil perder y no gritar
al juego de andar para llegar.

(It was you I was thinking of
when all around me,
everything was speaking of peace.
. . .
It was you who told me,
wait with determination
for the light of a new day.
. . .
Difficult to win,
difficult to lose and not cry out
in the game of walking to arrive.)
(33–34)

The precise nature of the relationship with her lost mother is difficult to ascertain, yet the imperfect tense ("decía") referring to what her mother used to say in conjunction with the lesson learned today suggests an imagined or recreated dialogue, a wish to fill a void, yet another marker of the losses and gains of displacement. Crucial as well is the title, a play on words with "fui," which can mean "I was" or "I left." Indeed, for Ilombé, being is interchangeable with leaving all in search for the lost mother. For all its imprecise geographic references, all the poems of *Ceiba* are filled with the anxiety of a lost topography, an absent-yet-present land that lies at the core of the poet's very being.

Ciriaco Bokesa is also a displaced identity seeker, despite his first poem quoted earlier, much more grounded in a precise geography than his later writing. Far more ironic, hermetic, and playful than Ilombé, in his postindependence poetry, he shifts away from the identity of the poet he once was, that man who wrote the Martí-sounding verses celebrating the moment of independence. After completing his studies in theology in Salamanca, Bokesa returned to Equatorial Guinea (Malabo) to become Francisco Macías's chaplain, a dirty job (as they say), but someone had to do it (as Bokesa might have said). Although he was jailed briefly by Macías, he stayed in the country even after the coup plotted by Teodoro Obiang in 1979. In 1980, however, he abandoned another (metaphorical) home, the priesthood, and his poetry reflects that rupture. His collection, *Voces de espumas* (Voices of foam) is heavily influenced (not with a great deal of anxiety) by modern Spanish poets who defied easy meanings of their works. Jorge Guillén, another exile poet and prominent member of the so-called group of 1927, appears as the voice behind the voice in the final series of poems from the collection, "Carta final." Here, as in all of *Voces*,

Bokesa signals, even celebrates, his indeterminacy. "A un indeterminado" (To an undetermined person) (85–87) begins with a tone of deep regret and despair. Aimlessly and joylessly, the poet laments his situation:

sin rumbo
ni nombre; sin objetivos

(without direction
or a name; without purpose)
(85)

Yet, about half way through this relatively long poem, the speaker reminds the troubled soul that life remains open: "¡De abanicos está la vida!" (Life is open like a fan!) (86). And "Yahveh" (Yahweh) is no longer worth waiting for (86). The entire poem is something of an awakening to the possibility that one might live not for God but like God: "un vivir a lo Dios" (a God-like life) ("¡Despierta!" 87).

That the "undetermined," ergo liberated, Bokesa is the same writer who joyfully anticipated liberty in the beloved "green island" of his youth and that this celebratory poem was written in the midst of the land that both formed him and limited him attest to the fluidity both of his poetry and of his persona. Indeed, Bokesa defies categorization, and he does so literally, almost as an act of existential resistance. Most indicative of this resistance is his commitment to remain uncommitted, that is, his insistence not to write or be interpreted as a political, ethnic, or even African(ist) poet. In "Umbral" (Threshold), the prologue to *Voces* (10), he characterizes the writing and reading of poetry as a search for poetic creation itself, and he goes on to criticize those who force poets into a political commitment. Particularly the African writer, he submits, is forced into a pattern of Africanism and commitment to a political landscape as a guarantee of his [or her] success, an attitude that is limiting in the least. In his words, writers who refuse to enter into the expected patterns see a "black" future (9). He goes on to state that in the lamentable case of Equatorial Guinea, exile writers are forced either into a voice of nostalgia or of revenge against political abuses, while the ones who stay at home extol the triumphs of the new society, in this case that of Obiang. "Umbral" also provides a warning to the reader: do not look for easy poetry; social, political, scenic verses are simply not the intention. Rather, Bokesa informs us that he writes to "express what lies within, abstracted from any concreteness" (10).

Bokesa is thus unique, not only because of his particular situation as a human being struggling both with and against his own "indeterminacy" but also because he defines himself as such. Preferring to distance himself from any easy categories as well as from what he seems to disdain in the direction of most of the writers in exile from his land, he creates his own niche, at times with playfully ironic consequences, as in the following lines from "La yuca" (Yucca):

La yuca es buena
pero los negros
van siempre antes
a por las patatas.
. . .
a por las blancas.
. . .
Y en mis andares
por mil Españas,
he visto cómo
a todo negro
le vuelven loco,
—negras de Hispania
o moras de Africa—
las toledanas.

(Yucca is good,
but blacks
always go
for potatoes.
. . .
for the white women
. . .
In my wanderings
through a thousand Spains,
I've seen
how every Black man
goes crazy,
—never mind Black Hispanic women
or Moorish ladies of Africa—
over the women of Toledo [Spain].)
(78)

A little honesty is in order, says Bokesa in this poem about one the most common edible products of all Africa. Yet, as in virtually any poem whose mainstay is irony, honesty is never earnestness, rather it is more Nietzschean than reformist or politically progressive. And in the mention of his "wanderings through a thousand Spains," there is yet another affirmation of the relativity, indeterminacy, and constant flux of exile and emigration; they constitute his asserted authority. "I have seen" many people and things, he asserts, thus turning movement and experience into his sources of authority.

A contrasting poetic voice to Bokesa's is embodied in Juan Balboa Boneke (b. 1938), a writer who, as much as any other Guinean cultural figure, represents African postcolonial exile in the modern sense. Balboa may very well be Bokesa's object of disapproval when the latter deprecates the politics of Guinean exile writing. Balboa's poetry is filled with political indignation, moral accusation, and an urge to vindicate those who have suffered the repressions of the two Guinean dictatorships. Typical of the exile writer, regardless of place, Balboa considers himself a witness to what went wrong, and his exilic "I" is a manifestation. In the colonial period, he left then–Fernando Poo to study in Granada, but when his country gained independence, he returned and, as a result, suffered the Macías persecution. He departed his country once again; this time he lived in Majorca (Baleric Islands of Spain) until the fall of the first dictator, after which he returned triumphantly to assume a government position. Upon seeing that Teodoro Obiang's regime would be more of the same, however, again he fled to Spain, the ubiquitous and ambivalent place of refuge for the majority of Guineans who leave their homeland.

As Benita Sampedro has affirmed, for Juan Balboa—I might add unlike both Ilombé and Bokesa—exile is an act of opposition, "a clear gesture of resistance, the resistance that will eventually give way to change" ("African Poetry" 206). Indeed, it is progress and change that Balboa longs for, and his "gesture" is an openly stated political act. In something of a signature poem, "¿Dónde estás Guinea?" a model for much of the anguish felt not only by fellow writers but also by many Guineans hoping for a democracy that the country has never experienced, the main rhetorical device is apostrophe, much in keeping with other exile poetry:

> Oh! Guinea Patria mía,
> hoy gimes y lloras de dolor,
> . . .
> en tus hijos buscas tu Libertad,
> pero
> . . .
> éstos dónde están?

(Oh! Guinea, my Country,
today you cry and groan with pain,
. . .
you search for Liberty in your children,
but
. . .
where are they?)
(Ndongo, *Antología* 51)

Exilic apostrophe is a constant in Balboa's poetry as he addresses himself to larger than life concepts such as "Libertad" (Liberty) ("Deseo de libertad" [Desire for liberty]), "Tiempo" (Time) ("Instantes de angustia" [Instances of anguish"), and again "Guinea mía" (My Guinea) ("Vencedores y vencidos" [Victors and Vanquishes]) (Ndongo and Ngom 144, 146, 151), all of which are the characteristic (if not conventional) expressions of loss, a rhetoric of mourning that contains an unstated hope of return to something better. Notions of death in Balboa are momentary because there always seems to be something beyond, a transcending force that is at once concrete and abstract.

Regardless of the familiar tropes of exile in Balboa's poetry, familiar, that is, in much of Western literature, the postcolonial foundation for that exile is crucial. In this regard, he shares with Ilombé and Bokesa an obsession with identity. Balboa is one of the few writers from Equatorial Guinea to have used the term *negritude* in a creative text. While the principal theme in this text, "Boloko" (Nostalgia), is typically exilic (Ndongo, *Antología* 50–51), the longing for the poet's familiar landscape on the beach village of Boloko on the eastern coast of Bioko (formerly Fernando Poo) is intricately connected to blackness:

Playa de Boloko
playa
de Negritude,
desde mi exilio
añoro tu calor;
tu fragante aroma
quiero percibir
y a la calidez de tu regazo
deseo retornar.

(Boloko Beach
beach

of Negritude,
from my exile
I desire your heat;
I want to sense/your fragrant aroma
and to the warmth of your lap
I wish to return.)
(Balboa, "O'Boriba" 51)

In previous verses of the same poem, the play of white (the sea foam "como perlas" [like pearls] 50) with the black hue of the sands is clearly a metonymic reference to Africa. Moreover, Balboa is exceptional among Guinean poets of his generation in his affirmation of his native language, Bubi, in the form of bilingual poems such as "Nka lokino [Me dormí (I fell asleep)]" and "N'ne Puacho [Volveré (I will return)]." The notion of exilic return for Balboa has much to do with a return to a lost language as to a mythic continent, the land of a dream, "Mi gran sueño" (My great dream) embodied in the "Unity" of Africa (Ndongo and Ngom 255). The final verse is "¡Creo en ti, Africa!" (I believe in you, Africa!) (255). Thus, remembering Gilroy, the Black Atlantic displacement is for Balboa more than a theme, it is the key to an entire subjectivity: to be African is to be fragmented (exiled from oneself), and *Zion* is not as much a place as a state of being, a condition, which is the focus of chapter 8.

The many and varied "Western" influences on Juan Balboa are representative of both the first wave of emigrants from Equatorial Guinea and the next wave informed by political circumstances. Younger writers will learn much from the ways in which Balboa molded his political frustrations into poetic expression. One of these is Donato Ndongo, the Guinean writer who has made the most extensive contribution to the life-work of exile. Ndongo is the Guinean emixilic model *par excellence.*

CHAPTER FOUR

Donato Ndongo

Model of Emixile

According to Donato Ndongo, in October of 1994, during a period of intense political repression in Equatorial Guinea, he was summoned to the headquarters of the then Secretary of National Security, Manuel Nguema Mba, Teodoro Obiang's uncle, known to be responsible for the incarceration, torture, and death of political dissidents. Mba placed a pistol on his desk and told Ndongo that if he didn't cease "criticizing" the Obiang government, he would be next in line as victim of the dictator's wrath. "If these things speak [indicating the pistol], you will be the next to die." At that time, Ndongo was head of the Africa bureau for the wire service EFE after having left his post as director of the Centro Cultural Hispano-Guineano. Mba's words gave him pause, since the security chief was (and remains) notorious, as evidenced in a piece that appeared in *Harper's* magazine by Ken Silverstein: "On August 22, 1993, Mba and another security official entered a hotel and broke down a door in order to beat Pedro Motú [a political opponent]. They then dragged him down the stairs, put him into a police van, and took him to Malabo prison where, according to the testimony of other people detained in the prison, Motú arrived unconscious. He died without regaining consciousness on the morning of the 23rd" ("Our Friend Teodoro").[1]

Ndongo's criticism of the Obiang regime was based largely on events such as the one described above. Pedro Motú was not the only person to have suffered abuses at that time; Ndongo was intent on reporting these cases as they happened. Recalling this period in his life, he points out that Mba had warned him several times but never until then to the level of a life threat. At that point, the author of *Las tinieblas de tu memoria negra* (*Shadows of Your Black Memory,* Ugarte trans.,) decided that it was time to leave, as much for his own well-being as for an act of personal resistance both to the Obiang regime as to the political, social, and cultural climate of his country since independence. Moreover, this series of events was by no means the only one that sent Donato Ndongo into exile. The threat was a part of a chain of circumstances and incidences ranging from his birth to the present. In this, Ndongo is not unique among exiles. Expatriates rarely leave their country for a single reason or event, as the departure becomes a liminal life-stage defined by what went on before and after. And in Ndongo's life story, as in the case of many Guinean writers, emigration/immigration is an integral part of the narrative.

In many ways, Ndongo falls into the patterns of Equatorial Guinean intellectuals and creative writers. He was sent by his family in 1965 to study in Valencia, Spain, and finish his secondary education. News of the 1968 independence was bittersweet; within months, the Macías "años de silencio" (years of silence) had begun to take their toll as news of the oppression—much of which was word of mouth—trickled into Spain. The Franco government, with Manuel Fraga Iribarne as minister of information and tourism, had devised a policy of classifying all information concerning Equatorial Guinea in the immediate years following independence, a policy known as "materia reservada" (classified information). Thus, the first of many exilic decisions was made: Ndongo would stay in Spain to do what he could to distribute information about his country. In 1969, he began his studies at the University of Barcelona (Central) with a concentration in African History. From 1972 well into the mid-1970s, his activities as a journalist brought him into the fray of the momentous events in Spanish history known as "la transición" (the transition from dictatorship to democracy). He wrote for several Spanish news journals, predominantly *Indice* (Index) and *Mundo Negro* (Black world), the latter of which remains an outlet for his writing today. In 1977, he turned some of his journalistic work on Equatorial Guinea into a book, *Historia y tragedia de Guinea Ecuatorial* (History and tragedy of Equatorial Guinea), which was at that time the only published information on the carnage of the Macías regime, due to the Spanish government's policy of "materia reservada."

In the 1970s and 1980s, Ndongo spent most his effort writing about Africa for the Spanish press: *Indice, Mundo Negro, Diario 16* (Diary 16), *Historia 16* (History 16), *ABC* (a news daily started during the Franco regime and still in publication), and the wire service EFE. During this time, he spent several years as the director of a residence hall close to the University of Complutense de Madrid, Nuestra Señora de África, which made an attempt to accommodate Africans studying in Spain by organizing cultural activities in addition to aid in dealing with Spanish bureaucracy. Dealing with the accommodation of African students was more than an occupation for Ndongo; it reflects his leadership role as an advocate of African issues and rights in Spain, a role that he would later assume as the director of the Hispano-Guinean Cultural Center in Malabo. As a person with firsthand experience with migration from Africa to Europe, he made that experience a collective one. Given the low numbers of Africans living in Spain at that time, the uniqueness of his condition as a Guinean dissident living in Spain made the focus on that activity all the more intense. Indeed, being black in the Spain of the 1970s was something of a "beginning intention" for his writing, as Edward W. Said calls it, a first thought that informs both his individual psyche and his status as a member of a group.

After the 1979 coup with Obiang in power, after returning to Spain from short visits to Niefang to see his family, despite the new dictator's deceptively cynical promise to establish democracy, Ndongo made a quixotic decision to return to his native land definitively in 1985 as the director of the Hispano-Guinean Cultural Center in Malabo (Bioko). That period of his life was filled with turmoil due to his reporting of incidents similar to the one described earlier. When in 1992 he left the cultural center to become a full-time journalist covering African affairs for EFE, a position that made his objections even more visible and hard-hitting for the Obiang regime, his situation in the country became more precarious than it had ever been, so much so that he fled from Malabo to Libreville, Gabon, where he spent another year with EFE before returning to Spain definitively in 1994.

However, for all of Ndongo's journalistic, political, and administrative activity, he has said that his prime desire is to write fiction, and that fiction is informed by his émigré status.[2] Undeniably, his narratives manifest the familiar tensions between politics and an invented reality, politics and its fictional representation, ambivalences felt by many exile writers as well as migrants. A man of political convictions with lasting connections to Spain, among the most important social developments in his life was the dissent of a post–civil war Spanish left, tired of dictatorship and determined to recover a socialist history and social "progress" broken by the war, as well as the movements for independence of former African colonies, in his case, the most important one being his native Equatorial Guinea. The fact that he begins to write fiction in the wake both of *negritude* (as we have seen) as well as the immediate aftermath of Franco allows him a certain distance from those two cultural-political phenomena. It also allows him a way of predicting the pitfalls of the newly achieved self-determinations, both Spain's and Equatorial Guinea's.

Still, Ndongo was and remains a resident of Spain, an African stranger in a familiar land, and as such he is intricately connected to the patterns of

Spanish intellectuals of his time, while remaining unique—other. Not that his fellow writers and friends—Antonio Ferres, Alfonso Grosso, Armando López Salinas, and Juan Madrid, along with a host of socialist politicians such as Alfonso Guerra, Fernando Morán, and Raul Modoro—were not interested in the writing of Aimé Césaire, Léopold Senghor, or Frantz Fanon. Ndongo was exceptional in that circle in the seventies because he was strange: a colonial subject of flesh and bone—we needn't forget skin. His writing manifests that subjectivity on virtually every page.[3]

Writing from the subject position of a black man is uncommon, if not completely absent, in the annals of Spanish literature. Ndongo's texts manifest a postcolonial otherness: he is at once in conflict with the political and social surroundings emanating from Francoism, and he is black. Fanon explored dual alienation in *Black Skin, White Masks,* a work that had a lasting affect on Ndongo:

> For not only must the black man be black; he must be black in relation to the white man. Some critics will take it on themselves to remind us that this proposition has a converse. I say this is false. The black man has no ontological resistance in the eyes of the white man. Overnight the Negro has been given two frames of reference within which he has had to place himself. His metaphysics, or, less pretentiously, his customs and the sources on which they were based, were wiped out because they were in conflict with a civilization that he did not know and that imposed itself on him. (110)

Put another way, like Fanon, Ndongo shares Fanon's sense of double alienation, the "metaphysics" with which he was nurtured, the belief system of his community, on the one hand, and the "civilization" of Spain, on the other. Ndongo could not be more ideologically different from his older fellow writers (Mijero, Ocha'a, Evita, and Jones Mathama), who extol the virtues of that civilization, albeit with a certain amount of tension given their own otherness. Ndongo's "tension," that is, his alienation, is laid bare from the moment he picks up the pen. He is a postcolonial other who presents himself as such and whose friends at "headquarters" profess to consider him the same as they (Lamming).

Nowhere is Ndongo's postcolonial otherness seen more keenly than in some of his early journalistic pieces. From 1972 to 1975, Ndongo wrote a series of six articles for *Indice* on Fanon (1925–61) on the eleventh anniversary of Fanon's death, all with the heading "Pensando en Frantz Fanon" (Thinking about Fanon). These articles are significant in a variety of ways, not only as indicators of Ndongo's changing perceptions (through Fanon) of his own identity as one of relatively few blacks living in Spain at that time but also as lenses through which we can revisit the historical transition in Spain from dictatorship to democracy. The writings of Fanon were circulating among the leftist youth in Europe in the 1960s and early 1970s—from personal experience, I know this was true of the United States as well. The Marxist view of the historical clash between urban workers, agents of revolutionary change, and the bourgeoisie, who would never give up power peacefully, was, with Fanon and others, becoming more complex in the light of colonial realities and the awakening of African yearnings for independence and self-definition. Ndongo's rendition of this historical qualifier as a revision of Marxist politics was not only political, it was personal and literary as well. It was an explanation of the complexities of race to a people—the Spanish—who still considered themselves relatively free of racial dilemmas of the Anglo-Saxon variety as well as a synthesis of global political happenings. These articles at once celebrate the work of a deeply penetrating intellectual and offer direct glimpses of Fanon's observations. Moreover, they manifest themselves in a Spain that at that time viewed itself as relatively free of racial bias: "It is difficult and risky to show the white man how torn one's soul can be when one is living on his turf. . . . How to show this to the farmer, miner or peasant, when for his entire life white culture has been hammered into him? Personally, I can assure that when one arrives into Europe from Africa, one must go through mental maneuvers to get beyond the conceptions that whites have instilled and to assimilate other new ones that other white people have tried to infuse" ("3. Pensando en Frantz Fanon, Fanon y el racismo" [Thinking about Fanon: Fanon and racism] 42).

These words, written in a year of political turmoil and protest against the Franco regime (1973), reflect, perhaps unwittingly, one of the crucial questions brought to the fore by the post–World War II (Marxist) left: the relationship between race and class in the struggle against oppression. Ndongo, again unwittingly, appeals to a sense of responsibility toward the other in his reading of Fanon. Assimilation and acceptance of the postulates that "whites have instilled" in an alien world are predicated on sameness, an erasure of the other. It is not as much that Ndongo, with Fanon as his ally, has prescribed a notion of African authenticity, as would the proponents of negritude. Rather, he points out how complex (if not precarious) the notion of solidarity against oppression can be when one side does not see the difference of the other.

Interestingly, Ndongo's writings on Africa for *Indice* were not only explications (personal and political) of Fanon's life and writings, they took on a topic of intense interest to Spaniards of the mid-seventies: the rebellion in Portuguese Africa initiated by General António de Spínola and a group of high-ranking colonial military personnel tired of quelling armed independence movements in Angola, Mozambique, and Guinea-Bissau, wars that were draining mainland Portuguese citizens economically and politically. This military rebellion led to the Portuguese "transition" from dictatorship to democracy just one year prior to that of Spain. Ndongo covered these events with precision, sangfroid, and, most of all, with an understanding of African history uncommon among Spanish journalists, their leftist inclinations notwithstanding. This was not surprising given Ndongo's own history, but what went unexplored (perhaps understandably given the Spanish situation) was his insistence that Spínola and the liberal generals were not as much interested in African liberation as they were in saving Portugal from economic collapse, a view that harkens back to Fanon's criticisms of the harsh consequences of African independence achieved through negotiation instead of a struggle (at times violent) in which the general populace participates. Ndongo wrote, "The main difference between Portugal and France is that the Iberian country is very poor and carries on colonial wars as well as 'the other war' against democracy in the world. Portugal—one cannot deny any longer, when secret reports are now coming to the fore—has supported a denigrating and cruel dictatorship. What Spínola has undertaken is a surgical operation to save his own countrymen" ("La crisis portuguesa" [Portuguese crisis] 24).

Significantly, 1973, the year in which these remarks about Portuguese liberals' real intentions appear, also marks the year of Ndongo's first literary publication. Deeply disturbed about Spain's official policy to censure news of the mass killings and torture that were going on in Equatorial Guinea as the two Iberian nations entered their respective periods of "transition," Ndongo turned to fiction. It seems that fiction served as something of a vehicle out of his desperation over the perils of his country and some family members who were suffering the oppression. Not an escape by any means, fiction, however, served as a way to ponder his own status as an immigrant-exile in Europe. His first piece was short, and it appeared in Camilo José Cela's well-known literary journal, *Papeles de Son Armadans*. After he submitted it, he got no reply from Don Camilo, just a copy of the issue with his story, "El sueño" (The Dream), and thus began his literary career. The narrative is not what one might think; that is, it is not a denunciation of crimes against humanity in the form of a made-up reality; it is far more subtle, more troubling. Its subject matter is something of a prophecy with touches of picaresque humor. It begins in Senegal on the banks of the Casamance River and tells of the epic trip of a young Senegalese man in search of the means to buy enough cows for a dowry: "¿Qué respeto te guardará una mujer por la que no has dado nada?" (What possible respect can you earn from a woman when you haven't paid anything for her?) ("El sueño," Ndongo and Ngom 205; "The Dream" 76). The search takes him first to a neighboring area in "el país mandinga" (Mandinga country) (205; 76), then to the city of Dakar, from there he goes to Las Palmas (Canary Islands) because he is told he can earn money in the Spanish city, then to the mainland (Algeciras), from there to Barcelona by train, and finally across the border into France. His end—his global north—is Paris. In the following passage, he thinks of the second woman he hopes to marry since the first one gave up on him:

> Si Dikate supiera que iba a pasearme por las calles de París, que vería con mis ojos negros la Tour Eiffel, y que visitaría al presidente de la República, y que hablaría con Napoleón. . . . ¡Eso valía más que todas las vacas del mundo! ("El sueño," Ndongo and Ngom 206)

> (If only Dikate knew I would be walking around the streets of Paris, that I'd see the Eiffel Tower with my black eyes, and that I'd get to visit the President of the Republic, and speak to Napoleon. . . . All that was worth more than all the cows in the world.) ("The Dream" 76)

In the manner of Lazarillo, albeit more innocent, this man's story relates an African experience of hardship, an all-too-familiar one given the future world situation—Spain would not begin to see the social ramifications of immigration for at least another decade. Yet, the narrative deals with far more than a typically African hardship. The end is a surprising short-narrative reversal (a la Cortázar) in which the reader discovers that the protagonist's journey has been a dream. This is a fortunate turn of events given that the protagonist is about to drown in a river on the final leg of the trip from the Spanish-French border to Paris. The perilous body of water is not the Casamance: "No sé si oirás, allá en el otro río, el grito de mi muerte" (I don't know if you can hear, over there in the other river; it's my death cry) ("El sueño," Ndongo and Ngom 207); "The Dream" 75–79). As a culmination, the reader discovers that throughout the dream, the protagonist has been at the side of a white woman: "Me desperté. Ella dormía junta a mí. Su semblante era risueño. Sus sueños no eran de la naturaleza de los míos. Sueños de blanca" (I woke up. She was sleeping next to me. Her face smiled. Her dreams were not like mine. They were dreams of a white woman) ("El sueño," Ndongo and Ngom 207; "The Dream" 79).

Fanon has come back to haunt. But in this case, we see the traces of the immigrant Fanon in the form of an all-too-common African man trying to make his way into the "civilized" white world. Here, Ndongo assimilates his readings of Fanon, along with his frustration about the events of his own country, through the words of this young man who can't seem to get enough cows to live happily, because it is clear that if he could, he would not have thought of leaving. But the ending subverts the reader's racial sensibilities, no matter if the reader is black or white. Does this story have a happy end? How could it be otherwise, given the situation? The black man in the form of an autobiographical subject, has awoken to his present reality comfortably resting in bed with a white woman. His dream is "not true": the cows, the nurturing flow of the Casamance followed by the treacherous waters of a European river, his back-breaking work for a dowry, the man who takes his money and passport on the way to France; all this has been an illusion, a nightmare. The "reality" of the story (ironically) is that he lives in a better world, a world in which work and determination pay off.

"El sueño" might be juxtaposed with the first paragraphs of the chapter of Fanon's *Black Skin* titled "The Man of Color and the White Woman":

> Out of the blackest part of my soul, across the zebra striping of my mind, surges this desire to be suddenly *white*.
>
> I wish to be acknowledged not as black but as *white*.
>
> Now—and this is a form of recognition that Hegel had not envisaged—who but a white woman can do this for me? By loving me she proves that I am worthy of white love. I am loved like a white man. (63; emphasis in original)

Ndongo is acutely aware of Fanon's irony not only in this story with an ironically happy end but also in his more literal reading of Fanon for his (predominantly white) readers:

> Fanon speaks of the black who wants to whiten himself at all costs. This desire cannot be realized by itself; moreover, its realization is impossible in the country of origin, given the colonial structure. Only the blacks who have crossed the border: as the Americans say, has the opportunity. Who is able to realize the miracle? Who better than a white woman? ("4. Pensando en Frantz Fanon" 44)

One wonders, however, if Ndongo's deceptively simple story has not gone beyond both Fanon's brutally honest depiction, albeit ironic, in *Black Skin* of social/racial relations as well as his own celebration of that depiction in his article. Does the protagonist "desire to be suddenly white"? As he yearns to see the Eiffel Tower and to speak to the president (perhaps even Napoleon), the humorous tone, as in any picaresque narrative, may belie that very yearning. Perhaps the underlying issue in this story, in addition to the notion of the white mask of prosperity, is the very existence of race as an empirical-biological reality. Does the reader know the race of the man whose dream is told? Do we know the race of the woman at his side? "Sueños de blanca" (Dreams of a white woman) may point to a wish, Fanon's notion of the "desire to be white" in contrast to those of the dreamer who feels the terror of being black. James Baldwin said, "As long as you think you're white, there is no hope for you" (*Price of the Ticket*). Out of context, these words could have been added to Fanon's chapter on sexuality in the black man-white woman relationship as a warning to blacks who seek power by becoming white. Yet, the "you" in Baldwin's famous dictum refers to white people.[4] Given Ndongo's circumstances as one of very few blacks writing in Spain in the 1970s, the possibility of the dreamer of his story being white is not inconceivable. Remarkably, Fanon's *Peau noire, masques blancs* was translated into Spanish as *¡Escucha, blanco!* (Listen, Whitey!). This unfortunate translation is an indication of the Spanish naiveté regarding questions of race regardless of the political sophistication. Ndongo's story, on the other hand, is in many ways another commentary on Fanon's work: it is as much about the construction of race as colonialism. In keeping with the double consciousness of the colonial and postcolonial subject, it is a story that challenges (intellectually, ethically, politically) facile perceptions as the same time as it denounces the idea of the European domination of Africa and all its aftermath.[5]

Clearly, along with the complexities of the construction of race, Ndongo's lasting concern in his fiction has been colonialism and its "dark" idea. Yet, perhaps due to the very power of this "idea" as it continued to manifest itself in Equatorial Guinea in its post-independence—one dictatorship followed by another of virtually the same ilk—it took Ndongo some time to publish his first full-length novel, *Las tinieblas de tu memoria negra* (1987), followed by *Los poderes de la tempestad* (The powers of the tempest) (1997), two volumes of a trilogy, the third of which has yet to be written. As "El sueño" shows, there is a need in Ndongo to maintain his distance between the political reality of postcolonial Equatorial Guinea, the development of events, the policies, the agents of its history, and the specific victims covered in his journalism and historical essays, on the one hand, and their symbolic representation, on the other. Thus, the notion of exilic memory of these realities, its haziness, the ethical questions it poses along with the issue of remembrance as a reliable tool to explore the colonial past, all come under intense scrutiny in these two novels.[6]

Typical of many émigré writers, Ndongo's narratives have gotten more attention outside of Spain than within. The de rigueur reviews in the Spanish press have appeared, but the more-penetrating articles of literary criticism on his work and sections of books have been mainly among academics working in areas of the world other than Spain (Fra-Molinero, Lewis, López Rodríguez, Ngom, Mengue, Nsue Otong, Otabela, Price, Zielina, Ugarte). It is perhaps an unstated opinion among academic critics of Spanish literature working in Spain or for cultural journals and supplements to news dailies that the very notion of a national literature of Equatorial Guinea is at best strange if it exists at all. Ndongo himself has referred to this possibility and has done a great deal to counter it by fomenting the production and the study of poetry, narrative, and drama from his country. Spanish dismissal of the very notion of Equatoguinean letters notwithstanding, Ndongo's writing, in all its double consciousness, bridges the semantic, social, and cultural divide between exile and emigration within a postcolonial perspective. With this issue in mind, the critique, albeit fictional, of Spanish colonialism and its aftermath is crucial. Indeed, Ndongo has expressed a certain indebtedness to one of Western literature's foundational texts of the workings of colonialism, *Heart of Darkness*.[7] As much through his fiction as through his essays, as a postcolonial subject trying with difficulty to convey his dilemma to the residents of the "civilized world," he submits that an understanding of today's blurring of national borders must involve the former realities of the colonies.

Tinieblas is first of all a bildungsroman, the story of a boy growing into manhood during the last years of Spain's colonial rule in Equatorial Guinea, and as he does so, the Spanish presence seems ubiquitous. Spain looms not only in terms of characters who represent Spanish institutions (the Church, the plantation economy) but also as a migratory destination of the protagonist: the yearned-for place that represents a life victory. In that regard, *Tinieblas* is also a book of memories: in the present of the narrative, the boy is grown and living in Spain as the reader moves constantly between Spain and Africa along with the narrator and the protagonist. The memories are themselves an exploration of how he arrived at the land that has become the object of all the tensions, quandaries, disquiet, and understated anger that fuel his introspection. It is tempting to read the novel as an autobiography, or at least as a narrative rendition of some of the most salient events in the author's life. When asked, however, Ndongo submits that his text is not autobiographical recreation of his life (Ugarte, "Interview" 231). It is only autobiographical in the sense that any text is not only a self-reflection of the author but also a rendering of his or her psyche. Still, it goes beyond the story of one individual in a unique set of circumstances; the narrator-protagonist's very identity is collective. Spain has made it so: the ongoing relationship between the Peninsula and Equatorial Guinea, between the life in the new land and life left behind, between the colonial subject and the colonizers, between the authorities (political and cultural) and the citizen, between the self and its other, all these interactions come to the fore in his fiction.

Two worlds are constantly juxtaposed in *Tinieblas,* not unlike the framework of the famed novel by Chinua Achebe—another emixilic African writer—in which "things" refer to an existence before the arrival of the Europeans, for as "things fall apart," Achebe's reader witnesses the collapse of a way of life, indeed the fall of "civilization." In this novel, we observe that collapse in the form of a subtle coercion of a boy into the priesthood and away from his tradition in deference both to the colonizers and to his father and mother, who are devout Catholics who have been well taught about the needed advancement (economic, moral, technological) of their native land. Fanon would say the protagonist's parents have been taught to wear white masks. Yet, throughout the novel, we find hints of resistance, which is, after all, the motive for the memories. Tío Abeso, a revered uncle and something of a counter-mentor to the boy, does not speak Spanish, he is a polygamist, he believes in the power of the tribe's ancestors rather than in Christ or any of the colonizers' deities, and he insists on providing his precocious nephew with the rituals that are the steps to manhood, including circumcision. In one of these memorable juxtapositions, there is an elaborate stream-of-consciousness description of the boy's circumcision followed in the next chapter by a more straightforward narrative leading to the protagonist's First Communion (chapters 2 and 3), all of which are remembered within the frame of the protagonist's present surroundings: again, Spain is present in these memories even when it is absent.

Remarkably, in what might go down in the annals of Spanish literary history as the definitive refutation of the Christian belief system, we see a cosmological debate between the protagonist's Christian mentor, Father Ortiz, and Tío Abeso; the former believes it is his apostolic mission to convert the latter due to his influence over the tribe, while the latter listens patiently and asks questions; and the questions win the debate. The impertinence of Tío Abeso, his daring to ask the priest if he abided by that Christian duty to be fruitful and multiply only exasperates Father Ortiz (*Tinieblas* 94). Yet, the protagonist's uncle does not let up: "Would you be telling me all this now if your mother and father were like you?" (*Shadows* 88).

Crucial in this cosmic, albeit humorous, debate is the presence of the narrator, whose role is to translate the questions and responses since neither of the two competitors speaks the language of his rival, his other. Similarly, it is the otherness of the narrator that is the force that defamiliarizes the Catholic practice of celibacy for priests, as the lad compares it to the practice of polygamy, through the encounter with Tío Abeso. Yet, it is a defamiliarization from both sides—Africa and Spain—from a man who, at the time that the memory is being recorded, is intimately cognizant of both belief systems. An interesting comparison is an equally hilarious scene in Achebe's *Things*

Fall Apart: there is an encounter between African Ibo villagers and recently arrived missionaries. The interpreter, although Ibo, speaks a dialect "harsh to the ears of Mbanta" [the village] and mistakes the word *myself* for *my buttocks:* "Your buttocks understand our language" (Achebe 102), says one of the villagers as he ridicules the translator's role as intermediary. Indeed, cultural understanding (or misunderstanding) is at the heart of the episode, for in Achebe's epic novel, this is the people of Mbanta's first glimpse of a white man, who, as the scene unfolds, proceeds to denigrate their entire belief system by asserting, "Your gods are not gods at all." When this was interpreted to the men of Mbanta, they broke into derisive laughter: "These men must be mad, they said to themselves" (Achebe 103). In the authorial voices of Achebe and Ndongo as formerly colonial subjects living in the land of the colonizers, both narrative episodes convey satirically the tensions within the eyes of native Africans on the Christianization of their land, all in a series of ridiculously incongruous intrusions.

Yet, if *Tinieblas* stopped here, if it were merely a series of these juxtapositions that serve as arguments in favor of the existence of an intricate African belief system and a "civilization" before the construction of Catholic chapels in Ecuatorial Guinea, Ndongo might be seen as the Spanish proponent of "negritude." Yet, as we have seen, the author is more interested in questioning the workings of power than celebrating indigenous customs and beliefs in all their blackness. "Blackness" along with the weight that concept carries with it is more complex than a nationalist celebration of identity. Notwithstanding Ndongo's critique of *negritude,* the title of this first novel comes from a poem by black nationalist pioneer Léopold Senghor, "Pour Emma Payellerville l'infirmière" (For Emma Payellerville, nurse), a tribute to a white nurse attending to black patients:

> Ton nom brisera les bronzes poudreux des gouverneurs
> . . .
> Sous ton visage lumineux, au carrefour des cœurs noirs
> Gardé jalousement par les ténèbres fidèles
> De leur mémoire noire.
>
> (Your name will shatter the powdery bronze of governments
> Beneath your luminous face, at the crossroads of black souls
> Jealously kept by the loyal shadows
> of their black memory.)
>
> (*Chants d'ombre* 27–28)

Yet, in many ways Ndongo's novel subverts the celebratory tone of Senghor's poem by juxtaposing the image of this innocent white woman ("Ta couleur de lait et d'enfant" [Your color of milk and child]) whose name will be enshrined in the memory of the blacks she looked after with that of a not-so-innocent Spanish priest.

Also crucial and unsettling in Ndongo's novel is the hybridity of the protagonist. Unlike the notion of racial mixing found elsewhere in Senghor's writing that posits the mixture as an ideal, in *Tinieblas* the lasting and defining influences of Spanish culture are explored as parts of an ongoing history. The reader witnesses growing disaffection from the colonizing culture on the part of the protagonist, a man formed by that very culture. In the last scene, as the boy observes a black man who rows the canoe that transports him and Father Ortiz to the ship that will eventually take them to the seminary, he points out that he cannot understand the black man's language because he comes from a different ethnic group. Even more disturbing is that he can understand the priest but not the black man: "y entendiste al padre y no entendiste al combe o bujeba" (*Tinieblas* 164) (and you understood the priest and not the combe or bujeba [*Shadows* 156]). While there is a rupture between the protagonist and his upbringing in this culminating scene, it does not make for a clean break; it suggests that any willing act of a separation from one's past may never be realized without a trace of that past. Thus, the lines of Senghor's poem seem deliberately taken out of context: what stands out in the novel is the history of that black memory.

While there are no draconian colonial figures in *Tinieblas,* colonization hovers above the setting. Father Ortiz, no matter how individually well intentioned (or "cariñosamente impertinente" [11]) (with loving impertinence [*Shadows* 3]), as the narrator first describes him, comes to represent the entire enterprise of colonialism. His annoyance with Abeso, his touch of pride, and his condescending interaction with the natives all humanize him, rendering his enterprise of conversion, in essence an act of cosmic destruction, within our reach. In the humanization of Father Ortiz, readers see how it might be possible for us, black and white, to participate in colonialist "othering." The characters (again black and white) participate as well, including the protagonist, who at one point actually dreams of becoming the priest who will baptize Tío Abeso, a scene worthy of a painting by El Greco (*Tinieblas* 34–35). Such fantasy is more than that of a boy with delusions of grandeur: it pinpoints the ambivalences of postcolonial exile and emigration, a search for independence in which there is an internal dialogue between self and other, white and black.

A more vivid picture of postcolonialism comes with the second novel, *Los poderes de la tempestad.* From the seemingly benign domination of Father Ortiz, his black cassock flapping in the wind as he scoots from village to village on his motorbike, we turn to something darker in the second. The object of the postcolonial critique this time is a character who might be seen as Ortiz's bastard son, "papá Mesie me Nguema Biyogo Ñegue Ndong" (24) better known to Spanish speakers as Francisco Macías. The typically exilic denunciations of the state of affairs that set off the departure are present on virtually every page of this second volume of the trilogy, with the same narrator-protagonist setting the tone. While Equatorial Guinea depicted in *Tinieblas* signals a nostalgic past—the lushness of the bush, the community of belief, a Catholicism syncretically mixed with traditional animism, flawed characters, objects of satire such as Don Ramón, the well-intentioned black schoolteacher who instills in his students what sounds like a parody of Francoist ideology—that same country of remembrance in *Los poderes de la tempestad* is all in ruins with the tempest of the postcolony. In this second stage of exile, the promise of return, it is clear that the lengthy stay in the colonizing country has served no purpose other than the awareness of a horrific situation.

In terms of the narrative technique, absent is the stream-of-consciousness dreamlike sequences of *Tinieblas,* the exuberance of prophetic visions, such as the old woman who appears several times in the protagonist's rapture during ritual experiences. The narrative motivation of *Los poderes* is that of indignation in the face of cruelty, political oppression, and all in the figure of an all-too-typical African dictator: descriptions of a series of horrific events beginning with the arrival on the island of the mixed-race family, an arrival filled with expectation and the naive idealism of the Spanish-educated Guinean lawyer who wants to participate in the development of his country. *Los poderes* is the story of a return to the mythical country of origin only to find the myth shattered. Upon his arrival, the protagonist is met by the personnel of a police state who frisk him, steal from him, and sexually assault his wife. The hope of landing a job that would lead to progressive reforms turns into pathos considering the country's state of affairs. The presence of his wife and child constantly remind him of his own otherness both within the country of his previous residence and the one he departed with Father Ortiz. The nation-as-prison metaphor is a particularly pervasive and intensifies throughout the novel, culminating in an epic escape from captivity, surprising only in that the protagonist, that innocent boy who dreamed of being a priest in the initial novel, does not die in the sequel.

Indeed, the representation of a concrete political "reality" is of paramount importance to Ndongo in this novel. Like *Tinieblas,* it is written from Spain; thus, memory is again a crucial factor in the construction of the novel and the marker of the protagonist's double consciousness. Yet, in *Los poderes,* exilic memory takes on a more concrete role: that of the eyewitness. In one of many detailed, graphic sequences, the protagonist, Angeles, Rut, and Lino (an old schoolmate) are walking along the Avenida de la Independencia in Malabo (the capital) when they observe the brutal death of a drunkard run down by a Mercedes Benz carrying the president to his luxurious residence (126–27). In another, on their way by bus from Bata (Río Muni) to the protagonist's unnamed town of origin—the setting for much of the previous novel—they are stopped by government militia and forced to witness the mass execution of ninety prisoners.

Here, the reader witnesses a horrific scene in which the lieutenant in charge of the executions repeats his actions nine times, killing ten people at a time as their family members watch: "one by one . . . the militiamen gathered the cadavers with rare diligence and threw them forcefully into the bed of the truck as a new line of prisoners was formed, another ten and another ten" (171; my translation). The second-person narrative ends the scene by drawing attention to the act of witnessing: "you saw how furtive tears streamed down" the cheeks of the family members (171; my translation). In this last phrase, the voice of the *I-you* manifests an African uniqueness (otherness) in Ndongo's storytelling. While the incidents he describes in this novel are rendered with the objectivism of an eyewitness, similar, one might say, to that of Rigoberta Menchú's first-person accounts of her life in Guatemala, in *Los poderes,* the testimony is embedded in a fiction that draws attention to the act of "seeing." "Viste" (You saw) is uttered by an inner voice not only directed to the protagonist (as in a Juan Goytisolo narrative), but it is also the community of victims as well who sees, the perspective of communal watching, a community of eyes. That the community of eyes might include those of the reader is yet another marker of Ndongo's exilic discourse of and about the other. Those of us who recall *Tinieblas* witness in *Los poderes* a return to the town of origin now in ruins: virtually all the lively characters of *Tinieblas* are now anything but lively—they are defeated, sick, skeletal. The thought that in the previous novel it would be the protagonist's role to "bring back the splendor of the tribe" (46) adds a certain urgency to the present of *Los poderes.* The narrator has forced us to watch (to testify to) the ruins of this "splendor," not only as a consequence of Spanish colonialism but now also of a more urgent reality, urgent not only because it is worse but because it is self-inflicted.

Here lies postcolonialism in all its "horror," as Fanon suggests in *Black Skins:* many of the winners of independence exceed the abuses of the colonizers. Their white masks are the force behind their horrific deeds; almost as an act of mimicry, those in control of the Equatorial Guinea depicted in

Los poderes commit heinous crimes against humanity. Whiteness/blackness is under constant scrutiny in this novel, not only because of the constant presence of the mixed-race couple and its offspring but also because of the descriptive psychological disquisition on the part of the narrator. Already, in the previous novel, the protagonist's mother (and indirectly his father) had considered the choice of a white woman as wife as a rejection of family and customs, and this reality is hardly ever out of view in the next novel. The entire ideological justification of those in power, an ideology clearly seen as harmful by the narrative voice, is to rid the "liberated" land of any trace of whiteness, that is, the Spanish influence, for in Equatorial Guinea, Spanish means white. This inward and outward racial conflict is seen from the very beginning of the novel when the family enters the country from Spain. As the military authorities check the family's passports, one of the authorities, an illiterate man, offers a political explanation of what he is doing:

> "¿Qué clase de pasaporte es éste?" me interpeló, siempre en fang.
>
> "Es un pasaporte español," aseguró el primero que había hablado. "Se ve que la señora es española."
>
> "Aquí no paña, oyes?" soltó enfurecido, el miliciano analfabeto en su castellano, como para que lo oyera Angeles. "Paña explotarnos dos siglos y ya somos independensia y expulsá de suelo patrio grasias a honorable y gran camarada y líder de asero su eselensia Mesie me Nguema Biyogo Ñegue Ndong." (30)

> ("What kind of passport is this?" he asked me, always in Fang.
>
> "It's a Spanish passport," the first speaker assured. "Seems the missus is white."
>
> "Listen here, no Spain," the illiterate militiaman uttered furiously in his Spanish so that Angela would hear. "Spain exploited us for two centuries and now we have independence and we threw them off our country's soil, thanks to honorable comrade and iron leader his excellence Mesie me Nguema Biyogo Ñegue Ndong.") (my translation)

Yet, at the same time, while these ideological pronouncements seem worse than wrongheaded, their underlying force penetrates the protagonist's consciousness throughout. The I-you protagonists asserts that he, too, feels guilty for adopting the manners of the whites, and this guilt, he submits "now constructs an impregnable wall between you and your people" (58; my translation). But this is not the only instance of guilt on the part of the protagonist. At another point, he turns away from his wife and child as all-too-vivid reminders of his own white mask: "I would have preferred that she, that neither of them [including the daughter] were at my side . . . a white woman who was my wife" (175; my translation). The political-psychological discourse of this novel is based firmly on Fanon's interrogations of whiteness and blackness, and it is at the center of Ndongo's exilic-migratory prose.

Fanon's sexual politics are also explored by Ndongo in this novel as yet another postcolonial representation of reality. One of the most memorable characters in *Los poderes* is a strange figure: a militia woman, Ada, who incarnates a certain sexual pathology rooted in racism and postcolonialism. Ada is the one responsible for the sexual assault of Angeles in the first scenes of the novel through an aggressive, if not grotesque, body search; later, she engages in a similar act in relation to the protagonist, an uncommon scene—not only in this novel but in any novel—in which a man is raped by a woman. After the protagonist suffers a tortuous interrogation by male militia members, Ada takes over; first she tries to arouse him sexually, and when she is unable, she removes her clothes, straddles his face, and achieves orgasm. One might ask how the rape is even possible in reality, let alone in a novel, yet the answer might be found in Fanon's masks: Ada is a black woman wearing the mask of the white male colonizer-rapist, a figure anything but uncommon both in reality and in fiction. Immediately prior to the rape, Ada affirms her politics to her prisoner, again something of an ideological parody of *negritude*: "'Nosotros somos africanos, abogado, somos negros. Nuestro mundo es otro, y debemos dejar a los blancos con sus cosas'" (257) (We are African, Mr. Lawyer, we are African. Our world is another one, and we should leave the whites to their own things.) Moreover, the protagonist's reaction to the rape, inadvertently to the ideology in all its hypocrisy, is as physical as the rape itself: not only is Ada's attempt to arouse him a failure, he vomits (257–60), a scene reminiscent of an episode in *Tinieblas* when the boy-protagonist throws up after being forced by a priest to eat a centipede-infested yucca (123). Indeed, both are bodily responses to colonialism insofar as their physicality has the effect of a reflex unmasking the whiteness. Ndongo, through Ada and the physical response to her, has extended Fanon's description of racial sexual politics by exposing the militia woman's black mask ("somos negros") (we are black) as an ideological justification for the whiteness of her behavior.[8]

Yet, for all the "horror" depicted in this novel, a "witnessing" novel par excellence, from the perspective of the ambivalences of exile and emigration, even more salient is the bridge it has attempted to construct between the author's country of origin and the adopted environs of his new nation, "new" in relation to his colonial past. Again, while there are aspects of *Los poderes* that suggest autobiographical intentions, the protagonist who marries a Spanish woman, has a child with her in Spain, and idealistically (nationalistically) returns to the newly "liberated" homeland is not a facsimile of the author or his life story. However, both *Tinieblas* and *Los poderes* do manifest another type of self-representation, a communal one. The voice of both narratives is collective both in its use of the second person and in its incarnation of the recent history of the native land. The vicissitudes of that land, its tenuous, intimate, nefarious, and dependent relationship to the old world of conquest and domination, lie at the core of the construction of both novels. Ndongo's identity, the essentialism of *negritude* notwithstanding, is part of his aesthetic posture as well as his ethical one. While identity itself, as an issue, is at the crux, it is never static. The presence of the other informs it, always looming above the collective author both as an exile and as an emigrant/immigrant.

The convergences of exile and emigration/immigration will be further issues of exploration as discussed next in Ndongo's writing in his next epic narrative, *El metro* (The Subway).

CHAPTER FIVE

El metro (The Subway)

Saga of the African Emigrant

To twenty-first-century Spaniards living in a city with a metro system, the following situation is familiar: a black man of indeterminate age carrying an enormous sack and a suitcase enters a subway car and stands toward the rear even though there are several seats unoccupied. His shade of blackness is deep, a blacker shade of black, almost purple, a darkness that highlights the whites of his large eyes. The predominantly Spanish-speaking passengers avoid staring at the man, notwithstanding a certain repressed desire to do so, as their brown, blue, hazel, and green eyes are blankly focused on what is immediately in front of them (as in all subway cars in motion from Los Angeles to Beijing) only to shift ever so discreetly toward the only "negro" in the car. Some barely notice him, seemingly more attentive to their own realities or those of the people they are traveling with than to those of the black man, such as, perhaps, a couple whose arms are wrapped around one another. The black man is wearing an orange cap whose visor shields his eyes as he gazes at his feet, faded and unwashed denim trousers, and a white T-shirt, too large for his average male physique, with the words "Chicago Bulls" on the front in block two-toned (red and white) letters that are framed by the horns of an angry-looking bull. His sneakers are old, the laces worn, and his socks threadbare and equally faded, most certainly filled with holes under the canvas footwear, although there is no visible evidence of the holiness. The subway riders do not know the contents of the sack at his feet or the suitcase, however they surmise it is filled with items for sale typical of subway station merchandise—sunglasses, CDs, T-shirts, toys, chewing gum, candy, cigarettes, mostly trinkets manufactured in any locale other than the one in which the black man resides at the present moment.

At the turn of the twentieth to the twenty-first century in Spain, it is striking how common this scene has become and others like it in any Iberian city modern and populated enough to have constructed an underground transport system, even a city as distant from Africa and as culturally homogeneous as Bilbao. And in relatively large concentrations of population without an underground transportation, such as Murcia or Almería, this very black man or a reasonable facsimile is likely to appear on a bus or walking down a crowded street on his way to work. It is often "illegal" work since the man probably arrived in the host city illegally. The moment this man spreads out his blanket to display his merchandise on a sidewalk or in a much frequented park such as Madrid's Retiro, having sighted a policeman on patrol, the items that constitute the black man's livelihood will disappear with lightning speed into the large white sack and suitcase. The man will also disappear into the crowd, as he tries desperately, although unsuccessfully, to become invisible among all the homogeneously white faces. It is these white faces, faces with their own conflictive histories and class backgrounds, faces of men, women, and children who must contend with the presence of this black man, this black migrant other, for in some ways, he is an intruder into their respective worlds. He seems to appear out of nowhere. The face-to-face encounter with the other, in this case the African other, is one of the mainstays of Spanish consciousness in the age of globalization, and it is the subject of much debate in a variety of contexts.

Much has been said in the previous chapters on emigration and exile but relatively little on immigration. While the Spanish news media have become intensely interested in the subject for the past few decades, rarely is the topic approached from the subject position of the emigrant/immigrant. Again, emigration/immigration has much to do with perspective as well as with the supposed authenticity, or lack thereof, of the accounts that describe the lives of immigrants in the new home. In his narrative of one man's journey out of Africa and into Europe, *El metro* (2007), the Guinean writer Donato Ndongo provides not only an antidote to the apparent silence of immigrant voices in the mainstream of Spanish thought but also an interrogation of that very notion of authenticity. This novel's unique perspective, however, is by no means isolated from the constant debates in Spain concerning immigration in a variety of contexts: newspaper reports, television documentaries, editorials, films, political speeches, laws proposed in Spanish parliament. It might be said that the incessant Spanish discussions about the new arrivals serves as one of the novel's central, albeit unstated, contexts.

Spain is seen not only by its own citizens but also by Africans as a gateway nation, a stepping stone for migrants to move illegally from Africa to Europe. From Felipe González's Socialist Party (PSOE) administration (1982–96) through José María Aznar's eight-year presidency to the return to power of the PSOE in 2004, many initiatives have been made to curb immigration in the form of physical, political, and cultural controls, including entering into agreements with Senegal and Morocco that restrict and/or normalize migrations to Spain from Africa. In what symbolically might be called the construction of another medieval "fortress" to repel invaders, the late twentieth and early twenty-first centuries saw the creation of many barriers including barbed-wire fences as detainment centers for people who had entered Spain illegally, preventing the Arab hordes from reentering the Peninsula (Agrela, "Spain" 13). These detainment centers, illegal crossings, and arrivals of new people, cultures, and religions have made for a lively, at times vitriolic, discussion on what amounts to the relationship of self to other. Indeed, what we perhaps too often call "Spanish national character" is now placed squarely in the fold of the relations of the self with and versus the other.

This discussion, however, is all too often monological; it lacks an essential side of the encounter with the other, or, as Emmanuel Levinas would say, an encounter always already in process from the moment we are born. The face-to-face relationship with the other presupposes a convergence of two faces with two histories, two sets of circumstances in all their complexity, contradictions, and plurality. Yet, the convergence presently in operation in the Spain of globalized economic and social realities, for the most part, only acknowledges the complexities of the host society. As seen in the introduction, the essays on African immigration into Spain by Mikel Azurmendi serve as a model for this one-sidedness, even though his stated intentions are quite the opposite: he is unequivocally in favor of integration, a word that for him represents both an ideal of coexistence in the age of globalization and a political program. Moreover, Azurmendi's views on immigration are representative of what many Spaniards ponder as they face this relatively recent reality. Typical of many Spanish voices, he is highly critical of "multiculturalism," as it leads, in his view, to the disintegration of society and to the lack of a communal spirit among citizens as well as to suspicion and resentment toward the other. When his discourse shifts from impressions of social problems to political philosophy, as it does every now and then, Jürgen Habermas's notion of democratic pluralism and the modern state is Azurmendi's foundational political and philosophical principle.[1]

As the introduction to the current volume discusses, Azurmendi, in his book, *Estampas de El Ejido* (Vignettes of El Ejido), offers a response to the anti-immigrant riots that occurred in this agricultural town in the province of Almería in 2000 by offering a practical solution to the problems of immigration: the immigrant must adopt, as soon after his or her arrival as possible, the culture, religion, ethnicity, and language of the new home:

> The real triumph of the African immigrant can only come about through his ability to change as a person and culturally overcome his pipedream of remaining in his tribal role. Unless he decides to return to his country of origin at the first possibility. This is not frequent, since the frustration he suffers keeps alive his desire to stay until he can amass what is necessary to go back home forever. Thus his integration into the new Europe is felt as less and less necessary since Europe is persistently hostile. This frustration opens paths to resentment and hatred toward Spain that can cause a certain slip into xenophobia. However, when the immigrant decides to establish a home and regroup his family within the new situation, he is taking the first positive—although not definitive—step against frustration. (303–4)

In a related work, *Todos somos nosotros* (We are all) (2003), Azurmendi furthers his arguments by alluding to the benefits of a break with the traditions that shaped the immigrant's culture before he or she emigrated:

> That they have come to us to better themselves also indicates in and of itself that they have already accomplished a certain break with the structures of traditions that force them to wait for someone or some mysterious force to ameliorate the harsh conditions of life in their land. To emigrate is already a great indication of cultural change, since it signifies the undertaking of life with hope, an opening of life to an uncertain, albeit better, future, coming from a certain individual audaciousness. (164)

Here again, the center of Azurmendi's notion of integration is modernity. Emigration is good for the emigrant because it represents a desire to be modern, to reject antiquated forms of life that have led to deprivation and oppression ("his pipedream of remaining in his tribal role," "traditions that force them to wait for someone or some mysterious force"). Both works, *Estampas* and *Todos somos nosotros,* analyze the social realities of migration from the perspective of an economically developed European center that provides the framework of understanding of those realities and thereby provide solutions. Curiously, perhaps incongruously, both works are also filled with anecdotes involving personal histories of flesh and bone, immigrants whose life situations confirm the author's arguments. Indeed, it is the desire to be modern, to become part of a modern society, an admirable wish in and of itself, that provides the impulse for Africans to embark on such precarious journeys out of the old land and into the new. Residents of the host countries should celebrate such desires and not rebuff them.

Yet, this treatment of immigration (the consequence of "emixile") too often deals disproportionately with the problems of the receiver society. As Azurmendi defends his position, he neglects the notions of critical thought that have made "multiculturalism" a prominent topic of discussion in a variety of places and contexts throughout the world. He does not consider immigration as an issue extending beyond European borders into the deepest reaches of Africa. Spain for him is, as for many Spaniards and Europeans, a fortress nation that protects the global north from the global south much as it was in the Middle Ages during the reign of the Visigoths. It needs a political will to fend off the "threat," as in Lucassen's *Immigrant Threat.* Indeed, Africa represents antimodernity, and, as such, it is either neglected or criticized as something undesirable whose population is made up of potential "illegals"; it is, in the final analysis, a place to abandon and forget. Again, as I have insisted throughout this book, the remedy for this neglect is to consider these immigrants, such as the black man who has intruded into the metro car, as exiles.

Ndongo's novel offers a variety of ways in which African immigrants to Spain might be seen as subjects forced from their land. The protagonist of *El metro,* Lambert Obama Ondo, a Cameroonian member of the Yendjok clan in the rural area of Mbalmayo thirty kilometers (about eighteen miles) south of Yaunde, must contend from the beginning of the novel with the exile from his traditions. The dialogue between tradition and modernity, at times a hostile one, pulling and pushing the protagonist along his journey, is felt on virtually every page. The consequence is the story of a man in exile from his homeland, his family, his village, and his way of life, an exile who eventually becomes an immigrant-intruder on the borderline of legality, much like the man I described in the opening of this chapter. Moreover, one may contend that it is the loss of traditions and the subsequent struggle both with and against modernity that serves as the unifying motif of the entire novel.

The story of *El metro* takes place on two continents and in several locales within both. As the setting of the novel moves from borderline to borderline, these geographical spaces provide the narrative's plot structure. The physical transitions from one place to another are not new to Ndongo's prose, as we have seen in "El Sueño," the story that initiated Ndongo's literary career thirty years prior to *El metro*. Lambert, the protagonist, decides to move from the Cameroonian village where he was born to the city of Yaunde; from there across the first national border to Dakar, Senegal, where he works to save enough African francs to buy an illegal trip to Europe through the machinations of "La Red" (the web, something like a syndicate of smugglers); then to Casablanca, Morocco; from there to El Aaïun in Western

Sahara, Morocco, where he embarks on a typically harrowing voyage via a "patera" (or motorized canoe) and arrives barely alive on the shores of Arrecife, a city on the island of Lanzarote, the Canary Islands. The arrival at the Canaries offers an apt transition from Africa to Spain at a little over the novel's midway point. This liminal midpoint is significant: it is at once symbolic of the longed-for destination as well as the convergence of the two continents. It is an ironic arrival, however, since Lambert's life journey must now continue within the confines of Spanish (European) sovereignty. The Canary Islands provide a liminal space between Africa and Europe, at once a real and imagined "thirdspace," as Edward Soja theorizes, whose politics and culture are Spanish yet whose geography is as African as are the many other islands that line the west coast of that other continent.[2]

As the journey continues, Lambert moves on from Arrecife to the Spanish mainland, but this time it is not Lambert who decides on the itinerary: he is apprehended by Spanish authorities and made to travel to Madrid by plane and from the Spanish capital by bus to Murcia and eventually Torre Pacheco, an agricultural town close to the southern provincial capital where he is illegally hired as an agricultural worker. Finally, he moves, this time through his own volition, back to Madrid in order to obtain a passport for a return to his place of origin. But Madrid will be as far as he is able to go on his return trip: at a metro station (the very station that began the journey), his travels are halted definitively by a group of Spanish skinheads who ram a knife into his lungs and end his life.

The underground rail system provides the center (both symbolic and concrete) of the novel's space and time; it is the site both of the beginning and the end. The metro allows the novelist a great deal of psychological speculation as well, for it seems to spark both the protagonist's inner thoughts as well as the actual occurrences of his life both in Africa and in Europe. In the opening of the novel, the reader observes the protagonist descend into the bowels of Madrid's subterranean world like a "groundhog," in his lexicon, "grombif":

> No podía dejar de sorprenderse cada vez que bajaba hacia el Metro: le parecía que se había transformado en un ser extraño, medio animal y medio humano, como un gigantesco grombif que cada anochecida buscara su madriguera bajo los túneles de la gran ciudad. (13)

> (He could not help but be surprised each time he descended into the Metro: it seemed as though he had been transformed into a strange being, half animal and half human, like a gigantic groundhog who at each nightfall looks for his den under the tunnels of the great city.)

The "grombif," a Guinean word not in Spanish dictionaries, refers to a frequently seen animal in west central Africa and is a persistent image. Its association with a variety of other images and ideas mirrors both the lexicographic and thematic intricacy of the novel itself: the act of a descent into an unfamiliar underworld, dehumanization of the protagonist, a fauna indigenous to another geography, a world left behind and utterly incompatible with the present surroundings, natural darkness contrasted by the artificial light of the underground city, the activity of digging into the ground in search of something, all this conjured up by a word alien to the language in which Ndongo is writing, a signal that the Western reader is in foreign territory. Ndongo, in something of a subtly subversive gesture, reverses the condition of the emigrant-exile's feelings of strangeness by inflicting that very strangeness or lack of immediate comprehension to the reader comfortably residing in the host country.

The narrative voice, a third person well within the mental frame of the protagonist, continues in this vein throughout the first section, but as the next chapter begins, we are taken to the native environment of Lambert Obama Ondo, his village, his extensive family members, and the conditions in which he lived as the son of "an important man in his tribe" (22). From that point, the linear temporal structure of his journey, five years from the departure out of his village to his death in Madrid, revolves around a search for stability and peace of mind unburdened by deprivation. This search is by no means undertaken for exclusively material motivations: Lambert Obama Ondo yearns to make his mark and to do what he deems is right according to the values taught to him by his community. In the frustration arising from the impediments to realizing goals that his village life has presented him, he seeks an outlet, he withdraws from his home life, as do many exiles, and initiates the search elsewhere. Again, like many personae non grata in their home environment who make a life decision to leave, the decision itself is a complicated one, motivated both by volition and forces beyond his control. In this, he is both an exilic hero and an exilic everyman, his quest is not only for better politics but for life itself.

The struggle between modernity and tradition is one of the mainstays of *El metro,* as in virtually all of Ndongo's writing. In many ways, it provides the understanding of the motivation for the protagonist's initial departure, a key for all of us gazing at the African other in the subway seeking to understand the origin of that person. Lambert possesses a complex history unbeknownst to his traveling companions: he is the grandson of a prominent tribal leader, Ebang Motuú, who is in turn the son of Guy Ondo Ebang. Lambert's father, contrary to the wishes of the grandfather, has become the village's Catechist, dedicating his life to the salvation of black souls. Thus, from the very beginning of the novel, clearly manifested are the struggles between the traditional cosmology and the modern one—ironically incarnated in Catholicism. This is a paradox typical of Ndongo's writing. While Lambert's father is a revered man in the community, the memory of his grandfather is equally powerful: Ebang Motuú (similar to Tío Abeso in *Tinieblas*) is the "último guardián de las esencias tradicionales de los fang en la comarca de Mbalmayo" (last guardian of the essential traditions of the Fang in the territory of Mbalmayo) (24), and he serves as a powerful presence throughout the novel. Lambert is thus the product of the conflict between generations as well as the conflict between African tradition and European modernity. Indeed he represents an uneasy (perhaps impossible) synthesis of vitiating forces.

The reasons for Lambert's primary departure are intricately related to the conflict between the old ways and the new, for it is a traditional belief that spurs his exit. Following the death of the protagonist's beloved mother, Dorotée Oyana, Lambert's father takes up with another woman whose daughter, Anne Mengue, is Lambert's lover, thus making Lambert's relationship with Anne an illicit one. The mutual, indeed rapturous, love between Lambert and Anne is seen as incest by the elders of the tribe, therefore Lambert's request to marry is denied based on tribal beliefs and taboos. Lambert reacts to the decision with the bitterness of a romantic hero whose limitless love is prevented from flourishing due to social contrivances. As the decision is made by the tribe's authorities, the narrator describes Lambert's reaction.

More than a shock, more than a disillusion, submits the narrator, the decision of the elders falls on the protagonist as an "immense tree" (170). It incarnates what Lambert sees as the wall preventing his happiness, and worse yet, it is the cornerstone of his tradition: "Tradition was shredding all that he had weaved together little by little patiently through the years in order to construct his life. . . . Incomprehensible norms . . . had splintered the security in which his very universe was established. . . . What to do? How to back away from such disaster?" (170).

At this determining moment, something of an epiphany in the protagonist's life journey, it is worth noting that Lambert's personal conflict is a collective one as well: the confines of what he sees as his oppressive village is at the same time a mark of his identity. Thus, it is a conflict very much within him and within all of those Africans desiring for modernity. "That very night," continues the narrator, "Lambert rid his spirit of the myths of the past in order to embark on a pilgrimage in search of new horizons"

(273). Indeed, *El metro* is the story of a "pilgrimage for new horizons." The notion of a sacred journey expands the protagonist's private decision to a public one as Lambert's life journey will become not only that of an individual but also the quest of many African youths in search of something better. The final image of this crucial episode, both an end and a beginning, offers a cautionary note both to the reader and to the protagonist himself. Lambert does not feel the nocturnal dusty breeze on his face, nor does he hear the hoot of an owl over the drone of the vehicle transporting him out of his village, a jalopy of a vehicle that "hacía notar su cansancio infinito, sobre todo, cuando iniciaba la ascención de la más leve cuesticita" ([a vehicle] whose weariness was noticeable above all when it began an ascent up a little hill) (173). Modernity's victory over tradition, or so Lambert believes at this point, is filled with dramatic irony, as the image of this tired transport vehicle attests. The epic quality of the departure ("pilgrimage") begun at the end of this chapter will become anything but a holy search, rather something akin to a *Candide* in reverse: while Voltaire exposed the pitfalls and absurdity of the old world, the "philosophical voyage" taken by Ndongo's protagonist will reveal the deceptions of modernity, a modernity with little or nothing to offer young black men filled ironically with a desire for something new.

As Lambert Obama Ondo moves from place to place within Africa (Yaunde, Duala, Dakar, Casablanca, and finally Aaïun in Western Sahara), his exploits are constantly scrutinized by the narrator in the form of both external and internal reflections on the part of the protagonist, his voice is often fused with that of the narrator. A novel absent of dialogue in the conventional sense, the dialogical imagination of Ndongo's narrative abounds: questions within an interior monologue in which Lambert ponders situations, thus creating a dialogue with an internal self, explorations of the mental states of characters other than the protagonist such as Madame Eboué, the spouse of a rich executive who uses Lambert as her gigolo (see chapter 11), disquisitions on African and world politics that beg for responses on the part of the reader, all this along with the entire thrust of the novel's discourse on emigration/immigration that connects to virtually every image and happening of the work.

Considering the theme of exile and its convergence with emigration, political discourse, almost by definition, looms above and around the novel's plot and content, not nearly as immediate as in *Los poderes de la tempestad* yet present nonetheless. The political content also allows the reader to further understand the protagonist's exilic-migratory trajectory. While in Yaunde, Lambert falls prey to a historical economic development that remains at the sociological root of much of the scarcity and ensuing emigration that plagues Africa today. Indeed, the narrator describes it as "plagues" in a tone that resembles at once the collective oral tale of a particular community as well as a universal epic. These are the years of economic structural adjustment brought on by the World Bank: "The extraordinary reduction in the value of money by half was a brutal blow that shook the foundations of the entire continent and made even the most solid economies tremble. . . . The main concern, the immediate one, was to divert the hunger in any way they could" (246–47).

As the narration of the economic crisis continues, unrest on the part the populace leads to repression: "The Army—in reality praetorian guards at the service of the powerful—was anointed by the Metropolis with ultramodern offensive equipment unleashed onto the street against the citizens" (249). These "plagues," a metaphor referring to a collective sickness, or "sicknesses," "flow" into the area just as Lambert has found a new woman, Sylvie, who might provide the antidote to the resentment he still feels for the forced break with his previous love, Anne Mengue. But the hardship is compounded by Sylvie's pregnancy coinciding with the economic collapse, widespread discontent, and police repression. Thus, the collective economic problems have lasting private effects: while Lambert feels responsibility for Sylvie and for their future offspring, his options for dealing with the problems are limited, if not nonexistent. Again, the interior monologue dominates the scene and eventually leads to the next departure: "The first thought that came to his mind was to ask himself what terrible crime he had committed to become the victim of such misfortune. . . . Was it his personal destiny or did it have to do with a collective disgrace? Because after a while, he recalled that a terrible agony had befallen the country" (259).

The interior monologue that closes this chapter allows Ndongo not only to explore the workings of his protagonist's mind but also to contextualize his experience and thus offer readers a perspective of African departures to Europe from inside the departure itself. From Lambert's view, the economic disaster is an effect with a cause. The cause, however, has as much to do with his traditional beliefs as with international economics. The crisis is cosmic; it has to do with the abandonment of the old ways. The remedy is a "collective act of contrition" for past wrongs (262). As Lambert continues his introspection, he recalls what one of the elders of his tribe, now dead, declared about the conditions of Africa:

> El viejo Nso Endaman había anunciado con claridad su propia muerte a través de las mil desgracias que padecían ahora los miembros de la tribu y el conjunto de todas las tribus. . . . Había sentenciado que la decadencia de la estirpe se había

iniciado el día que los negros abandonaron sus tradiciones para abrazar las creencias y costumbres de los albinos llegados más allá del mar, y Africa seguiría postrada mientras no se realizara un acto de contrición clectivo en recuerdo y homenaje a todos sus hijos muertos fuera de su tierra por la traición de sus propios hermanos. Ese testamento se refería a los acontecimientos de antaño, a la esclavitud y al colonialismo propiciados por la ambición y el egoismo de ciertos jefes que vendieron a sus hermanos, pero también a hechos presentes . . . pues algunos africanos encumbrados por los blancos seguían vendiendo a sus hermanos y manteniéndolos en miseria y en la opresión, era necesario un exorcismo púbico y general para aplacar las iras de los muertos para que todos los idos encontrasen la paz y se conviertieran en espíritus benefactores. (261–62)

(The elder Nso Endaman had clearly announced his own death through thousands of misfortunes endured by members of his and many other tribes. . . . He had declared that the decay of the race was initiated the day the blacks abandoned their traditions to embrace the beliefs and customs of the albinos who had arrived from over the sea and that Africa would remain prostrate until there was a collective act of contrition in remembrance and in homage to all her fallen in alien lands as the result of their own brothers' treachery. That testament referred to events in the past, to slavery and colonialism propitiated by the greed and ambition of certain chiefs who sold their brothers; they also referred to present events . . . since some Africans empowered by the whites continued to sell their brothers and keep them in misery and oppression, a public exorcism was necessary in order to pacify the ire of those no longer with us so that all the ancestors could find peace and become spirits for the benefit of all.)

The political discourse of exile here becomes the story of a fallen tradition. The force driving the people from their land is at once political and cosmic. A belief system that must cope with present realities remains deeply embedded in the protagonist's consciousness. Yet, at this moment, as he faces the birth of his child in the midst of tremendous material hardship, and as he recalls the wisdom of his elder, Nso Endaman, Lambert remains ambivalent. Introspection at the time of extreme adversity is, after all, irrelevant to the material deprivation: "Había llegado el tiempo de actuar" (The time for action had arrived) (262), which for him calls for another exit. The exilic migratory departure is at once the action he must take as well as the force that drives his life. Taking leave is also the principal impetus of the novel itself. The chapter ends with Lambert's arrival in Dakar from Yaunde three days later (156).

Thus, the political and existential discourse of Ndongo's novel is structured around a series of departures related to the exploration of identity—introspection coupled with concrete experience. This exploration, however, does not end with the discovery of ethnic or racial authenticity. Authenticity as put forth by the proponents of *negritude* is hardly the motivating force behind the protagonist's travails. The originating point of the journey, the village in Mbalmayo, is not a symbol of a mythic return, as in Odysseus's Ithaca. Rather, it is a marker of the protagonist's past; it embodies a set of cultural, political, and economic circumstances, circumstances that indicate anything but geographic or ethnic stability. Lambert's journey from the global south questions that stability; his crossings have the effect of obliterating the borders regardless of their seeming impermeability.

Among the most telling, indeed harrowing, indications in *El metro* of the porosity of those borders (despite the European Union's attempts to create official barriers) is the near-death experience of the trip via patera ("kenús" is the word Ndongo uses) (334) from El Aaïun to Arrecife, the African-Spanish port of entry par excellence. The protagonist's passage to Europe provides a fictionalized version of a happening reported in Spanish and other European news outlets almost on a daily basis. The fiction notwithstanding, the narrator's depiction of the crossing has the appearance of a reality less partial and more poignant than any supposedly disinterested news report because it provides a context (chapter 15): Lambert's dealing with the smugglers of migrants, the ways in which money is exchanged, the description of the vessel and the passengers, the use of women's bodies for a place on that vessel, the twenty-seven men and nine women ("all black") (336) who are the central character's traveling companions, the storm and the ensuing "mountainous waves" (341), the word *tierra* (land) (345) uttered as the vessel approaches Lanzarote Island, and the final lunging from the canoe into the water and onto the shore, all reminiscent of the documentary *Tarifa Traffic* (see the introduction in the current volume) yet far more expansive and thorough an explanation of the global reality that surrounds the crossings.

Lambert has not only seen how his fellow Africans cross into Europe, he has lived it with them. The same could be said of Lambert's creator, a Guinean who has also crossed borders both in his life and in his writing. Ndongo did not arrive in Spain by way of a life-threatening boat ride, yet his exile is equally bound by specific political events that "plague" his country, as the current volume's previous chapters show. There is no doubt that *El metro* may be read as an extended sociological treatise that counters Spanish conventional wisdom on immigration (such as that of Azurmendi). Yet, this narrative is more than that. Ndongo's protagonist crosses borders; allied with his narrator, he obliterates them. With the emigrant-exile's double consciousness as his aid, he defies these frontiers at once by entering a new environment and by participating in it in a variety of cultural contexts. Moreover, that these contexts make readers uncomfortable given the material and political situations that define them begs ethical questions regarding the relationship between self and other. It is perhaps a facile response to the reality of African immigration in Europe to rely constantly on enlightenment principles and on the promise of modernity as a palliative to the reality of these exilic border crossings, again noting Azurmendi. For it is modernity itself that lies at the crux of emigration/immigration as we gaze at Lambert and others like him riding in the metro.

In his exploration of the "Black Atlantic" (*The Black Atlantic: Modernity and Double Consciousness*), Paul Gilroy argues in essence that the Lamberts of the world might be seen as the cornerstone of modernity. Since the nineteenth century, argues Gilroy, black writers and thinkers have lived and worked in cultures that are transnational by definition, and it is this de facto dual consciousness blending cultures and blurring national boundaries that lies at the heart of modern thinking. Interestingly, Gilroy is critical of Habermas (Azurmendi's model) in his view of the "unfinished Enlightenment project" that defines both the modern and postmodern world because it does not sufficiently account for slavery and other forms of colonial oppression of a good part of the entire world. For Gilroy, it is not that the Enlightenment is "unfinished," rather the entire project is thrown out of kilter by the border crossings of which slavery is the prime model (46–58). Similarly, the ambivalence vis-à-vis Gilroy's understanding of modernity that *El metro* manifests throughout its pages is not necessarily an indictment of modernity and all that Habermas's (and Azurmendi's) Enlightenment Project signifies. Ndongo's character's double consciousness—his rejection of tradition and embrace of it, and, inversely, his thirst for modernity and rejection of it—is more than anything an affirmation of plurality and difference, something that, as we have seen, is not embraced by Azurmendi and others of like mind. Indeed, it is the exilic-migratory journey that accounts not only for the dual consciousness but also for Lambert's and Ndongo's knowledge of both continents from within. In Gilroy's words: "In focusing on racial slavery and its aftermath we are required to consider a historical relationship in which dependency and antagonism are intimately associated and in which black critiques of modernity may also be, in some significant ways, its affirmation" (48).

The final scenes of *El metro,* although tragic if not pathetic, as Lambert lies bleeding in the depths of Madrid's subway as a result of knife wounds inflicted upon him by skinheads, the overall effect of the journey has not been entirely without a hopeful message. For in his final recollection, Lambert imagines both his mother, "la siempre anhelada Dorotée Oyana" (the always-longed-for Dorotée Oyana) (457), along with his grandfather Ebang Motuú, who tells him not to be afraid: "al fin has llegado al puerto de destino, y tu muerte no será una muerte anónima" (458) (at last you have arrived at your destined port, and your death will not be anonymous). Moreover, the ending is a synthesis of the dual consciousness of both Gilroy and Du Bois, at once pathetic and hopeful: pathetic because of the strikingly dramatic irony of the revered chief's words, since we can only imagine the headlines in the next morning's newspapers tucked away in the metro section—"Death of a Black Man of Uncertain Origin"—and hopeful because according to traditional belief, Lambert has passed on to another life in which he will be anything but anonymous. He himself has become an "ido," an at-once absent and present ancestor anything but anonymous. The fusion of both worlds in this last image is yet another manifestation of all the beauty and horror of the Black Atlantic.

In a public lecture on this novel in Madrid on May 24, 2007, José María Ridau, novelist and commentator for the newspaper *El País,* referred to *El metro* as a "contra-épica" (counterepic), thereby emphasizing the pathetic finale. As the other presenter of the novel, I referred to the protagonist as an African Ulysses yearning for a return to an evasive origin. In retrospect, I think the slightly different readings are due to Ridau's understandable insistence on the irony of the last image. The patriarch's words stressing that Lambert's death will not be that of an anonymous man are filled with pathos in view of the reality of Lambert's anonymity in Western eyes, a man as nameless as the one described in the opening of this chapter. However, in Ebang Motuú's world, the African resting place of the ancestors, Lambert is anything but anonymous. Indeed, the patriarch's prediction, according to a specific subject position, has come true. Obama Ondo will be known for his struggle to arrive at something—anonymous in one world, famous in another. In the underworld of the metro, Ndongo has fused both cosmologies within his writing and within his own double consciousness.

CHAPTER SIX

Between Life and Death

The Macías Generation

In a novella by exile Guinean writer Joaquín Mbomío Bacheng (b. 1956, Niefang, Río Muni), titled *El párroco de Niefang* (The parish priest of Niefang, 1996), a character who dies as a result of political incarceration during the Macías regime (1968–79) comes back to life momentarily to make contact with the protagonist, Father Gabriel. This dialogue is part of the *mibili,* a ritual in which a spirit takes the form of a living member of the community to offer (haunting) advice. These spirits are said to possess great knowledge due to their ambivalent state of being—at once dead and alive. In this instance, Patricio, the spirit, declares that all people are prisoners of existence, to which the intellectually and existentially perplexed priest replies: "Pero Patricio, la existencia no puede ser una cárcel" (But, Patricio, existence cannot be a prison) (52). Patricio responds with a disquisition that includes an assessment of the historical transition in Equatorial Guinea from colonialism to dictatorship.

All was fine in the colonial days, Patricio explains, everything was "agreeable, luminous." The patterns of life were simple, although not without their contradictions, such as the "prettiest women" of the village becoming "lovers of the whites, the priests, and the rich men." Patricio describes the voice of the priest as that of a "comediórafo" (comedian) as he delivered the sermon, "but that didn't matter, because the most important thing was the white bread we would all receive at the altar as we squeezed ourselves into a long line behind the backside of the woman immediately in front." It was another world, all part of what he calls "colonial theocentrism." But this world fell, continues Patricio, with independence and Macías; with the new ruler came the deluge and the end of an era of stability: "Para mí fue la cárcel la muerte, y así descubrí la existencia" (For me, prison was death, and that's how I discovered existence) (52).

Indeed, there is wisdom in the voice of spirits. As a past prisonmate of

Father Gabriel, Patricio's ghost has insights into the vicissitudes of existence, even more so than his friend, due to his liminal status between life and death. He has expressed in essence the conscience of his generation. He tells us that the "theocentrism" of the colonial period led to exile, prison, and death during the Macías regime.

Mbomío's *Párroco de Niefang* expresses the frustrations of those who lived the colonial years during adolescence and early adulthood hoping for self-determination along with freedom of religious, ethnic, and linguistic self-definition. While the novella's similarities to Donato Ndongo's *Tinieblas* (Shadows) have been pointed out by critics, equally of note is that Mbomío's and Ndongo's entire generation of Guinean writers and intellectuals is shaped by virtually identical political and cultural experiences.[1] It is not only political repression, first as a Spanish colony, then as a country under dictatorial siege, that gives rise to the disquiet of these writers. It is also the condition of ambivalence, again a double consciousness expressed poignantly in Patricio's words. The light-hearted, if not nostalgic, recollection of Catholic rituals he was made to participate in years ago belies the narratological fact that the one who is remembering them is engaged in another ritual, the *mibili,* which stands in opposition to Christian belief. Moreover, we note the black-white contrast as the pretty women of the village flaunt their elegance with full knowledge that their haughtiness comes from their relations with white men, priests, and the wealthy. As Patricio's spirit suggests, power is derived by race, gender, and money. Acknowledgment of these patterns heightens the tension of the novel, a tension embodied ultimately by Father Gabriel as he is released from prison after Macías's death only to find himself in an extremely compromising condition. While he begins to question his faith, the faith of that "other world," as Patricio's voice calls it, he is designated by none other than Pope John Paul II for sainthood. All this is compounded by the emergence of a new dictatorial regime and by what seems like a permanent condition of exile. Clearly, the most salient theme of this novella, as in virtually all the writing and thinking of Mbomío's generation, is the otherworldliness of exile.

Joaquín Mbomío's case follows the patterns of many of his generation: he was educated in the continental area of Río Muni and obtained a higher degree in Spain where he studied Spanish philology to become a secondary-school teacher. During the Macías regime, he was imprisoned in 1978 after having been accused of being a "traitorous student" (Ndongo and Ngom 456), sentenced to hard labor in Bioko, and released after Macías was killed in the coup plotted by his nephew Teodoro Obiang.[2] In a journalistic piece published in "Diáspora," Mbomío describes his experience:

> I began to observe this sociopolitical phenomenon [punishment for political beliefs] a few years ago when I was in prison in Black Beach in 1978. One day, someone named Cayo, then a member of the Popular Militia [the police force], who was recently named Director of Prisons, furiously began to strike one of the prisoners who was named Aranda (from Sao Tomé). [A] corporal from the National Guard, Alée, immediately came toward him . . . to tell Cayo that only political prisoners should be mistreated, "the ones who have spoken badly of the government." Not the ones like Aranda who are there for robbery." ("En Guinea")

Clearly, the prison experience has shaped Mbomío's life as well as his writing. His case is illustrative of exiles of the twentieth and twenty-first centuries, not only from Equatorial Guinea but also from virtually any nation that has had similar histories and in the foregrounding of the place of writing: reconstruction of a lost environment, expulsion from a former locale, and memory.

In 1980, Mbomío moved to Lyon, France, where he became a journalist. With guarded skepticism, he returned to Equatorial Guinea in 1988 to work as a correspondent for Agence France Presse. But, in 1990, once again he was forced into exile by the Obiang regime. He has been as critical of Equatorial Guinea's second postindependence dictatorship as he has been of the first. And in both cases, his criticism is deepened by the double consciousness of a former colonial subject, a man educated in a language not his own, albeit something he embraces. In a short statement that precedes his novella, he affirms the legacy of Spanish culture coupled with that of Africa: "Spanish colonization has been assimilated by our people, not without sacrifice, but there has been, however, what he calls an "entronque" (convergence) between the cultures of the two communities, the Hispanic and the African" (*El párroco* 8).

While Father Gabriel of *El párroco de Niefang* is no copy of Joaquín Mbomío, there are certain autobiographical resonances, much as in Ndongo's *Tinieblas* (see Fra-Molinero, "La figura ambivalente") but not so much in the details of a life as in the existential, religious, and identity crises that the novel narrates. Specifically, the protagonist's dilemmas center around the questioning of his faith as a result of political imprisonment. This theme is reminiscent of canonical generation of 1898 writers, such as Miguel de Unamuno in his *San Manuel Bueno, mártir* (Saint Emmanuel the Good, martyr) whose memorable protagonist priest agonizes over his inability to believe in God. Similarly, Mbomío's Father Gabriel is torn between his spiritual disillusion (both with Christian doctrine and with the Church) and the necessity of responding to the needs of his community. His people are in need of heroes, as his fellow priest Father Matanga, tells him (*El párroco* 29). Moreover, there is talk of his becoming a saint after his death for the suffering he endured at the hands of Macías's attempts to rid the country of all symbols of Catholicism as tools of imperialism. Again, the intertextual relationship between Mbomío's novella and that of the Dean of Salamanca, as Don Miguel was called, is more than a coincidence. The author's prologue shows how indebted Mbomío says Guinean letters are to Spanish literature (*El párroco* 8). *El párroco,* however, centers on an internal crisis enhanced by the crossroads between African culture and that of Europe. In order to save his people from the emptiness of atheism that the Macías regime incarnates, it is necessary to show them that the Lord is still capable of miracles and that the miracle must be made flesh to the African. In a defining scene, Father Matanga, Father Gabriel's learned companion from the seminary, reasons with him as if he were putting forth a theological argument, not without a certain anthropological authority:

> ¿Te has fijado en el comportamiento de un africano cuando se encuentra frente a una obra de arte? Pues el negro no se contenta con la simple contemplación. Siempre toca, palpa, manosea y acaricia la obra para poderla apreciar. Es decir, que el africano necesita sentir la obra en su propia carne, en su ser más profundo. Este contacto crea un lazo, el africano crea una historia de amor con la obra y entonces la valoriza.... Sólo de esta forma nuestro pueblo volverá a creer y a vivir según el Evangelio. Te pido, padre—concluyó el teólogo—que hagas un milagro si quieres que el pueblo vuelva a creer en Dios, a salvarse y llegar a la vida eterna. (*El párroco* 62)

> (Have you noticed the behavior of an African when he finds himself in front of a work of art? The black man is not content with mere contemplation. He always touches, feels, strokes, and caresses the work so that he can appreciate it. In other words, the African needs to feel the work in its own flesh, in its most profound state of being. This contact creates a link, the African creates a love story with the work, and then he values it.... Only in this way will our people again believe and live according to the Gospels. I'm asking you, father—the theologian concluded—to perform a miracle if you wish the people to believe in God again, to be saved and thus arrive at life everlasting.)

Matanga's words might be read as an ars poetica of Africa in relation to "Western" notions of high art. In this view, the work of art must be made flesh, not metaphorically shaped into something "palpable" or described as something sensuous. Rather, there must be a direct, tangible link between the work and the person or community to whom the work is directed. Yet, in Mbomío's novella, the dilemma unfolds in the reluctance of the protagonist, indeed his disbelief, that such connection is viable or even possible. Matanga is asking him not as much to perform a miracle as to pretend to perform one.

Father Gabriel's crisis, both in Unamuno's sense and in that of the African who has seen and assimilated a reality other than the one recognized by his community, straddles two worlds, and it encapsulates the impetus for much of the thinking and writing of the Equatorial Guineans who came of age during the transition between the colony and independence.

In a subsequent novel, *Huellas bajo tierra* (Footprints under the earth) (1998), Mbomío sets out to describe firsthand the atrocities of the Macías regime, through the eyes of Juan Ndong, a character who could be seen as an archetype of the victim of these "years of silence." He is the illegitimate son of Girolla, a similarly typical Catalan business man, who makes his fortune in colonial Equatorial Guinea through the production of palm oil. With independence and Macías's attacks against all Spanish institutions, particularly the landowners, Girolla is forced back to Barcelona. As the story opens, Girolla recollects the day the son he did not know visited him and left behind his diary, a manuscript that becomes the interpolated text of the novel. Mbomío's signature fascination with the connections between those living and the dead manifests itself in the creation of yet another character representative of Equatorial Guinea's postindependence history, Mba, a character who represents the common Guinean citizen, "el guineano" (the Guinean) (15). The description of the workings of the mind of a man who became Macías's prime henchman is revealing: Mba was at one time a loyal and trusted worker in Girolla's palm oil business who abruptly turned into a killer. He was honorable and generous, a man who practiced the ethical teachings of his village elders who had told him that Europeans were all spirits, "blacks who had died only to return to life as whites." And when he came across a bad white person, he identified him "as an old enemy of the tribe" (16). Yet, Mba is also described as a "good Christian" (17). Indeed, in Mbomío's rendering of this all-too-typical Guinean character, a decent man who becomes an enthusiastic executioner, we see before us a man with his own unanalyzed double consciousness: he was "unworried" about the profound divisions between the two world views, that of the Europeans and that of his tribe. Mba's error is precisely that—unlike Mbomío, an exile and emigrant who understands both worlds from within, in all their incompatibility, Mba makes the tragic mistake of the assimilation of the white man's world into his own. Suffice to say that the Clarentian priests never taught him to read Levinas.

Clearly, Mbomío, along with many cultural figures of his generation such as Ndongo, Francisco Zamora, Justo Bolekia, María Nsue, J. M. Davies, Julián Bibang, Jerónimo Rope, Antimo Esono, Marcelo Ensema, and Eugenio

Nkogo, experienced exile and emigration in a way that conditioned their writing.[3] Indeed, there is a consciousness of a generation in these writers as one of the poets, Jerónimo Rope Bomaba (b. 1953 in Malabo) states in the prologue to his *Album poético* (Poetic album): his is a "lost generation." He goes on to state, in a poetic spirit reminiscent of Zamora's picaresque style, that it is precisely this loss, this lack of belonging, that serves as the main impetus of his work: "It is the cause of the pain I express in my poetry, no matter if I sing or complain. But I am not discouraged. I have not wished to write pessimist poetry. Between the pain arise laughter and jokes" (13). The experience of political pain—a malady both celebrated and lamented—also has to do with a dual identity (cultural and linguistic) that merges the geographies of Equatorial Guinea and Spain. The merger, however, as seen in Mbomío's novella, is anything but an easy one. In this younger generation's writing, few homages or praises are sung to the Spanish cultural legacy left in the African tropics by Spanish priests, colonial government officials, or traders, as was the case in some of the texts written by the older writers: Chema Mijero, Ocha'a, Jones Mathama, and the one who never left, Evita. Indeed, the experience of the elders has been more migratory than exilic. Their cultural ambivalence is presented at times subliminally in their very attempts to overcome it. The Macías generation, on the other hand, is far more conscious of that ambivalence, more aware of issues related to blackness and their colonial double consciousness.

One of the most telling manifestations of this open ambivalence—an aggressive one—is the multifaceted writings of Francisco Zamora Loboch (b. 1948 in Annobon). Zamora is one of the most prolific Guinean writers of his generation. Son of a prominent Annobonese teacher and intellectual, Maplal Loboch, whose life was made miserable by Macías for having criticized the postindependence regime, Zamora went to Spain after secondary school to study economics but was unable to return due to the first dictator's seizure of power. He stayed in Spain and became a journalist and simultaneously began to write poetry and essays, much like both Ndongo and Mbomío. Zamora, however, parts ways from his codissident writers in that his tone is often acerbic. Ironically, perhaps the most well integrated among those of his generation into Spanish life—he is a prominent staff writer for the well-known Spanish sports journal *As*—the double consciousness manifested in his writing approaches that of a man suffering from (or in his case celebrating) a split personality. The following poem, "Prisionero de la Gran Vía" (Prisoner of Gran Vía [a Madrid boulevard]), is included in an early anthology of Guinean writing.

Si supieras
que no me dejan los días de fiesta
ponerme el taparrabos nuevo
donde bordaste mis iniciales
temblándote los dedos de vieja.
Si supieras
Que tengo la garganta enmohecida
porque no puedo salirme a las plazas
y ensayar mis gritos de guerra.
Que no puedo pasearme por las grandes vías
el torso desnudo, desafiando al invierno
y enseñando mis tatuajes
a los niños de esta ciudad.
Si pudieras verme
fiel esclavo de los tendidos,
vociferante hincha en los estadios,
compadre incondicional de los mesones.
Madre, si pudieras verme.
(Ndongo, *Antología* 131)

(If you only knew
that they don't allow me
to wear my new holiday loincloth
where you embroidered my initials
as your old-lady fingers trembled.
If you only knew
that my throat is rusty
because I can't go out into the street
and practice my war cries.
That I can't go out for a walk
on the great boulevards
with my bare torso, defying the winter
and showing off my tattoos
to the children of this city.
If you could only see me,
loyal slave to the bleachers,
loud fan in the stands,
unconditional patron of the taverns.
Mother, if you could only see me.)

The speaker is a "prisoner" forced into assimilation of Spanish life. However, the poem's references to Gran Via, one of the main boulevards of Madrid, along with the sports stadium and the city's adversarial winter make the "imprisonment" indicate a not altogether disastrous immigrant experience. The tension in the poem is not as much in the present condition of the poetic voice but in the lurking presence of Africa in the form of the mother, the old woman with her trembling fingers whose presence is embodied as the implicit reader of the poem, as if the speaker were writing her a letter from his new urban residence. The connections between the old world (the tattoos, the loincloth, the war cries) and the new one of Madrid are markers less of nostalgia than a dual reality, a physical understanding, as in the African's necessity to touch the work of art, as Mbomio relates. Thus, Zamora conceives his writing from the standpoint of two separate realities at once. Indeed, the emigrant-exile's departure must have been a difficult one, as we, the outside readers of this "letter," can only imagine what life was like prior to that departure. The ironic self-deprecation in the reference to the "new loincloth" that the speaker dons for festive occasions is at once humorous and pathetic. It allows readers an inroad to otherness.

A more hermetic expression of displacement comes to the fore in Zamora's collection of poetry *Memoria de laberintos* (Memory of labyrinths) (1999). Javier Reverte, in the prologue, describes the collection as "perfumed by bitter-sweet song." It contains the laments of an "expatriot," because the poet "is as much Spanish as Guinean, or perhaps he is a stranger between two homelands, although to one he may owe his birth, and to the other his word" (7–8). This description of Zamora is no doubt accurate: like virtually all the Guinean writers of his generation, he is caught in an uncomfortable middle ground dividing two continents by power and exploitation—perhaps the same could be said of most African writers who lived colonial and postcolonial experiences. Yet, I would qualify Reverte's assessment by adding that birth and language merge in Zamora's writing. *Memoria de laberintos* expresses the strangeness—at one point he calls it absurdity (39)—of living in a land other than that of one's birth. The circumstances call for an attempt, however strained, to mix the two worlds. How can it be otherwise? Birth and language go hand in hand. Thus, what we find in Zamora's poetry are words that harken to an elsewhere, an other world at once familiar to the poet and separate from him. An illustrative model for this merger of asymmetrical elements is the poem whose title is also the title of the entire collection, *Memoria de laberintos*—"Memory of labyrinths."

Desde la humildad del gemido
en una esquina
observo no sin impotencia
el suicidio de tu memoria de rocío
los paletuvios
cada vez que la solitaria dama
de gasas blancas sobre fondo oscura
ataviada
derrama la miel en el asfalto
incapaz de resolver
el secreto del laberinto
en la humedad de los zarzales.

(18)

(From the humility of a cry
in a corner
I observe not without impotence
the suicide of your dew-like memory
in the trees
each time the solitary lady
dressed
in white gauze over a dark background
pours honey on the asphalt
unable to solve
the secret of the labyrinth
in the humidity of the brambles.)

The poem evokes the dreamlike nature of memory, something hidden in a labyrinth within the speaker's remembrance. Memory seems to be haunting him, as from the spirit world, in the form of a lady dressed in white gauze, yet he cannot grasp it. Indeed, the poem has a gothic quality: the "trees" ("paletuvios") and the "humidity of the brambles" ("la humedad de los zarzales") amidst the poet's cry from what seems like a street corner ("asfalto"). Thus, the mixture of unlike elements—the physical impossibility of being in two places at once—is not only the cause of the poet's consternation but perhaps also the impetus behind the entire collection, clearly an exilic inclination.

Elsewhere in the collection, Zamora offers his readers indications of his specific Guinean circumstances: his allusions to Clarence, the city named by the British that is today Malabo (54, 64), the "hombre de Mmo" (something akin to a medicine man) (38, 64), "eludiese Sevilla de Niefang" (eluded Seville from Niefang) (28),[4] Annobon's ecological destruction (36), "the age of Nubia" (41) "Dyoba, Nguema, Bokesa" (poets whose work was read from textbooks by elementary school students and in Ndongo's *Tinieblas*) (32), the prison of Black Beach or Blaybich (60). Yet, in each of these cultural references, the situation in which they appear is nearly always tempered by another reality, often that of Spain. The emigrant-exile's experience must always be subject to these kinds of unlikely comparisons, contexts, and mergers of cultures. A related marker of Zamora's poetry, common in the writers of his generation, is the fusion of words and place names of his native land with the language that colonized him, as in the poem "Anita Awawoo":

> Camino a Yaba
> entre Ikoy y Cemetary Street
> alguien
> . . .
> me habló de vuestra decadencia indiferente
> en los muladares de una urbe atroz, africana
>
> (57)
>
> (On the way to Yaba
> between Ikoy and Cemetery Street
> someone
> . . .
> told me about your indifferent demise
> in the trash heaps of an atrocious city, African.)

The atrocious city is Malabo, and the woman whose "indifferent demise" (or is it that the news of her downfall was told to the speaker indifferently?) is Anita Awawoo, the matron of an eating-and-drinking establishment frequented by many residents of the city. What stands out in Zamora's labyrinthine remembrance of this woman is not only the pathos of the "trash heap" in which she and her memory are buried but also the synthesis of African and "Western" place names: "Cemetery Street" (no doubt named by the British) and Ikoy, as well as the internal rhyme of the name itself, Anita Awawoo. This technique is reminiscent of Nabakov in *Speak Memory* as the famous exile Russian writer plays with sounds of names in his recreation of the past.

The complexity of Zamora's poetic absorption of exile and colonial dual consciousness does not allow for facile readings; he seems to assert himself in his poetry by defying the conventions of exile. Certainly, the "sterile complexities of exile politics"[5] enter into Zamora's poetry in *Memoria de laberintos* as in "Encuentro de vida o muerte en el estadio de Santa María" (Meeting of life and death in Santa María Stadium) (60–61), in which the poet describes the infamous stadium that served as an internment camp as well as a center of torture and execution under Macías. Again, we see the traces of that liminal state between this world and that of the spirits. But exile and cultural displacement seem also to transcend those complexities and horrors as in the following poem appropriately titled "Exilio" (Exile), even though there is much of an immigrant's writing in the texts of Francisco Zamora as well:

> Cuando el absurdo
> embutido en su gelatina
> de exilio y frío
> miseria y nieve
> lloraba en la almohada
> era posible a veces
> afirmar
> alguna cabeza de puente
> sobre islas de madréporas
> y entre colonias de anémonas
> aferrarse a la vida
> alimentándose
> de la carne sobrada de pseudópodos
> del paramecio y la vorticela.
>
> (39)

> (When the absurd
> mixture, the gelatin
> of exile and coldness
> misery and snow
> was crying on the pillow
> it was possible at times
> to affirm
> some bridgehead
> over coral islands
> and between colonies of anemone
> cling to life
> nourishing themselves
> of the remaining flesh of ameba
> of paramecium and vorticella.)

Here, exile coagulates into a gelatin. Yet, the scientific terminology counters the exilic desperation ("coldness" and "misery") as if the affirmation of life in defiance of this "absurd mixture" were something primordial in the form of ameba or coral (both plantlike and animal-like). Moreover, the poetic voice resists the snow of exile with these coral islands. In this way, Zamora universalizes exile in a manner that virtually any emigrant/immigrant can understand. While in another poem Zamora calls the circumstance of being away from one's birth place "absurd," in these verses the absurdity is universal.

Poetic and linguistic complexity notwithstanding, the clarity of Zamora's critique of his former colonizers is at times striking, not only in his poetry but also in his book-length essay on Spanish racism "Cómo ser negro y no morir en Aravaca" (How to be black and not die in Aravaca) (1994). The book's intention is to respond to an ugly incident that occurred in the well-to-do Madrid suburb of Aravaca in 1992. Lucrecia Pérez Matos, a black woman immigrant from the Dominican Republic, was killed by three skinheads directed by a member of the federal police force, the Civil Guard, in a dance club called the Four Roses. "Cómo ser negro," however, only mentions Lucrecia Pérez by name in the dedication (7) and in the several references to Aravaca, in the text itself as well as in the title, with Aravaca as a place of death for blacks. Thus, the connection between Spanish history and this particular crime is situated within a larger context of social, cultural, and historical relations. Yet, beyond the specific references to the "crime of Aravaca," as it was called in the press, the essay may be read not only as a protest against the crime but also as a response to the many reactions the crime aroused on the part of Spaniards.

Indeed, the circumstances of this murder—that the assassins were known for their hatred of immigrants and that the young men were incited by a policeman acting on his own—led to a major public outcry against racism in all Spain. There were demonstrations attended by thousands of people, songs composed in (pathetic) memory of Lucrecia, and public discussions on immigration and racism.[6] One of the more self-reflective examples of this pubic indignation was an editorial by novelist Juan José Millás, one of the most prominent commentators in the Spanish press. In a November 23, 1992, piece that appeared in *El País* shortly after the murder, he reminded his readers (in his signature literary style) that some time ago, Spaniards were the ones fleeing the misery of their homeland for the promised land ("isla de Jauja") of Germany "Cuando los españoles éramos los árabes de los alemanes." He continued by describing what he imagined (and what a reporter investigating the circumstances of the crime had told him) as Pérez's journey from a village in the Dominican Republic to the Aravaca suburb:

> Lucrecia did not know what a faucet was, or an elevator, or a bathroom. In other words, one day the poor girl was in Vicente Noble, her hometown, trying to figure out a way to cope with hunger, when an employment monger sold her a dose of the island of Shangrila-Aravaca, and suddenly, as if she had shot herself up with something hallucinogenic, she found herself flying and crossing things they called borders, moving around through spaces where there were no bananas or coconuts, working in a house with faucets and electric washing machines and hot water, and maybe one of those appliances that squeezed juice out of the fruit. In other words, a hallucination, a nightmare, an illusory trip taken to rid herself of the addiction to hunger, to detoxify herself of poverty. (*El Pais,* 23 Nov. 1992; my translation)

Millás's poetic expression of the tragedy of Lucrecia Pérez, particularly as it is mediated by similar experiences suffered by Spaniards not long ago, is noteworthy, as are all the lamentations and appeals to the national sense of justice that were aroused by the crime. Yet, at the same time, one wonders if this attempt to deal with otherness lacks a larger historical context. Moreover, the association of Lucrecia's dream of Aravaca with a drug addiction is an interestingly counterintuitive protest against her slaughter, given stereotypes of immigrants as drug dealers. It is equally interesting that Millás seems to see Lucrecia Pérez's downfall as a problem related to modernity: she does not know what a faucet is. He never asks himself how modernity itself coupled with racism might be part of larger historical processes. While he provides a pertinent historical commentary on Spanish immigrants in Germany in the 1960s who were in similar conditions as those endured by Lucrecia and others like her, he does not do the same for the history of the Dominican immigrant, who is portrayed as a person yearning for "bananas and coconuts." By contrast, "Cómo ser negro," coming from a man who asserts and embraces his own otherness in the face of those who categorize him as a person without modernity, extends Spanish history vis-à-vis the other and thereby provides a response not only to the murder but to all the Spaniards calling themselves progressives.

The Guinean's indignation about the victimization of Lucrecia Pérez manifests itself in a way quite different from that of Millás: "Cómo ser negro" is a humorous essay, albeit black humor. Zamora offers a tongue-in-cheek history of racism in a country whose people have constructed a self-concept of indifference to skin color as a marker of identity:

> The Spanish have known how to keep their monster dormant in camphor and mint, wrapped in silk sheets and draped in a fine table cloth, making several generations believe that there is no racism in a country whose patron saint is St. James—aka the Moor Killer—the land of Cardinal Cisneros [the Inquisitor

> of Castile], Torquemada [the Grand Inquisitor], the Catholic Kings, Quevedo [known for anti-Semitism], Pedro Blanco [a notorious slave trader] or the Duke of Santoña [known to have fathered a slew of illegitimate children in Cuba]. (21)

Zamora's voice in this essay is that of a stand-up comic, as the chapter titles indicate: "Trabajar como un negro" (Work like a black man), a Spanish commonplace that designates working as hard as blacks (slavery notwithstanding), "Por qué el blanco es tan listo y el negro tan lerdo" (Why whites are so smart and blacks so slow), "Músculo negro versus músculo blanco" (Black muscle versus white muscle), "Pene blanco–pene negro" (White penis–black penis), and so forth. In a subchapter titled "Fórmula para trabajar como blanco siendo negro" (Formula for working as a white while black), the Ecuatorialguinean poet parodies at once the classified section of newspapers as well as a host of progressive Spanish political commentators and writers:

> Wanted: a black writer for an overwhelmed white writer: interested Ugandans should courteously contact whites such as Antonio Gala, Francisco Umbral, Emilio Romero, etc. (36)

All of these writers frequently voice their opinions defending the oppressed. The final section of this chapter is a (faux) classified ad that is a description of an idea for a new videogame consisting of an emigrant/immigrant's trip to Spain beginning on the coast of Morocco and ending in Aravaca (the prize). But to get there, the player must grip the joystick so hard that it turns black, as he or she undergoes storms, sharks, and cold weather, and when they arrive at Tarifa—we are reminded of *Tarifa Traffic*—they must elude police as well as pistol-wielding white thugs, faces covered (39). Thus, as the liberal intellectuals (Azurmendi included) cope with the problem of immigration as an unsettling blemish on the national character, a topic that weighs heavy on the conscience of Spaniards, Zamora mischievously calls for a reflection that transcends facile condemnations of the errors of others, as if to say, "Liberal commentator, heal thyself, of racism."

The entire project that encompasses this hard-hitting, albeit playful, commentary on Spanish culture and history, arises from Zamora's own double consciousness. We are reminded again of Paul Gilroy, who calls it "the special stress that grows with the effort involved in trying to face (at least) two ways at once" (3). It is precisely this "black Atlantic" voice that Zamora raises loudly (albeit humorously) not only in this historical essay but in virtually all his writing. Indeed, "Cómo ser negro" is difficult to categorize, for despite the ironic, at times overstated, assertions, it is also a serious book of history, erudite at times, as the author discusses Spanish literature and history of a variety of genres and periods not without authority. His words, for example, on the differences between Quevedo and Cervantes in terms of racial discourse are worthy of an academic treatise (101–7). Yet, the reader is unsure exactly what to make of the essay given the overarching irony of the entire book. "Is he serious?" one might ask, but the answer is not an easy yes or no; it has to do with reading his essay as a manifestation of double consciousness. The final section is anything but a conclusion, rather something as inconclusive as a dictionary, "Diccionario racista" (Racist dictionary) (151–72), in which the author lists over two hundred words from A to Z to which he gives nuanced meanings all having to do with race, as in the following:

> apartheid: Spanish invention (caste society) perfected in South Africa functioning in the following way: the white screws the mestizo and the black; the mestizo screws the black. If the black complains, he's a bastard and deserves hanging. (154)
>
> basketball: Sport that whites see as tragic and cold (Bird), and blacks as happy (Magic, Jordan). (155)
>
> dollar: $Racism$. (159)
>
> Madrid: fascist city par excellence, taken over by Ultrasur [an organization of soccer fanatics], skinheads, and doormen wearing hats who won't let you hang out, no matter what color you are. (167)

I note that Zamora has lived in Madrid for several decades.

Beyond the humor of these final pages, it is unclear if the author intends this "racist dictionary" as an ironic statement that his own words are racist or as a critique of racism. To end the essay with the ambivalence of a series of double entendres is fitting: Zamora's readers think they know the meanings of these words, as they perhaps believe they know the author's intention, but given the black perspective, both the words of the dictionary and the essay as a whole escape a facile meaning. The reader laughs, yet the laughter is tempered by a realization of the existence of the other. One might say that Zamora (generously) offers a way for us to be included in his double consciousness.[7]

As the works of Zamora and Mbomío attest, an ambivalent consciousness leading to an awareness of European and African cultures is at once an important unifying thread of the Macías generation even though the writing of this group spans many genres, themes, and styles. The struggle (both inward and outward) between indigenous languages versus the languages of colonial power, mainly Spanish, is another important feature of the generation. Already in the writing of Juan Balboa, one of the earlier poets of the transition between the colony and the independent nation, this theme emerges in his *O'Boriba* (see chapter 3). Yet, in the works of Justo Bolekia, Julián Bibang, and J. M. Davies, the language of birth is not only a theme, it is one of the defining elements of their writing. As a linguist at the University of Salamanca, exiled from Equatorial Guinea in 1973, Bolekia is deeply interested in language as a marker of self. His collection of poetry *Löbëla* (a title referring to a Bubi goddess) is intended, he submits, for readers of the Bubi language. However, this stated intention is tempered in his introduction by the admission that in the reading and assimilation of the poems, the reader may feel the urge "to transfer the interpretation . . . to his or her social surroundings, using experience as a point of departure." What Bolekia intends in his poetry is not to exclude from his readership those who do not belong to his ethnicity, rather he requires of his reader the very double consciousness that motivates African writers. He goes on to remind us that his intention counters the creation of "a static world anchored in times gone by in order to justify the absence of movement or collective volition." This experience, he goes on to say, is both "individual or collective [and] should not be extrapolated to other dimensions contrary to the historicity of each individual" (8). Indeed, stasis and singularity, identities frozen in time, are precisely what Bolekia avoids, as he argues for and creates a state of constant flexibility. Moreover, the movement he promises in his poetry is predicated on the tension between reality and desire that, in the final analysis, provides the impetus behind the life of anyone who embarks on a migration.

In *Löbëla,* Bolekia delivers on his promise. While the familiarity with Bubi, not only the language but also the collective structure of belief in that society, is a factor in the assimilation of the verses, it is not imperative. What is crucial, however, is the recognition of the "historicity of each individual," a recognition of movement and change. Indeed, Löbëla itself, both the collection and the goddess, is the embodiment of this fluidity. The work is divided into three parts: "Gritos plegados" (Folded screams), in which the poet recreates his ancestral past; "La ondina Löbëla" (Ondine Löbëla), poems addressed to and about the goddess; and "Versos furtivos" (Furtive verses), where the poet melds a remote past with an immediate past, thereby creating his vision of the present. Each section is introduced by a prose-poem offering readers not as much an explanation of the poems but a taste of them, an orientation that leads in several directions at once. In his description of Löbëla, the second section, the poet characterizes her as an entity capable of transformation. Indeed, she is many spirits at once: "la diosa amante y madre" (love goddess and mother) and at the same time "el dios hombre que posee y desgarra impío cual joven doncel apresurado" (the male god who possesses and scratches like a young bachelor in a hurry). She is a life force, an object of desire (both male and female), all and nothing. Bolekia ends the prose poem with a question: "¿quién es Löbëla?" (Who is Löbëla?) (33). Perhaps unwittingly, this Bubi poet is celebrating his own diasporic consciousness with the assertion of a fluid identity. If there is anything that seems to characterize Bolekia's beloved goddess, it is not only that she seems to incarnate an African Dionysian spirit, but also her very ability to change identities, thereby questioning the notion of identity itself as the poet asks who Löbëla is.

The uses of indigenous languages in the texts of the exile members of the Macías generation underscore the issues of identity and authenticity that characterize much postcolonial African literature. It is common in the works of Zamora, Davies, and María Nsué (whose novel *Ekomo,* as chapter 8 shows, is unique in Guinean literature for its feminine authorship) to employ words and phrases from the author's upbringing. Moreover, several members of the group are actively involved in the linguistic codification and recovery of these languages: Julián Bibang's *La migración fang,* Bolekia's several works on the Bubi language, Jerónimo Rope also works on Bubi linguistics (*Album poético* 14). The issue is tempered, however, among the members of this generation, due to the first dictator's attempt to obliterate Spanish. One might even say that for the Macías generation, Spanish was seen as something of a language of unwitting resistance. It is not that Spain or Spanish culture is celebrated in these writers—notwithstanding a few exceptions—rather it is accepted as the lingua franca in the face of a crude and anti-intellectual attempt to negate its status. Ndongo describes the postcolonial language policy during the Macías regime in the following way:

> [Macías's] repression was generalized and indiscriminate; above all it was directed to all who were able to think on their own. It is necessary to underscore that with the return of tribal customs as a counterpoint to values acquired from Spanish culture, Macías—like Idi Amin in Uganda, Sekou Touré in Guinea-Conakry, Mobutu in [then] Zaire, and so many others on our continent—did not really promote indigenous cultures but deculturation. . . . Thus, deprived of all cultural support, what was put forth was the denigration of the individual and insecurity. . . . [Guineans] were forced to abandon European culture and what it represented as a universal path to progress, deprived as well of the deeply imbedded meanings of their rites and ancestral beliefs. . . . As a result of Macías prohibiting both the teaching and the very use of Spanish, since it was considered an "imperialist language," illiteracy went from ten percent to seventy percent in the eleven years of his regime. ("Literatura moderna")

How then is the need to recover the "deeply embedded" traditions and rites reconciled with the use of Spanish? As we saw in the poetry of both Zamora and Bolekia, the use of Spanish as the principal means of communication does not preclude an African vision. Indeed, it is precisely a marker of the African vision to see the world from the point of view of not one but in some cases several languages. What distinguishes the African from the Spanish is an acknowledgment that the latter represents the circumstances of colonization, as in the following lines from Zamora's poem "Retrato de damas coloniales" (Portrait of colonial ladies) (*Memoria de laberintos*):

Mujeres de pálidas nervaduras
como de flores muertas
Senõras de mítica oquedad
. . .
Mujeres que uno jamás volverá a sorprender
en aquel inaccesible abandono

(13)

(Women of pallid veins
like dead flowers
Ladies of mythic hollowness
. . .
Women who one will never surprise again
in that inaccessible abandonment)

While the above text does not refer to language specifically, Zamora's poem reveals a unique form of crepuscular writing vis-à-vis colonial times in which Spanish was the language and the vision of power embodied in the "damas." As the poet watches them, then and now, he realizes that there is something about them that will never return, a sense of loss both nostalgic and liberating—again we see the tension between reality and desire. The flowers of the Spanish language, like those of these ladies, are dead. Abandonment, however, of Spanish would be akin to a negation of the historical reality of colonialism and its legacy.

Similarly, in Rope's poetry, language is an object of consternation as in the following poem "No hablo bubi" (I do not speak Bubi), in which communication is a prime marker of identity.

"No hablo bubi"—dices.
Gracias te doy porque no.
Para llegar a lo que tú,
¿qué ha de serse, sino mitad?

¡Quiróptero a tu suerte
abandonado
en la encrucijada del ser auténtico!
. . .
Pobre diablo, ¡no tienes identidad!

(75)

("I don't speak Bubi"—you say.
I thank you for not [doing so]. In order to become you,
what can one be, if not half?
a bat abandoned to fortune in the crossroads of authentic being!
. . .
Poor devil, you have no identity!)

Rope's ethnicity is Bubi, and this factor figures prominently in these verses. A situational poem, "I do not speak Bubi" re-creates an exchange of words between the poet and an interlocutor. That the object of address (the "you") should declare proudly that he does not speak his own language triggers an ironic series of invectives—the poet calls him an "abandoned bat," a "poor devil," and ends by depriving the interlocutor of identity. He is only half of something, in the middle of authentic being. Perhaps unwittingly, Rope has described himself as well: he is in "the middle of the crossroads of authentic being." Moreover, he suggests that this middle state may be a universal one.

The following poem is from the same collection, in which Spanish and Spanishness are by no means abandoned. Almost as if he were countering the Macías regime's attempt to obliterate all traces of Spanish culture, Rope writes a poem, "Canto a la hispanidad," reminiscent of the older generation whose veneration for all things Spanish (Chema Mijero, Ocha'a, Mathama Jones) was one of the prime movers of their writing:

Por tí, augusta madre, España,
por tu gloria preclara,
. . .
Por la fe y lengua que nos unen,
Pueblos de América
Pueblos de Africa y del mundo entero
¡juremos sobre la tumba del Atlante
del Inca y del Esclavo
que duermen en la tromba oceánica
el sueño glorioso de la paz,

conjurar juntos el agobiante tercermundismo
en cuya ríspida senda tanteamos
la órbita secreta de un futuro más venturoso!
(111–12)

(For you, august mother, Spain,
For your illustrious glory,
. . .
For this faith and language that unite us,
Peoples of America
Peoples of Africa and the entire world,
Let us swear on the grave of Atlas
of the Inca and the Slave
who sleep in the oceanic downpour
the glorious dream of peace,
conjure, together, oppressive thirdworldism
in whose rough path we decipher
the secret orbit of a more fortunate future!)

Swearing on the grave of "the Inca and the Slave" is a collective act that acknowledges the unity of Spanish-Guinean culture, an act that will lead to peace and progress. This poem is not necessarily inconsistent with the previous one, for it seems to affirm a linguistic ideology: both Spanish and Bubi as a crossroads, as a half of something or a half of nothing.

The writing of the members of the Macías generation remind us of the question of the use of indigenous languages in African writing posed by famed Kenyan writer and expatriate Ngugi Wa Thiong'o, a question that has spurred an engaging polemic. In the essay "Return to the Roots: Language Culture and Politics in Kenya," Wa Thiong'o has argued eloquently that African writers should make use of their indigenous languages as an assertion not merely of identity but of freedom in all senses, liberation from colonialism and postcolonialism as well as freedom of (political) expression. To use the language of the colonizing power—English, French, Portuguese, Spanish—is a way of "colonizing the mind." Those who disagreed, major figures such as Chinua Achebe and Wole Soyenka, among others, countered by asserting that writing in a certain language is less a matter of choice than a given: the language of articulation comes from something primordial, and any attempt to preclude a certain idiom is itself a curtailment of real freedom of expression. Ezekiel Mphalele, a South African writer, pointed out that during the apartheid regime, an attempt was made to encourage the use of indigenous languages and thereby relegate native African writing to the vernacular, that is, to submerge it into a ghetto and ensure that it not be disseminated to a wider audience (Mphalele qtd. in Wa Thiong'o, "Return" 54–55).

In what seems today a matter easily resolved by simply allowing for the individual writer to write as he or she sees fit, it is important to scrutinize Wa Thiong'o's perspective, for the issue is not as clear-cut as one might assume. In his view, language is related not only to expression but also to class and history. It is not only a vehicle of communication but what he calls a "memory bank" and goes hand in hand with independence and self-determination:

> Languages in their particular forms arise historically as social needs. Over a time, a particular system of verbal signposts comes to embody both continuity and change in their historical consciousness. It is this aspect of language as a collective memory bank of a given community which has made some people ascribe mystical independence to language. ("Return" 57)

Considering Wa Thiong'o's individual experience of prison and exile from the postcolonial regime of Daniel rap Moi (1978–2002), one might explain his insistence on indigenous languages on the desire to recover a past. The forced separation from his culture (as is the case with virtually all exile and even emigrant writers from Equatorial Guinea) has been a defining factor in virtually all his work. Moreover, the tendency in African writing to retell stories of a specific community and the need (at times explicit) to extend the oral tradition of their past to a present in which writing is an individual creative act as well as a collective performance is clearly manifested in the writers not only of the Macías generation but perhaps in all Guinean writers and cultural figures.

On the other hand, one wonders if Wa Thiong'o's arguments belie the double consciousness that he himself upholds as he writes in another essay, "Literature and Double Consciousness," which begins with a reference to W. E. B. Du Bois's characterization of "'double consciousness through which African American life and thought have evolved'" as "'a peculiar sensation . . ., this sense of always looking at oneself through the eyes of others'" (37). In what might be seen as a Marxist extension of Levinas's discussion of the other, the Kenyan author states in the same essay, "In all societies, the images we have of ourselves in relation to other selves, or the images we have of other people in relation to ourselves are dependent on the place we occupy in the entire system of organization and control of wealth" (38). Wa Thiong'o seems to conclude from this, however, that the images that wealth and power create of the self must simply be discarded. In my view, his writing, along with that of Mbomío, Ndongo, Zamora, Bolekia, and Rope (along with other Guinean writers both younger and older), shows that not only are those images part and parcel of the double consciousness itself but also that to discard them may very well turn into a vain enterprise. They remain as traces of memory, "memoria de laberintos," and in many cases arise in conjunction with counter images, images of exile such as those of Wa Thiong'o and many other African writers. Thus, it is not as much that Guinean writers in their uses of Spanish are asserting their dissent from Wa Thiong'o's view—indeed, Bolekia and Zamora, above all, would be the first to agree—"a particular system of verbal signposts comes to reflect a particular people's historical consciousness," as Wa Thiong'o says in "Return to the Roots" (57). Rather, they seem to be engaged in a reworking of Spanish, perhaps a deformation of the colonizing language, particularly as an act of defiance not only of the colonizing power but also of the continuation of that very power in the form of the tyrant who, ironically, wants to do away with Spanish.

Language itself is at the heart of the issue, and it comes back to haunt again and again just as did Patricio, the ghost whose words open this chapter. When Macías arrived, he declares, he began to speak in another language, pretending that the new idiom was the authentic one (Mbomío, *El párroco* 52). But Patricio's spirit knows better, as do all the members of the Macías generation.

CHAPTER SEVEN

Exiles Stay at Home

Much has been said of the concept of "inner exile," particularly in relation to cultures and nations that present obstacles to the expression of dissidence against the governing bodies of those cultures and nations. The nation of Equatorial Guinea is at once unique and typical among contemporary societies suffering from direct governmental restrictions (overt and covert) on the flow of information as well as on commentaries on that information—typical among African nations dominated by dictatorships and unique in its history of colonization by Spain, which itself has had a recent dictatorial past. As citizens of a former colony of Spain, Equatorial Guineans are familiar with the dictatorial history of the ex-colonizers, a relatively recent past in which a dialogue between those forced out of their land, on the one hand, and those choosing to stay (in some cases, forced to stay) is a definitive marker of the culture. Of course, I am referring to the cultural politics of Franco's Spain, the very politics that led to the creation of Equatorial Guinea's dictatorship.[1]

This is not to say, however, that Guineans have always shown animosity, or even awareness, of the societal pitfalls of Francoist dictatorship. An indication of Guinean political sensibilities is Donato Ndongo's memorable character in *Tinieblas,* Don Ramón, the native teacher who drilled into his impressionable students the high ideals and virtues of Franco and everything the "caudillo" (the chief) symbolized: Franco and his supporters were the saviors of the Spanish nation when it was being threatened by a red scourge intent on burning down churches and convents (24–29). Similarly, chapter 1 of this study shows many of the early writers and intellectuals from Equatorial Guinea, almost without exception, identified with those virtues. While not as blatantly as Don Ramón, the writing of people such as Mijero, Jones Mathama, Ocha'a, and Evita seems to avow an open espousal of Spanish imperialist, authoritarian ideology. However, the events surrounding the Macías dictatorship, the circumstances of the emergence of the country as an independent nation, and the subsequent failure to create a viable democracy meant a significant change in those sensibilities. With Macías's virulent anti-imperialist ideology directed especially against the Spanish colonizers, those who spoke or wrote with reverence or even nostalgia toward any aspect of Spanish society were met with daunting obstacles including imprisonment, torture, and execution, all part of orchestrated accusations of treason against the independent state that Papá Mesié, as Francisco Macías was called, had forged.

Thus, anticolonialism comes of age—or one might say it is deformed—in Spanish Guinea with a reign of ultranationalist state terror.[2] In 1979, with the coup against Macías successfully carried out by his nephew Teodoro Obiang, the state-driven ideology becomes even more convoluted. The official reading of the history of the first ten years of Guinean independence is highly critical of the uncle and everything he did as ruler. In Obiang's own rendition of his coming to power, *Guinea Ecuatorial: país joven* (Equatorial Guinea: A young country) (1985), the lambasting of the previous regime is paramount as a justification for his own rule. The view of the statement that the "época de triste memoria" (period of sad memories) (45) was a sorry episode of the nation's history and became part of the "imagined community" (as Benedict Anderson might say), the official story of how the nation's recent past has been shaped into a present and even brighter future. In his book, Obiang calls Macías's Equatorial Guinea a nation "sin ley" (without law) (45–63) and lambastes his uncle for the destruction he caused; at one point he calls it "una serie de holocaustos" (a series of holocausts) (52). The critique, however, has a dual intention: while it condemns the former regime for its human-rights abuses, it puts forth an impression of indignation toward such abuse, thereby solidifying its own legitimacy as the authentically redemptive government intent on correcting the ills of the previous one. Thus, by accusing Macías and his henchmen—one of whom was ironically (and pathetically) Obiang himself—the new leader puts forth an image of national identity and respect for a democratic governmental process and the rights of the individual.[3]

A young generation of writers, however, provides a vehicle by which to debunk the image. Note, for example, the words of a preface to a novel by Juan Tomás Ávila Laurel (b. 1966), *Áwala cu sangui* (Awala with blood)[4] (2000) in which the author offers something of an allegory of the change from Macías to Obiang that is indeed more of the same:

> Y cuando todos los nativos creían que se había acabado todo, que se había despedido el representante de Macías, pues el barco había subido las escaleras y había emitido los tres pitidos de despedida y se había puesto en marcha, vieron cómo giró y dirigió de nuevo su proa amenazante sobre la isla y volvió sobre los mares ya navegados. Todos los isleños llevaron las manos al pecho, sin acertar en la causa de su extraña vuelta. ¿Qué habrá olvidado el representante de Macías? . . . Venían a tierra ¿A qué? Todos temían. Quizás sea por mi edad de entonces que no llegara a mis oídos la causa de esta inesperada vuelta. . . . No sé. (iii)
>
> (And when all the natives thought that everything was over, that Macías's representative had bid farewell, since the gangplank had been pulled back and the ship had blown three whistles signaling its departure and had fired up its engines, they saw that it turned back aiming the bow menacingly at the island and making its way back over waters that had already been navigated. All the islanders brought their hands to their chests, without knowing the cause of the strange return. What could Macías's representative have forgotten? . . . They approached land. For what? Everyone was afraid. Maybe it was because of my age back then, but the reason for their surprise return was not communicated to me. I don't know.)

In many ways, Ávila Laurel (the most prolific of Guinean writers) expresses here the conscience of his generation. He is a model for others of his age, such as José Siale (b. 1961) and Maximiliano Nkogo (b. 1972), all of whom convey in their writing a profound dissatisfaction with the state of affairs of their country. Indeed, many ask, what had Macías forgotten on his way out? The curious answer is "I don't know."

The presumed lack of knowledge is somewhat disingenuous, not in a malicious sense but in the sense of someone who knows of their own demise yet is unable to resist it openly, other than through indirect allusion. There is much of the picaresque in the narrative of Guinean inner exiles. While not always humorous, Ávila Laurel's first-person perspective of events paradoxically is a way of skirting the criticism he offers to a Guinean society led dictatorially by Obiang and his lackeys. In *Awala cu sangui,* the object of the description is the life of the people of Annobon during the Macías dictatorship (specifically, 1977). It is a story told from the perspective of one who was there, as the third-person narrator occasionally becomes a first person. Yet, the preface and an occasional reference to the present coyly remind the reader that perhaps the real object of criticism transcends Annobon during a specific year. While a relatively short text, *Awala cu sangui* offers an epic rendition of Macías's rule, the work written as if the storyteller were relating a legend. All characters suffer, not only the Annobonese but also the "subversives," whose only crime is to point out the lack of basic living essentials such as soap, and those who attempt to escape into a hostile ocean, that is, those who saw "'la muerte del mar'" (the death of the sea) (55). The phrase has a dual reference: the escape from Macías's Annobon and beyond that the countless deaths of Africans as they set sail for Europe.[5]

Yet, for all the indirectness of Ávila Laurel's criticism, it is also true that what gives rise to his suggestive prose is not only the despotism of his government but also his literary sensibilities—the verbal winks of the eye and a certain playfulness of language that is itself an attempt to bring thoughtful attention to the realities of his society. The contrast, for example, between his essays and his imaginative works is important. In *Cómo convertir este país en un paraíso: Otras reflexiones sobre Guinea Ecuatorial* (How to turn this country into a paradise: Other reflections on Equatorial Guinea) (2005), the criticism is open, perhaps even defiant. It consists of commentaries on the politics and society of Equatorial Guinea, all written in the style of a hard-hitting editorial one might find in a news daily. The list ranges from "Agua" (Water) to "Tabaco, el alcohol, las drogas" (Tobacco, alcohol, drugs) arranged alphabetically in the table of contents, so as to direct the reader to virtually any social problem he or she may think of including but not limited to: agriculture, China, city hall, Cuba, demagogy, democracy, enemies, the flag, freedom of expression, God, Korea, press, radio, sex, soccer, torture, tourism, TV, and youth. The author's words are acerbic and at times sardonic as in his mocking description of the government's discouragement of the use of tobacco, which, according to Ávila Laurel, far from a manifestation of a genuine concern for the health of its citizens is in reality an unintentional parody of similar measures in countries of the global north: "And this imitation of the customs or laws of foreign countries reveals how servile servitude of some governments are, in our case it comes from attitudes filled with paradox and demagogy" (54). Further on in the same commentary, he points out the hypocrisy of the familiar warning, "Sanitation authorities caution that use of tobacco can lead to serious health problems" (55). In view of the fact that there is no medical equipment in all of Equatorial Guinea capable of detecting cancer and that no one knows the causes of countless hospital deaths—Ávila Laurel works in a hospital in Malabo—it is patently clear that the "public service" slogan is a sham (55).

Yet, the more serious critiques of governmental practices appear with somewhat more earnestness when the subject deals with an activity as hideous as torture (15–16). The entry begins with a discussion of the Macías years in which the practice of "Atar" (Tying up) (15) was used as a method of dealing with "subversives," those who, according to the rulers, were intent on destroying the newly formed independent state. The ones who suffered this form of punishment or interrogation were bound as if they were a "bundle of wood" (15). Many have lived to tell of the experience, asserts the author, although he does not describe specific cases. Significantly, an allusion is made to the same practice that goes on in Ávila Laurel's present: "As seen recently among different cases of convicted people who have shown signs of having been tied cruelly, we recover a previous memory [the Macías years] so that we can speak of the treatment of detainees in the penitentiaries of Equatorial Guinea. In these places detainees are beaten, in all the prisons there are various forms of physical punishment" (16). There is a similar comparison in the entry on "discursos" (speeches) (34–35) in which the author mocks Macías's political harangues and compares them to those of the present day, speeches that no one understands despite the applause: "El cambio de régimen no aportó ningún cambio en este tema" (The change of regime did not bring a single change in this situation) (35).

Thus the overriding theme of this work is the insistence on the continuity of dictatorial rule, an assertion that the promise of the end of a horrific period of Guinean life has not been fulfilled. However, while the previous regime was known for its isolation from the "West" in its embrace of the nonaligned nations during the cold war, in Ávila Laurel's present political reality, the developed nations—those that triumphed with the end of the cold war—are complicit. The situation is different, but the social reality remains virtually identical: economic misery, lack of potable water or support for public education, corruption in the highest circles of government, a corruption linked to multinational corporations (63–64). Indeed, one wonders how such a diatribe was allowed to circulate, given the very situation described in its pages. Again, a comparison to the Spanish state during the last decade of Franco's rule may serve as an explanation. Equatorial Guinean society, for all its anticolonial attitudes, still keeps Spain in its historical memory, and the patterns of the flow of information are an indication. One notes that in Ávila Laurel's criticism, there are no mentions of specific cases of prisons or human-rights abuses, and when the subject turns to the economy, there is barely a discussion of Equatorial Guinea's most lucrative national resource: oil.[6] Yet, the most likely explanation of the paradoxical publication of "How to Turn This Country into a Paradise" is its lack of readership. While the literacy rate is relatively high (85 percent, according to UNESCO), dissemination of written texts by Guineans is virtually nonexistent. The rulers learned from the Franco regime that criticism can be controlled, and its occasional circulation can be used as a sign of tolerance, albeit repressive. Teodoro Obiang seems to have taken lessons from Manuel Fraga Iribarne, whose infamous censorship laws of the 1960s were designed to redact all comments on the regime that were not positive.[7]

Both the beginning and the end of "How to turn this country into a paradise" are telling indicators of the nature of the criticism as well as its intentions. Unlike the preface that announces the beginning of *Awala cu sangui*, the initial words of these essays are straightforward. The author speaks of the difficulties of disseminating ideas such as the ones expressed in his text, given the political circumstances. Almost as an act of resistance against the repressive tolerance shown by the publication of his works, he states that the curative intention of his words will not be fully realized until they are allowed to be uttered in the public square (7), thereby affirming the importance of orality in his community. Even more notable is the final entry, "Resumen" (Summary) (78–85), which is more a statement of purpose, something of a Guinean "What is to be done," than a synopsis. Here, he states unequivocally that the solution to Guinean society's grave problems is not a regime change. The deleterious effects of the previous coup that brought about the present change are reason enough; the victims were not as much the previous rulers since many have remained in power. Those who suffered the most were Guinean citizens of all ethnicities. He alludes to an aborted coup supposedly plotted by a group of first-world oil profiteers, among whom was Mark Thatcher, son of Margaret, in alliance with a prominent leader of the Guinean opposition in exile, Severo Moto.[8] Although Ávila Laurel expresses his skepticism that such a coup was a real threat, his more important concern is that any armed action in his country would result in disaster (83) and that ultimately the solutions to Equatorial Guinea's problems must come from the Guineans themselves acting en masse and in protest: "El cumplimiento de las promesas electorales es el que legitimiza un sistema democrático. Para ello, el pueblo tiene que existir. Tiene que manifestarse mediante reclamaciones puntuales y justas" (The fulfillment of electoral promises is what legitimizes a democratic system. For this, the people must exist. [The people] must demonstrate by way of just and precise demands) (82). He goes on to conclude that silence is not an option, especially in a world in which the demands for human rights are growing. Defiance, as in the very pamphlet that the reader has in his or her hands, is what the times require: "We know that no one wants to be silent. Also that no one should do so. To the thousands who do not remain quiet, we add our voice and again we turn our backs on the shameless violation of human rights as a reproach to that behavior" (85). Again, regardless of the political passion that emanates from these concluding words—themselves worthy of a speech in the public square countering the empty promises of the officials of the two dictatorial regimes—the clear statement in opposition to armed insurrection, as well as a rejection of foreign mercenaries who presume to take power, is perhaps something that those in power might welcome. Clearly, Ávila Laurel has been a thorn in the sides of Guinean leaders. Yet, the most feared consequence, a repetition of the very coup that brought the two dictatorships to power, will certainly not come about by the efforts of this Annobonese writer, at least not according to a straightforward reading of this text. Notwithstanding the political rhetoric of "How to turn this country into a paradise," this text is representative of the ambivalent voice of an inner exile, an outcast relegated to the margins of power. The author's frustration at his own marginality is as much a motivation for his political writing as it is a desire for change.

While Ávila Laurel is not a wandering political exile, such as Ndongo, Mbomío, Bolekia, or Zamora, he has spent time outside his country. In keeping with the patterns of writers, professionals, and other intellectuals from Equatorial Guinea, he has resided in Spain, if only for a short time. In 1998, he was in Valencia for three months studying techniques for the cultivation of bacteria. Thus, Ávila Laurel is familiar with immigrant life in Spain, not as much as a seeker of refuge from African material realities, that is, not with the hope of staying permanently, but as a student with a professional interest in the host country. Yet, for Ávila Laurel, an imaginative postcolonial writer, the time in Spain was more than a period of professional advancement; it was a time of observation, and the object of observation was the colonial power that had shaped both his own life and that of his country. Moreover, for an internally exiled writer who feels a responsibility to oppose the social and political realities of his country, the stay in another land makes those observations of another country all the more intense and complex.

The literary text that best exemplifies Ávila Laurel's reading of Spain is *El desmayo de Judas* (Judas's faint). The title, according to Lewis in his assessment of this novella (189–92), comes from "a religious group whose purpose it seems is to reinterpret the role of Judas in biblical mythology. . . . The pro-Judas group maintains that this apostle was carrying out the will of God" (190). Set in the late 1990s in the old quarter ("Casco Viejo") of Valencia, not far from the banks of the River Turia, the narrative deals with the lives of Spaniards coping with difficult family relations and all the social ills that afflict modern life in a first-world country. It begins with a birth, that of Judas Garamond, the illegitimate child of Ana Garamond and Juan, a young man suffering from mental instability. That disequilibrium, as well as the family dysfunction into which Judas is born, allow the author a vehicle by which to articulate a series of outrageous statements on that "other" (for him) world. While Ana lives in the same apartment complex as Juan's family, there has been little contact until Juan's mother and father learn of the birth of their grandchild. We later learn that Ana herself suffers from epilepsy due to having been the victim of abuse. Family relations, then, an important fabric of Guinean society, are inspected from the eyes of an African, who in this text observes his Spanish surroundings as if he were a voyeur, suggesting to his reader that the people in this land are not only odd but that they, too, suffer from social ills.

The prime example of oddity is Juan, who becomes involved with a "Brotherhood" (Hermandad) or sect that believes that Judas Iscariot is the prime model for the human condition, the one who betrays Christ but repents for having done so—thus, the name of his child. Juan is eventually cast away from the sect and becomes a street wanderer shouting incomprehensible warnings and pronouncements into the Valencian air. There is an attempt on the part of the narrator to expose this oddity in a sympathetic light; Juan is something of an idiot savant decrying the ills of a world gone mad. In many ways first-world modernity is one of his targets: "'Ahora estoy aquí en este pedestal, mirando las cabezas de las vérgenes y de los apóstatas del comunismo. . . . Ahora veo vuestras intenciones gastando millones en putas y ladrones. Alguien ha dicho que soy loco, y no sabe que veo todo desde aquí'" (Now I'm here on this pedestal, looking at the virgins and the apostates of communism. . . . Now I see your intentions spending millions on whores and thieves. Someone has said that I'm crazy, and they don't know that I can see all from here) (65). And while the character rants on, we as readers might laugh as would the one who passes by this "ambulatory schizophrenic" (as the modern therapeutic community might say), yet in the hands of this African writer, Juan's insanity, somehow, seems not so insane. Like Ávila Laurel, Juan is a marginal member of society, tossed into a world that seems both strange and daunting to him.

However, this seemingly unfamiliar first-world environment is not altogether unknown to the author. Typical of African double consciousness, Ávila Laurel represents the lives of his former colonizers both from within their society and from the outside. The narrative voice begins the tale from the perspective of an omniscient third person, yet as it progresses we note (as in other works by Ávila Laurel) a suggested first-person presence who throws the perspective of the all-knowing storyteller out of kilter. While the narrative "I" never appears explicitly, the story line is interrupted at times with comments about the society and the specific city in which it takes place. Thus, Spain is described as an unfamiliar place, as if the describer were speaking at once to a group of tourists from a distant land and at the same time to Spaniards themselves, showing them how "others" see them, not without the typically African questioning of modern society. One of the narrator's many disquisitions on today's consumer society is that all cities seem the same: "there is no difference between a girl lounging in a easy chair in her house in Zaragoza and another one, who, with her tits pointing upward, looks at her own Valencian sky; all skies are the same." With all the talk of each city's peculiarities, he goes on, "No one can tell any city from another when sitting in front of a pitcher of beer" (36).

Interestingly, Marvin Lewis sees this work as having a "certain metafictional quality" (191). Indeed, these authorial interruptions also allow for social commentary from a postcolonial perspective as the narrator defamiliarizes the all-too-typical Spanish café banter, better known as the "tertulia," always with the beverage of choice serving as the inspiration behind the not-always-coherent opinions:

> ¿De qué hablarían los tres hombres frente a sus vasos de ginebra, cerveza o coñac? . . . De la contaminación, de la delincuencia, de las guerras, del paro del proletariado, del fútbol y la dictadura de los políticos, o sea, de la democracia. . . . Si los coches Ford tienen que dar trabajo a miles de tudescos, francos y lusos cerrar una fábrica porque su humo contamina es firmar un contrato con la miseria. . . . Y esto se puede decir porque se sabe que no se puede arreglar nada, que pese a las verdades y mentiras con alcohol, mañana, cuando nos miremos en el espejo creeremos que hemos hecho el ridículo. (38–42)

> (What could these three men be talking about in front of their glasses of gin, beer, or cognac? . . . Pollution, crime, wars, unemployment of the proletariat, soccer, and politician's dictatorship, that is, democracy. . . . If Ford cars must bring employment to thousands of Germans, French, or Portuguese, the closing of a factory because it causes pollution, that means that you're signing a contract with misery. . . . And you can say all this because you know that you can't fix anything, in spite of the truths and lies that come with alcohol, tomorrow, when we look at ourselves in the mirror, we'll think that we've come out looking ridiculous.)

Here, as in the entire novel, Ávila Laurel is at once demonstrating his own knowledge of Spanish life and exposing its artificiality and absurdity, particularly as it is seen by one who also knows the misery of the third world from within, as we have seen in his political essays. Despite the author's brief stay in Spain, his familiarity with the society goes beyond that of a visitor. Indeed, he is telling Spaniards who they are as he invites them to look at themselves from the perspective of the African other.

Yet, Africa is not absent from this "Valencian" text. Occasionally, Africans appear in the story, almost furtively, as when Juan encounters a pair of blacks walking along the banks of the Turia. It is revealing that this crazy-sane person, who has become a "vagabond" in the city, is able, despite the language barrier, to strike up a relation with them, which suggests a kinship between Juan and the equally out-of-place people from that "other" continent (58–59). Yet, more important is the Guinean novice, María del Carmen Abang, a character who also comes into contact with Juan and whose story appears toward the end of the narrative, again as a monstrance of an unlikely affinity between Juan and Africa. Born in a village in the continental area of Equatorial Guinea, Abang finds herself in Spain in fulfillment of a religious vocation as a nurse, indeed something of a countermissionary coming to a first-world country from the third-world to do God's work. In another intervention by the narrator, we learn that María del Carmen dutifully performed her tasks at the Valencian hospital but that the only task difficult for her to perform, if not impossible, was the attention to the dead. For as the author interjects, the religious authorities were unaware that in her culture, women are not allowed proximity to corpses (97–100). So much so, that she suffers what one might call a nervous breakdown, making it impossible for her to continue in Spain. She returns to her native land and is cured by a shaman ("curandero") whom she ends up marrying and with whom she has "robustos hijos" (robust children). That they lived happily ever after, asserts the narrator playfully, is the end (and future) of her story (100).

María del Carmen Abang's interpolated tale is connected to the story line of *El desmayo de Judas* in an indirect way. For a reason perhaps only understandable to crazy people (and to this black author), when Juan sees her, he attempts to bite her ear. For this, he is summoned to the police station for interrogation. Thus, Abang is the cause of Juan's demise through no fault of her own. The more intricate connection between the two, however, is thematic. They are both marginal figures in Spanish society, and both are seen, according to conventional norms, as people who need help, either from some sort of therapeutic community or a benevolent organization that will take care of them. The outcomes of both, however, could not be more diametrically opposed. While María del Carmen enjoys a fairy tale end as she returns to her birthplace to be cured according to the practices of traditional society, the last image of Juan is pathetic. He meets both his wife, Ana, and child, Judas, in a charitable establishment for the homeless; his joy is palpable as he cries out, "'Es mi hijo'" (It's my son) (105). Ana, however, in one of her epileptic fits, unable to cope with the encounter, is taken away by an ambulance. Juan, also incapable of confronting the reality, goes back into his world, leaving his son alone and in effect orphaned, just as destitute as his father.

Ávila Laurel began writing *El desmayo de Judas* in Valencia and finished it upon his return to Malabo. It is a work that expresses at once the sensibilities of an inner exile and those of an immigrant intellectual far from home. The evocations of Valencia, its natural atmosphere, the cold of January unfamiliar to an African, the narrow streets of the old quarter, all this despite the assertion that all the cities in Spain look the same to the narrator (35), are further manifestations of the double consciousness that shapes Equatorial Guinean writing in exile, both inner and outer. And in Ávila Laurel's case, the double consciousness is exacerbated considering the added factor of inner versus exterior exile. That Ávila Laurel and others like him carry on a dialogue with those who have left contributes to the ambivalence of exile. In an interview conducted worlds away from both Africa and Spain, Ávila Laurel and Donato Ndongo enter into that very dialogue.[9] Both manifest a certain solidarity among exiles while acknowledging (perhaps unwittingly) the difficulties of maintaining that united front of (exilic) resistance. When asked about the condition of exile, Ávila Laurel asserted:

> I know that Donato lives in exile and that I live in Equatorial Guinea, and I know the circumstances of his exile. I don't think a special category [of exile] is merited. It is painful to be in exile, but not so much as to assert that there is a tremendous difference between one who is outside and one who is inside.

to which Ndongo responded,

> Yes indeed. I agree with Juan Tomás, at least in the case of Equatorial Guinea, there is no difference. That dichotomy has not yet come about because we have a shared reality that has forced some of us to leave. Because exile is not voluntary. They have obligated us to leave the country five minutes before they were going to kill us. That's reality. And those who are on the inside, for whatever reason, continue to be exiles within that immense concentration camp called Equatorial Guinea. (Rizo, "Una conversación" 269)

But, of course, there is a difference. Despite the assertions to the contrary and despite the experience of political and social alienation felt by both, the exilic experiences of the two writers are not the same. Ávila Laurel expresses the pain of his own inner exile, a pain that by definition arises from a series of circumstances different from those of his older brother in the family of exiles. As Ndongo spoke of having been forced to leave minutes before someone in power was going to pull the trigger, he was referring to his own case (see chapter 2 in the current volume). And the metaphor of the nation–concentration camp is something he feels from the outside, while Ávila Laurel experiences it tangibly, perhaps not as metaphorically. That both are exiles is indisputable, but this does not preclude different (indeed very different) experiences, a distinction that manifests itself in their writing.

Nowhere, however, is the ambivalent dialogue between those who have left and those who stayed more apparent than in the story "Todo llega con las olas del mar" (All arrives with the waves of the sea) from the collection *La revuelta de los disfraces* (The disguise's revolt) (2003) by José Siale, a Guinean writer living in Malabo who is of Ávila Laurel's generation. Siale's status as inner exile is problematic given that he has worked within the government of Teodoro Obiang as a magistrate of Equatorial Guinea's Supreme Court and as legal advisor to the office of the presidency. His writing, however, is by no means an apology, much less a justification, of governmental policy at any level. His most extensive work, a first novel, *Cenizas de Kalabó y termes* (2000) (Kalabo ashes and termites), is a bildungsroman with a first-person narrator not without touches of the picaresque, as in the following masterful first sentence:

> Lo acepto, que me corten la lengua ya, desde ahora, que me metan "iboga" por todos los orificios hasta reventar sin previa extrema unción, si lo que divulgo a continuación para el conocimiento público, deviene de una tergiversación de los hechos acaecidos en la villa de Santa Isabel el día dos de febrero de mil novecientos y pico. (19)

> (I accept it, let them cut out my tongue, starting now, let them fill all my orifices with "iboga" [a hallucinogen] until I burst without having received the last rites, if what I reveal here for everyone to know, comes from a deformation of the events that took place in the town of Santa Isabel on the second of February around 1900.)

The exaggerated insistence on the exactness of his rendition of events, ironically and picaresquely, leads the reader to skepticism. While the focus of the protagonist's life becomes the Macías dictatorship and all its abuses, the suggestion that the regime continues in the form of another (however unnamed) tyrant resides uncomfortably and coyly in the mind of the reader, and, as such, it provides a haven from possible recriminations from the authorities. Even more politically ambivalent is "Todo llega con las olas del mar," a story set in a time and place not immediately clear to the reader. Its main intention, notwithstanding the nebulousness of the geographical and temporal references, almost as if it were a fantasy, manifests (with *Las cenizas*) a wish to carry on a dialogue with the exiles.

Cenizas and the stories of *La revuelta* are both written within a literary context of repression, that is, they are both openly aware of the very social-intellectual context that comprises virtually all the factors surrounding emixile. While *Cenizas* is filled with episodes that remind us of Donato Ndongo's *Los poderes de la tempestad,* the story "Todo llega" is an undisguised (as in the title) commentary on that very work. The first work is filled with specific historical references to the Macías regime, as in a section narrating a political trial in which a citizen who has spent time out of the country is accused of subversion (*Cenizas* 164–73). This episode echoes similar situations throughout Ndongo's *Los poderes,* although in the former, the narrative is immediate, as if it were told with the aid of a real trial transcript (not implausible given that the author is a lawyer):

> ¿Quieres decir que vuestra facción activista no tiene medios financieros? ¿Cómo actuáis? ¿Cómo os movéis? Que te conste que estas preguntas son de pura rutina, lo sabemos todo.
>
> Yo no tengo ninguna facción activista ni pertenezco a movimiento político alguno. (*Cenizas* 166)

> (Do you mean to say that your activist group has no funds? How do you function? How do you move about? Keep in mind that these questions are pure routine, we know everything.
>
> I do not belong to an activist group nor any kind of political movement.)

By contrast, "Todo llega" is illusive about its historical reality and specific about its literary allusions. From the opening of the story we meet dreamlike characters who are "alive"—although even this may be questioned—only in the sense that they have lived in other works of recent Guinean literature. Indeed, these characters also provide geographical specificity by allusion, that is, they have appeared before as characters in literary works about Equatorial Guinea. Moreover, all the characters and works that constitute the immediate referents appear within the context of exile. The story is something of a roman à clef, and the dedication is the first clue: A Francisco Zamora, Justo Bolekia, Donato Ndong [Siale's spelling], Juan T. Ávila Laurel, Joaquín Mbomío . . . y todos aquellos que cuentan nuestras historias" (To [. . .] . . . all those who tell our stories) (69). However, not all these writers receive equal attention. The dominant (pre)text that serves as Siale's point of departure is Ndongo's *Los poderes de la tempestad.* The main character of "Todo llega," Mbo Abeso, is a secondary—albeit important—personage in Ndongo's novel: Primo Mbo, the cousin of the protagonist of *Los poderes,* is the one who meets him at the airport and accompanies him through much of the ordeal of the exilic return (see chapter 2). We recall in *Los poderes* that the cousin dies in the novel at the hands of Macías's brutal armed guards because the main character, the unnamed "yo-tú" of his trilogy, refuses to carry out the order to kill his cousin. In Siale's story, however, Primo Mbo is much alive, so much so, that when he is confronted by his literary demise, he questions it, much like Unamuno's Augusto Pérez in *Niebla* (Mist) and the characters in Luigi Pirandello's memorable *Six Characters in Search of an Author.* What saves Primo Mbo in the story, or so he thinks, is that he had not read beyond page 299; his death arrives on page 301 of the *Los poderes* novel. The absurdity of the situation is exacerbated in the light of the context of his conversation with another character, none other than Judas Garamond, the infant in Ávila Laurel's novella. Equally unreliable as a vehicle to reality and equally fictional, Judas Garamond (Siale's re-creation) also refuses to accept the story of his counterpart in *El desmayo de Judas* (Siale 96–99). When Primo Mbo, who has read the work, summarizes the plot to him, Judas responds much the same way as the "dead" cousin: "'¡No es mi historia!'" (It's not my story) (99). Indeed, the story is a parody in the classic sense.

Yet, it would be misguided to read Siale's story as a spoof of the exile literature of his country, a text whose intention is to establish a barrier between his own work and that of not only Ndongo and Ávila Laurel (an avowed inner exile) but also Zamora, Bolekia, and Mbomío, all of whom make cameo appearances through references to their works. Given both the anthropological and literary importance of the dead as crucial (indeed living) forces in shaping the present and future, the figures masking as characters of Siale's story are more manifestations of homage to the exiles than a debunking of them. In many ways, Siale's story is a vehicle to carry on the tradition of the ancestors, in this case a clever vehicle, postmodern in its literary references and verbal winks. Yet, perhaps more important as an unstated thematic reference is the "mibili"—the ceremonial phenomenon profoundly connected to a belief system in which the ancestors come back to life to intervene in present situations. As we have seen, this phenomenon is seen directly in the works of Ávila Laurel, Mbomío, indirectly in Ndongo's constant mention of ancestors as primal forces, as well as in the poetry of Bolekia and Zamora.[10] In this sense, the thrust of Siale's statement in "Todo llega con las olas del mar" has to do with the arrival on the Guinean shore not only of the exiles themselves but also their spirit-characters, at once dead and alive, as are the elders who now occupy another life.

On the other hand, one cannot help coming away from this text perplexed. The strange happenings, characters, and conversations notwithstanding, the reality of the Guinean carnage of 1968–79 and continuing (albeit not as horrifically) into the twenty-first century is, after all, the motivation of Guinean exile and emigration, a circumstance that Siale attempts to counter with his writing. But does the author call in this particular text for the return of the exiles? Does he yearn for their presence in a sacred parody directed toward them? Is he suggesting that his government—after all, he works for it—will welcome the exilic homecoming? It seems that the playfulness of

"Todo llega con las olas del mar," a tendency not altogether missing from the other stories of *La revuelta,* belies the lamentations of exile. It is also worthy of note that on its own, that is, the story of the newly conceived Mbo Abeso along with the other characters, is not a self-contained narrative—it cannot be. Were it not for *Los poderes* and other texts, we would not have a story. Thus, the intended readers of this work are primarily the exiles themselves. In a work of social criticism, the kind that inner exiles tend to write, one must at least ask if this is enough.

Similar to Siale's is the case of Maximiliano Nkogo and his only published novel *Adjá-Adjá* (Hustle [slang, Equatorial Guinea]) (2000) among the most adroitly constructed narratives of Guinean exile-emigration literature. Born in 1972 in the continental area of Equatorial Guinea in Nfulunkok-Yenkeng, he lived in Malabo during his adolescence. At the age of seventeen, with the encouragement of Donato Ndongo, who was the director of the Hispano-Guinean Cultural Center in Malabo from 1985 to 1992, he began to dabble in the art of fiction, and the result, *Adjá-Adjá,* a collection of short fiction, was felicitous: "Adjá-Adjá y compañero en una jornada ordinaria" (Adjá-Adjá and company on an ordinary day), "Adjá-Adjá y compañero en un tres de agosto" (Hustle and company on August third), and "Emigración" (Emigration) are all three included in the title *Adjá-Adjá y otros relatos* (Hustle and other stories) (see Lewis's description 66–73). Nkogo, according to his then-mentor, seemed to have the predisposition to become a writer. Like many of his generation, he spent time in Spain as a young man, in his case studying Spanish literature and philology at the Universidad Complutense de Madrid while residing at the residence hall Nuestra Señora de Africa. Notwithstanding the critical success of the collection—Nkogo was awarded a literary prize for the collection by Malabo's cultural center—he did not complete his program of study in Madrid. Instead, Nkogo returned to Equatorial Guinea to work for the government. He is now minister of welfare. Thus, like Siale, Nkogo's status as inner exile is tempered by his position in the Obiang government.

Of all the narratives written by the young generation of inner exiles (if we accept that category for Nkogo), *Adjá-Adjá* is the most clearly and consistently picaresque. The very title could not be more roguish. It is a vernacular pidgin English expression in Equatorial Guinea that refers to the attempt to get something for nothing through illicit or illegal behavior; deceit is virtually always involved. An American English equivalent might be *jive* or *hustle,* although both of these do not take into consideration *adjá-adjá*'s most salient feature: the bribe. Extortion may also be part of the activity, yet *adjá-adjá* is more a petty transgression than part of "organizational crime." As a practice, it is by no means exclusive to Equatorial Guinea; there is more than enough evidence for it in the so-called first world. But in African countries, as well as in Latin America, this kind of activity is as much cultural as it is juridical or criminological. *Deviance,* as it is understood in developed countries, would not pertain to *adjá-adjá,* because it is not exactly extraordinary or exceptional, it is simply a technique of survival. There is a Spanish word on which *adjá-adjá* is derived, migaja, which comes from *miga* (crumb or morsel), referring to what an urban pigeon might pick up off the street (*Adjá-Adjá* 48).[11] Thus, *adjá-adjá* also connotes something unclean in a moral sense as well as tangible.

The real names of the protagonists of *Adjá-Adjá* are never revealed, only their nicknames, "adjá-adjá and company," a designation that defines them according to their unsavory activity. The designation *adjá-adjá,* according to the narrator of the second story, was contrived when the characters were in the military where a cadet devoured four bread rolls that belonged to an officer. And when this became public knowledge, the narrator tells us, the other cadets began to call him "Adjá-Adjá" or morsel-morsel (48). After their time in the military, they become traffic police, and, as such, their social function enhances both the nature of the activity and its transgression: they are policemen, not high-ranking officials, common "cops," having a difficult time surviving in a social structure that makes it extremely difficult to do so. Thus, in many ways, they are not exceptional; the author's choice of policemen as protagonists exposes the criminality of the entire society, a criminality of which no one is spared. The two policeman, however, are perhaps more directly responsible for the persistence of officially sanctioned criminal activity since it is their social function, conventionally defined, to do precisely the opposite.[12] Like a picaresque tale, *Adjá-Adjá* asks ethical questions on the individual's complicity in a social system that counters what we accept as honorable behavior. Also like the picaresque genre, the text exposes certain social realities that allow the reader to ponder, perhaps even condemn, the injustice and inequality of that society. And in the context of Guinean society of the 1990s, the picaresque is an apt outlet of criticism for inner exile, as it was for the anonymous author of *Lazarillo de Tormes* in the sixteenth century and for Camilo José Cela, author of *Pascual Duarte,* in the twentieth, both of whom might be seen as inner exiles in their own right.

While the general object of commentary of "Adjá-Adjá y compañero en una jornada ordinaria" and "Adjá-Adjá y compañero en un tres de agosto" is contemporary Guinean society, that is, Obiang's Ecuatorial Guinea and indirectly other postcolonial African dictatorships, the immediate focus is quotidian reality.[13] Both stories take place in a single day—Aristotle could not have been more pleased—and the happenings are seemingly insignificant: two policeman get up in the morning and set off for work; after the day is done, they come home. Their work consists not as much of maintaining law and order as finding something for nothing to complement their miniscule wages by using their petty power over the citizens they come across, always pointing out some kind of irregularity, threatening arrest or legal action, and finally, if all comes out according to plan, accepting the bribe. The physical descriptions of Malabo, the conversations with ordinary people, the market place, the movie theater still playing *Star Wars* and interrupting the session several times, no doubt due to the ill-functioning equipment (24, 35), the bar in which Adjá-Adjá and company enjoy a glass of wine for free by complaining (and threatening) that the glasses are dirty (32–34), all these happenings in their minimalist depictions, are in reality not minimal in the least, they are part of the author's strategy for laying bare the ills of Guinean society in its postcolonial and post-Macías reality. The roguish humor notwithstanding, Nkogo's day-in-the-life rendering of his Afro-Spanish world is anything but trivial.

As in the veiled social criticism of much inner-exile literature (and in picaresque literature as well), the self-conscious narrator is implicitly included in his own critique. While the narrator of these two stories is a third person, the perspective is limited by the eyes of the two main characters. Adjá-Adjá y compañero seem to be telling their own stories. The very doubling of the protagonist(s) is an indication: they seem to complement one another, almost as if they were speaking in one voice. They seem to share all experiences in precisely the same way; they even finish each other's sentences:

> "Y le aseguramos, señora, que si no fuera por este señor que está ahí en la puerta . . ." le dice Adjá-Adjá
>
> "lo hubieramos acabado de otra forma" agrega el compañero. (33)

> ("I assure you, Madame, that if it weren't for that gentleman over there by the door"—Adjá-Adjá tells her,
>
> —"we would have solved this in another way," adds his companion.)

While the united front established by Adjá-Adjá and his "company" is designed as a barrier between the police and the citizens, it is also apparent that the two petty officials are citizens as well. They are not spared their fellow Guinean's hardships; they, too, must survive in a society in which scarcity is the mainstay of everyday life. We note a certain sympathy in their portrayal despite their devious and bullying activity. The opening image of the first story describes the protagonist—one of the few scenes in which Adjá-Adjá is without a companion—in his meager home with his wife and children. Life in Equatorial Guinea for these policemen is "days without joy," not a great deal to eat, "just a bunch of bananas not yet ripe" (13). Nkogo's description of life questions the complicity of all Guinean citizens in a society replete with corruption. The moral questioning continues throughout "Adjá-Adjá y compañero en un día ordinario," despite the satirical tone. In the culminating episode of the story (40), the narrator intervenes with an ironically moralizing discourse pointing out the guilt pangs felt by both characters at all they have done on this "ordinary day." Yet, like the more engaging picaresque tales, the reader is unsure if these policemen are genuinely remorseful. Indeed, remorse is for the reader to determine. One senses that all participants in the story—characters, author, narrator, reader—are included in the interrogation.

More politically bold is the second story, which continues virtually all the features of the first: the setting is the same, as are the main characters and the twenty-four-hour time frame; even the secondary characters appear as parts of the same cross-section of society. The important difference, which will not amount to a major difference in the policemen's routine, is that the second story occurs on a national holiday: "en un tres de agosto" (August third) refers to the commemoration of Teodoro Obiang's liberating coup that supposedly freed Guineans from a "despotismo sangriento" (bloody despotism) (43). The depiction of the festivities and the reasons for celebrating are rendered in the same voice as in the first story, thus the reader can not help wonder how straightforward these seemingly uncritical depictions are. Indeed, there is a hint of parody when the narrator portrays the historical events that provide the motive for the celebration. A historical monument was erected, he asserts, "commemorating those altruistic martyrs . . . who, at the moment of truth decided to offer their souls for the common cause" (43). Clearly, the rhetoric is bombastic, and its effect, particularly in the light of what went on the previous story and will continue in this one, is to debunk the highfalutin discourse of the Obiang regime, which is never named yet understood on virtually every page. That the activity of "adjá-adjá" has continued on this day like any other day, that the promise of development by means of Equatorial Guinea's petroleum (71), its most lucrative resource, is not in the horizon, and that Malabo's "lujosas chabolas" (luxurious huts) (57, 72) seem to be the citizens' most common dwelling places, all point to a contradiction in the portrayal of the "Third of August" as a symbolic and heroic day. In other words, the picture of the country painted by the narrator through the eyes of these "cops" stands as a dialogical counterpoint to the official discourse of the nation.

Still, the most disturbing feature of both stories, beyond the social reality of Obiang's Malabo, is the ethical commentary that closes the two, almost in symmetrical relationship. In "Adjá-Adjá y compañero en un día ordinario" Adjá-Adjá and his partner are bothered by what they have done or at least they begin to question their own behavior: "Van pensando en las circunstancias y vicisitudes de la vida, y profundamente sienten remordimientos por todo lo que han dicho y hecho hoy" (They are thinking of the circumstances and the vicissitudes of life, and deeply they feel guilt over all they have said and done today) (40). Yet, like virtually all the instances in which the reader begins to sympathize with the main characters—again the comparison with *Lazarillo* is apt—the narrator puts a stop to the sympathy with more cynicism. In the last analysis, says the narrator further on, our two policemen have had no recourse, for after all, their wives and children have to eat: "Los dos agentes creen que tenían que hacerlo, tenían que actuar como han actuado, pues, por lo menos, han tomado algunas copas hoy y sus mujeres y los niños picarán algo esta tarde" (The two officials believe that they have had to do it, they have had to act in that way, because, at least, they were able to have a few drinks and their children and wives will have a little bite to eat this evening) (40). And in "The Third of August" we find the very same guilt as if in a narratological desire to round out the happenings of both stories, thereby offering the reader a sense of an ending: "Ni él ni su compañero sienten remordimiento ninguno, pues hoy no han molestado a nadie" (Neither he nor his companion feel any remorse at all, since today they have bothered no one) (75). The irony of these words resonates in light of the very behavior we have witnessed, a series of acts all meant to get something for nothing by "bothering" those around them. The reference to "no one" (nadie) might be read as the other's other, that is, the main characters are marginal by virtue of their lowly status within the society and are even more lowly in the eyes of the world. But they, in turn, marginalize their own "others," in a seemingly perpetual chain of face-to-face encounters.

The implicit moral discourse of these two stories is even more pronounced in the third, "Emigración" (Emigration), a narrative that situates Equatorial Guinea in a world context. Nkogo, like any citizen of Equatorial Guinea, is well aware of the ubiquity of the remedy to the problems that plague the country—departure, the reality that many Guineans want to leave if they have not already done so. From the self-conscious cynicism of the first two stories, the author changes the tone of the third to pathos, a sentiment familiar to those who face the possibility or obligation to leave the home. The narrator, however, does not dwell on nostalgia or the recreation of the lost place of origin, as in many exile narratives—Ovid being one of the first masters of the genre. The place conjured up in "Emigración" is not the land of the past but that of the future, a geography that will relieve the characters from the hardships they are forced to endure. Moreover, in this story, in keeping with African double consciousness, Nkogo globalizes his narrative by juxtaposing his environment with that of the (other) white culture.

"Emigración" is the story of Miko, a youngster, typical resident of Malabo in that he and his family live "imprisoned in the cage of their own destiny" (79). Indeed, the story is about destiny, the almost certain possibility that whatever Miko does to improve his situation and that of his mother, he will fail. From the moment the story begins, we learn that Miko can no longer attend school, because his father was killed in prison for political reasons. Yet, while the protagonist has become the breadwinner selling trinkets in the Malabo market, expectations for a better future arise: a Spaniard working for an NGO not only buys many articles in Miko's vending stall, he befriends him. Although the relationship is genuine, it is clearly built on a dependency, an economic exchange, albeit not devoid of affection. But, as the reader suspects, the situation can not continue: the Spaniard is transferred to Kosovo, not without having offered Miko hope by his mere presence and his attention. Nacho, the Spaniard, is the benevolent neocolonialist who feels compelled to remedy the problems that his society has had a hand in bringing about. The implicit commentary on the NGO, as a symbol of first-world benevolence, is a further marker of pathos: while Nacho's intentions are honorable, both their causes and their effects belie the benefits. Again, as in the first two stories, the issues of complicity and culpability are dominant thematic features of "Emigración."

Perhaps as a result of his relationship with the Spaniard, the fact that Miko has tasted a bit of prosperity and, more important, that he has come to know first-hand a representative of that prosperity, the Guinean decides to embark on the typical migratory trip to Europe, or Eden, as the narrator calls it (89). The promised land of Europe is conjured up by Miko not as an afterlife or as some sort of spiritual dwelling place but as something real, and this supposed reality forms the mainstay of the story's pathetic irony. As Miko childishly describes his longed-for ideal, the reader hears a cautionary voice as well, a warning that the particular Eden is more fantasy than fact. "I'm off to Europe," says Miko to his family, because he is under the impression that his friend will land him a job (89). This pronouncement is addressed particularly to the protagonist's mother, who has tried to convince him to stay. Of course, that cautionary voice wins out in the battle for reality, given the outcome. In a harrowing boat ride reminiscent of a similar episode in Ndongo's *El metro,* Miko, along with his fellow beleaguered travelers, dies in a storm. In a description worthy of Juan Rulfo, Nkogo underscores the fatality of the situation, a tragedy in which the very heavens seem utterly indifferent to the suffering. As the waves rise over the vessel on its way to "Eden," and the winds blow, the narrator interjects, "La bola luminosa nocturna, que está en su fase llena, les porciona una luz tenue, y las estrellas, más alejadas, apenas se enteran de lo que ocurre" (The nocturnal luminous ball in its full phase, provides a tenuous light, and the stars, more distant, barely know what is happening) (94). Yet, while the tragedy may appear natural, it is clear that Nkogo's intention is to implicate more than the moon and the stars. It seems no one is left innocent at the culmination of "Emigración." In a final sentence that reminds us of the last words of the voice-over of the documentary *Tarifa Traffic,* as we saw in the introduction, "Alguien tiene la culpa" (Someone is to blame), the narrator asks an uncannily similar question: "¿Pero de dónde saldrán los que acaben con estas tragedias?" (But where are the people who can put an end to these tragedies?) (95).

Nkogo's moral discourse, his indictment of Guinean society through the portrayal of his two policemen, his extension of his immediate surroundings to those of the entire globe including those that force his characters into emigration, a journey that, in this case, is nearly identical to exile, and the indirect style of putting forth that discourse, all hearken back to the beginning intention of the inner exiles. As in Ávila Laurel's questioning of what Macías thought he left behind on his allegorical way out of the country—"¿Qué habrá olvidado?" (What could he have forgotten?)—Equatorial Guinea's stay-at-home writers ponder that very departure. For in many ways, they have left without leaving. They observe the exiles, as does Siale in his metafictional commentary on Ndongo, and they watch the emigrants die in the waters of the Atlantic Ocean and the Mediterranean Sea without having anyone to confirm their deaths as their bodies lie in the bottom, and as they do so, they observe themselves.

CHAPTER EIGHT

Gendering Emixile

The Mythic Return

Femme nue, femme noire
Vêtue de ta couleur qui est vie, de ta forme qui est beauté
J'ai grandi à ton ombre; la douceur de tes mains bandait
    mes yeux
Et voilà qu'au coeur de l'Eté et de Midi,
Je te découvre, Terre promise, du haut d'un haut col calciné
Et ta beauté me foudroie en plein coeur, comme l'éclair
    d'un aigle.
. . .
Femme nue, femme noire
Je chante ta beauté qui passe, forme que je fixe dans l'Eternel
Avant que le destin jaloux ne te réduise en cendres pour
    nourrir les
racines de la vie.

(Naked woman, black woman
Dressed in your color that is life, in your form that is
beauty!
I grew up in your shadow. The softness of you hands
Shielded my eyes
and now at the height of Summer and
Noon,
From the crest of a charred hilltop I discover you, Promised
Land
And your beauty strikes my heart like an eagle's lightning
flash.
. . .
Naked woman, black woman
I sing your passing beauty and fix it for all Eternity
Before jealous fate reduces you to ashes to nourish the roots
of life.)

—Léopold Senghor, "Femme noire"

The verses of this oft-quoted canonical poem "Femme noire" by the pioneer of "negritude," Léopold Senghor, address the black woman as if she were a deity. The poetic "I" speaks as a male yearning to recreate something primordial, a lost essence that manifests itself in this deity of black womanhood. The description of the naked black woman also evokes a sense of place, a geography: the woman is a "promised Land" that penetrates the heart of the speaker, as she appears to him high on a mountain pass. The mother figure stands out as well in the image of the nurturing and gentle hands that have allowed for the growth of the poetic voice—in French, there is an added sense of aggrandizement ("J'ai grandi"). She is a life source ("racines de la vie"), she offers the male "I" a glimpse of the eternal. In this way, Senghor puts forth his vision of Africa in its entirety in the figure of the black naked body.

The association of the black woman with the essence of Africa and the yearning for a return is not unique in African writing or in popular sensibilities in relation to the image of Africa. Similarly, in "The Rivers of Babylon," a well-known song by the Jamaican reggae musical group the Melodians, the poetic voice intones a nuanced rendition of Psalm 137 about the memory of Zion. The song invokes "the rivers of Babylon," as the speaker says, "he wept, when he remembered Zion." And later, he asks, famously, "How can we sing King Alpha's song in a strange land?" (Melodians). The biblical text on which this is based is nearly identical: "How shall we sing the Lord's song in a strange land?" In Rastafarian cosmology, King Alpha is another name for the emperor Haile Selassie I, who is also seen as a deity, and his place of rule, Ethiopia, is the yearned-for destiny of all displaced Africans. In the song, the word *strange* is extended for several beats, stressing the out-of-placeness not only of the speaker but also of his entire group, tribe, or family, now in captivity in the oppressive world of Babylon. The singer, as he takes the form of this displaced person, plays the roll of a traditional *griot,* the storyteller-minstrel whose duty is to entertain, to teach, and, ultimately, to tell the people what is happening in their community and thereby offer guidance.[1] The situation evoked in the song is clearly archetypal, as in Ulysses' haunting memory of Ithaca and his eventual return. Yet, for diasporic communities, the return to a form of Zion is intensified by concrete political and historical circumstances. Thus, captivity of Babylon may be read as the effects of slavery, a cosmic uprootedness grounded in the tangible historical reality of slavery. The desire to go back to an origin, however constructed, becomes part of an act of resistance and an affirmation of identity.

The return, then, is an object of desire, the fulfillment of which will constitute an ending place of rest, a nurturing center once fragmented. Or so the story goes. Yet, as we have seen, both the end of resistance and the achievement of an integrated self in the form of an identity is more part of a process—a signifying process—than a product. One of the most telling dimensions of that never-ending recreation of the journey home is the figure of the mother. The mythic, essentialized "Mother Africa" is a symbol of that return, the site both of the beginning of the journey outward and the turning inward toward the place of origin. By extension, the figure of the mother becomes a figure for womanhood itself, a limiting figure against which there has been some significant criticism. According to Florence Stratton, who has written extensively on African women's literature, the Mother Africa trope is ubiquitous and follows two lines of development: an African essence based on shared values and a "sweep of history" in which the African woman symbolizes that story of Africa through time. It is what Fredric Jameson (and others) have called a "national allegory" (qtd. in Stratton 41). As a figure deeply embedded within African consciousness, Mother Africa comes under intense scrutiny among feminists—African, European, and American—not without a variety of interesting tensions and disagreements.

Notwithstanding the discrepancies, for the phenomena of exile and emigration/immigration, African womanhood is particularly important in terms of the vexing possibility (or impossibility) of return, as seen in the syncretic reformulation of Psalm 137 in which the very customs of the old forms of life (not only songs but also by implication marriage, family, and birth and death rituals): "How can we sing our songs in a strange land?" I read "songs" as the entire gamut of community life. Being away from the land (the motherland or familyland) feels unnatural, especially when the departure has been forced. In the case of emigration, the mythic return is no different than it is for exile; both have to do with waiting. We are reminded of Mikel Azurmendi's description of the African immigrant in Spain whose life consists, unfortunately for the Spanish social critic, of working not for assimilation into the life of the adopted country but to earn enough for a return—one might add a triumphant return, which is the object of immigrant desire. The exile's condition of living in the metaphorical "waiting room," with the suitcases close at hand, is almost identical. The line separating emigration/immigration (the economic) and exile (political) is blurred in the light of the political economy of most African countries in the postcolonial period: abject poverty enabled by corruption and political repression. Thus, the return home is seen in both cases as more than a material-political solution to a problem but as a reason for being, a form of redemption in which the family group embodied in the figure of the mother, and by extension all women, is primordial.

Equatorial Guinean cultural figures in exile or who have emigrated are not exceptional among African postcolonial writers in their re-creations and reflections of the mythical return. Again, perhaps the most telling model is Ndongo. The mother figure of *Tinieblas,* both as a character of flesh and bone and as an incarnation of a value system, is a crucial dimension of the entire novel. The development of the protagonist's relationship with his mother and father is constant, it lies at the heart of the coming-of-age story. The boy is caught between the antagonistic impulses of tradition and modernity, yet the conflict between the two is not always binary, for at times the two notions overlap. The relentless tug of Africa is represented not only in Tío Abeso, the man who refuses to give in to the demands of the Church (see chapter 4) but also in the protagonist's mother. To see the mother and father (especially the latter in his celebration of the modernizing capitalist work ethic [71–74]) as an unmediated pro-Western influence is to ignore the equally strong pull towards Africa represented by the mother.

Indeed, all the women in *Tinieblas* stand more as symbols than as individuals. The episode that narrates the protagonist's circumcision is one example. As the women observe and cooperate, they seem to stand in the background. Yet, at the same time, one senses that it is they for whom the ritual is set into motion. On the fateful day of the circumcision, the I-you narrator catches a glimpse of his mother as a "figure" in the midst of a collectivity of women: "esas mujercitas se pasan la vida lloriqueando por todo y por nada, y a mi abuela, Mamá Fina, meneándose parsimoniosa y como dominádolo todo" (those little women go through life whimpering about everything and nothing; and my grandmother, Mama Fina, was strutting around sternly as if she were controlling it all" (*Tinieblas* 42; *Shadows* 34). And, later, as the boy's blood dampens the earth after the severing of the foreskin, the narrator takes the opportunity to offer what might be read as an incantation: "la última gota de tu sangre se perdió en la tierra madre tierna y cálida y desde entonces roja, fecundada por tu sangre" (the last drop of your blood vanished into mother earth, tender and warm, reddened, inseminated by your blood) (*Tinieblas* 45; *Shadows* 37). The words "tierra madre tierna y cálida" are more than prose poetry, they are a performance of the ritual itself, an affirmation of a connection between the tribe manifested in the boy and "mother" earth.[2] The ritualistic style of parts of the narrative in which certain phrases are repeated as in a prayerful incantation hearken to the central figure of the woman. The vision of the grandmother Mama Fina, during and after the circumcision, along with the repetition of that very vision as she morphs into an old seemingly blind woman (*Tinieblas* 59) are further indications of the importance of womanhood in the construction of the boy's life journey.

Moreover, as a human being who, like any human being, does not fit into the symbol ascribed to him, the protagonist's mother insists on the boy's return as he embarks on his journey to the land of the whites with the priest. While she and the father remain proud of their son for having been chosen to become a priest (although she perhaps less so than the father), it is the mother who consents to the departure on a condition that will temper the entire novel, indeed the entire trilogy: "no nos traigas una blanca" (don't bring us home a white woman) (*Tinieblas* 70; *Shadows* 64). While this command is uttered by the father in a letter that will be written after the departure, it is clear that he wishes to speak for the moral voice of the mother: "no le des un disgusto a tu madre" (your mother wouldn't be able to handle it) (*Tinieblas* 70; *Shadows* 64). The man has deferred to the mother in matters of central importance to the family, as if to assert that the real transgression is to defy the mother's hopes for integrity and harmony. Indeed, the entire departure that the novel leads up to is built upon this condition: not only a return but a return intact, that is, not married to a white woman.

The opening of the next novel in the trilogy, *Los poderes de la tempestad,* counters the family command, albeit with a great deal of trepidation regarding those instructions. *Los poderes,* as I have insisted in chapter 2, is the novel of exilic return, yet the gendered underpinnings of that return are essential to its structure. Years after the farewell at the port of Bata that constitute the final images of *Tinieblas,* the protagonist is on a plane about to land in the capital of his country. A married man with a child—the wife is Spanish, meaning white—he contemplates the reception he will be given, particularly in the light of the wishes of his mother, a want that is repeated in a textual reference to his father's letter of years ago: "como un estribillo repetía no me traigas una blanca no le des un disgusto a tu madre" (as a refrain I repeated [the father's words] don't bring us home a white woman, don't disappoint your mother) (*Los poderes* 10;). The protagonist has committed a transgression. More important than not having become a priest, which is perhaps more the father's wish than the mother's, he has not delivered on the promise he made when he was a boy. Granted it was an unstated promise—he was perhaps too young to have made it with conviction—yet the conflict of dueling identities (double consciousness) has taken its toll. In many ways, Mother Africa has been morally violated. And this violation is part of the complex nature of the political violation as well. Throughout this narrative of a return from exile, the ethical voice of the protagonist is heard throughout. It is not only his repugnance and indignation at what the dictator is doing to his land and his people that defines the moral discourse, it is also his own misgivings at having spent too much time in the land of the whites and, transgression of all transgressions: having married a white woman. This is not to say that the character feels remorse about committing a sin, for just as behaviors that were proscribed to him as a child by the Church are no longer objects of guilt, his mother's "disgusto" (her not being able to handle his love relationship) are, in the final analysis, not morally justified given his new consciousness. The "rightness" of his love relationship is a matter of ambivalence: while he has betrayed Mother Africa in a specific way, the dominating motif of the betrayal of Africa is that of the new rulers.

Indeed, Africa is the constant victim of violation in Ndongo's writing (and in that of myriad other postcolonial African writers). In both the early story "El sueño" and in the novel *El metro,* in many ways an extension of the story (see chapter 2), the ultimate goal of return obsesses both protagonists. Both characters emigrated for reasons beyond their control. In a sense, they were expelled by an Africa that was not acting according to its own moral and social dictates. In the first, the man's inability to amass enough cows for the dowry to please the wife of his choice and her family, as well as the playfully disparaging remarks about bicycles as replacements for cows ("en la gran ciudad las mozas ya no querían vacas sino bicicletas" (in the big city, young women no longer wanted cows, just bicycles) ("El sueño 205; "The Dream" 76), all coalesce as the force pushing the man out of his home. In the second, Obama Ondo leaves as a form of protest against the stringent communal rules that proscribe a legitimate (for him) love relationship. His subsequent departures (from Dakar, Western Sahara, and the Canary Islands to Madrid) are all part of a global sweep over which he has little power even though he is acting as an agent in his own destiny. In both narratives, a harmony has been broken, and the responsibility of restoring the harmony is shaped by the constant possibility of return, an insurmountably difficult one in both cases.

In addition, figures of women in the form of actual mothers and potential mothers stand as embodiments of predeparture Africa. To make Africa whole again, there must be a realization of the return. Africa is the magnet, a haunting force that occasionally shows itself in the form of ancestors, customs, religious beliefs, and family relations, yet all these entities hearken back to the idea of maternity as a life force. Contact with the family after the departure is unremitting: the migrant of "El sueño" on more than one occasion yearns for contact with home, as when he speaks of his wish that the second lover and potential wife and mother, Dikate, could (only) see Paris: "Si Dikate supiera" (if she knew) (Ndongo and Ngom 206). The situation is reminiscent of the proverbial English phrase "if she could only see me now." Yet, in the African's case, it has more to do with wishful thinking than reality, for he is nowhere near Paris. Similarly, albeit more pathetically and somberly, Obama Ondo's anxiety at having left, the unresolved conflict between him and his community, is heightened with every contact and every memory of home. In this regard, his mother is crucial. In the mind of the protagonist, the mother figure is a constant. He remembers the photos of her, that she seemed to give birth with "meticulous regularity," and that she treated her husband with respect, "a quality she struggled to instill in all her offspring" (39). Dorotée is the mother figure incarnate as she gives birth every two years with extreme generosity, self-sacrifice, and subservience. Her death will contribute to the protagonist's departure (36), and her memory to his urge for return. She stands as a moral symbol, less a woman of flesh and bone than a model of behavior, an icon.

The pathos of the tragic end of *El metro,* as suggested in chapter 5, rests on the abrupt end to a journey cut short. That Obama Ondo had made his decision to return and that his life was seemingly changing for the better so that the return might actually be realized makes the final images of the violent death on the metro at the hands of hatemongers appear as the end of a novel of romantic disillusionment. The longed-for integration and, in his case, reconciliation between himself and his homeland cannot be consummated due to a mishap. Yet, the mishap seems to have been planned from the beginning; it was his social and racial destiny. All this is made even more pathetic considering the immediate motive for the return: Obama Ondo's acceptance of his responsibility for his child and his child's mother.

The idealization of the African woman as mother figure in Ndongo's work, however, is not identical to that of Senghor in "Femme noire." The difference is based not merely on the conventional distinction between poetry and prose, the former being more predisposed to economy of language and allegorical articulation and the latter to elaboration and detail. There is a qualitative difference as well: contrary to Senghor's unquestioning essentialism, Ndongo's maternal images are filled with trepidation and complexity, not due as much to the complexity of the women themselves as to what they are destined to represent. Along with the protagonist's mother in *Tinieblas* is the father, the male figure of complicity with the white man's ways. His cooperation with the colonial power structure rests on his life companionship with the mother (the one who represents the traditional ways as well), and this, in turn, throws the binary opposition between male and female out of kilter. In *El metro,* the many and varied women who populate the novel serve to question the African Mother myth. Sylvie, Madame Eboué, Anne Mengue, indeed all of Obama Ondo's love relationships, are cases of women with a specific set of problems and characteristics that ultimately reflect on the journey out of Africa and back, a "globalized" Africa whose postcolonial connection to Europe has turned it into something unrecognizable.

The same sort of ambivalence is found in other Guinean emigrant-exile and inner-exile writers. Justo Bolekia's poetry in *Löbëla* serves as one of the most telling indications of this ambivalence. The haunting presence of the "mother goddess" Löbëla ("nuestra diosa madre") (33; see chapter 3) is the force that structures the entire collection of poems. However, as Bolekia insists in many suggestive ways, Löbëla is chameleon-like. She appears in different names and performs various functions. Moreover, she is both female and male:

> Löbëla es Wewèöpö, es Wésëpa, es Uri; es la diosa amante y madre. También es nuestra diosa madre, y a su vez es el dios hombre que posee y desgarra impío cual joven doncel apresurado. Es el marido anciano trepador que descubrió a las doncellas casaderas poseídas en la poza de las teñidas aguas rojas; es la anciana cuyos pies nunca pisaron el suelo, la guía de mujeres y zagalas, la reina de dios Wedye. Es a su vez amante de no sé qué furtivo dios llegado de las tinieblas donde mora Sitòböro. Pero . . . ¿quién es *Löbëla.* (33)

> (Löbëla is Wewèöpö, is Wésëpa, is Uri; she is the love goddess mother. Also, she is our mother goddess, and at the same time she is the man god who irreverently scratches like a young man in a hurry. [Löbëla] is the ancient husband trickster who discovered the brides-to-be in the red colored well-waters; [Löbëla] is the old woman who never stepped on the ground, the guide of women and lassies, the queen of the god Wedye. At the same time she is the lover of who-knows-what furtive god appearing out of the shadows of the dwelling of Sitòböro. But . . . who is Löbëla?)

The elusiveness of this description, the definition of a name that defies total understanding, the answer to a question that ends in the very same question, invites conjecture, and, I might add, it counters an essentialist embrace of a single entity that engulfs an entire continent and an identity.

Still, Löbëla the entity is anything but an immediately recognizable human being with all the social reality that accompanies the human of flesh and bone. Her defining attribute is her Dionysian force and the variety of qualities she is able to evoke: motherhood, desire (male and female), fertility, movement, change. And central to all this is that for the poet, Löbëla is both universal and specific; she represents a lost past, a desire in conflict with reality. In a correspondence with the poet, responding to my own version of the question asked in the above definition (Who is Löbëla?), Bolekia answered like the griot that he is, as if to say, "Let me tell you a story":

> Cuando yo era niño (y lo fui hace más de medio siglo ya), mis ahora ancestras (abuelas, tías, madre, etc.) me legaron el acervo cultural que sólo la sabiduría familiar o comunitaria guardaba. En sus relatos (hoy llamados cuentos, leyendas, etc.) figuraban como personajes destacados esas mujeres que yo he elevado a la categoría de diosas. Por una sencilla razón: eran las protagonistas, las heroínas, las madres, etc., porque el hombre aparecía muchas veces elidido, ausente, como un mero inseminador.
>
> Además, desde el momento en que es el ser humano el que define su destino (aunque no siempre), creo que no viene mal incorporar nuevas diosas en nuestra mitología y no limitarnos a reconocer como diosas a las que nos fueron legadas por la colononización.
>
> (When I was a child [over half a century ago], those who are today my female ancestors [grandmothers, aunts, mother] bestowed on me a cultural legacy that only family and community wisdom could keep intact. In those narratives [today called stories, legends, etc.], the main players were women whom I have elevated to the category of goddesses. The reason is simple: they were the protagonists, the heroines, the mothers, etc., because men seemed eclipsed, absent, they appeared as mere inseminators. Also, from the moment human beings define their destiny [although not always], it's not a bad idea to add new goddesses to our mythologies and not limit ourselves to the recognition of the goddesses given to us by colonization.)

Indeed, Löbëla embodies a lost past stripped away by colonialism. While there are no specific references to the exilic return in Bolekia's poetry, his verses are filled with the anxiety of a loss. The recuperation of the loss is the narration of Löbëla, which may be read as his attempt to return vicariously to the lost land. One of the poems in the collection, "La balada de Löbëla" ("Löbëla's ballad") (44–45), is a song that tells Löbëla's story. It is a celebration of her heroic feat and her interactions with other gods. The culminating lines offer a glimpse not only of the poet's intention in singing Löbëla's praises but also of his at-once collective and personal connection to the goddess:

> Yo cuento mientras alguien escuche,
> Cuento la misteriosa vida de Löbëla y Wewèöpö,
> . . .
> Yo narro lo que nadie logró enterrar
> Porque cuento y canto la Balada de Löbëla. (45)
>
> (I tell the story as long as someone listens,
> I tell the mysterious life of Löbëla y Wewèöpö,
> . . .
> I narrate what no one has been able to bury
> Because I tell and sing the Ballad of Löbëla.)

In a word, Bolekia's exilic return is itself the narration of the story of Mother Löbëla.

Virtually all the writers covered in the previous chapters allude in some way to a primordial connection between a mother figure and a return from exile/emigration. When Siale's first-person narrator in *Cenizas de Kalabó* arrives home after having been forced to wander the world in exile, the presence of the mythical mother could not be more clear. As the protagonist offers the mother the fruits of his wanderings in the form of an envelope filled with money, he affirms that the relief he felt for having rid his mother of material misery made him feel "like a genuine son of this earth." Indeed, he says it reinforces his sense of obligation not only to his own mother but to all the "mothers of Africa" (218). Similarly, in Nkogo's story "Emigración," the mother of the protagonist, Miko, represents the force of unity and integration. She tries desperately to convince her son not to set off for that (falsely) promised land, and given the outcome, it is clear that among the author's intentions, his urge to demonstrate the good will and wisdom of the African mother is paramount.[3]

The mother trope is so pervasive in its symbolic evocation of a lost home that one must ask where the Equatorial Guinean writers are who transcribe women's exile-emigration experience in ways that expose women as women and not as myth. While one might argue that "real" women populate the texts of the exile-emigrant writers of Equatorial Guinea, even though their appearance is hardly ever as protagonists (with some exceptions, discussed later), there is a case worthy of mention in the story "Bea" by Francisco Zamora (Ndongo and Ngom 191–94). Bea is a Senegalese woman living in Madrid whose uprootedness is apparent from the beginning to the end of the story. She is displaced spatially, spiritually, culturally, and most of all, climactically. When the Madrid winters bring temperatures never felt in Senegal, not only is she uncomfortable but she also becomes sick. Almost as a palliative to the infirmity, a condition that will cease the moment spring arrives, she seeks the warmth of the man who is telling the story. She becomes pregnant but can not endure the thought of bearing the child. In an act of desperation, she seeks a gypsy woman to relieve her of the pregnancy. She survives the abortion—a word never mentioned in the story—but the result is devastating. She leaves her man to become a prostitute, only to be assaulted by a black man, and finally decides to return to Senegal, better a disgraced woman in her own land, she declares at the end, than having to put up with the Madrid cold (193).

Yet, even in this superbly crafted narrative, worthy of famous realist Spanish writers such as Pío Baroja or Emilia Pardo Bazán in all its naturalist implications—the sickness, the climactic inadaptability—the figure of the African mother coupled with a return to something "natural" looms behind all the stark realism. One might even suggest that the protagonist of the story is not Bea but the "I," who knows her intimately, a fellow African: "Africans lost in the big city" (191). Countering Madrid's or Europe's or advanced civilization's indifference and inhospitality is the voice of the narrator himself, whose loss of Bea is perhaps the most important element of the story. Bea's hardships stemming from the absence of her land are a replication of those of the narrator. One might even say that the narrator's pathos is even more pronounced because he seems resigned to his present reality, a reality too far from his homeland. Like Bolekia, Zamora's return is vicarious: he experiences it through his writing of "Bea" (or writing Bea). That Bea's motherhood has been torn away by the city does not only signify the loss of his own child but the loss of the mother of his child. The dominating symbol of the story could not be more romantic: a bird.

> Madrid había iniciado su irremisible carrera hacia el caos. Sus pájaros, son sus pulmones contaminados, heridos por el agobio letal de los escapes, arrojados de los parques y los arrabales por un irracional ejército armado de feroces bulldozers, grúas y excavadoreas, iniciaban una agonía lenta cada arremetida de invierno.
>
> "Madrid no es ciudad para pájaros." (191)

> (Madrid had initiated its irremissible race toward chaos. Its birds, with their lungs filled with pollution, wounded by constant lethal emissions expelled from parks and fields by an irrational army of fierce bulldozers, cranes, and mechanical shovels, initiated their agonizing retreat as winter attacked.
>
> "Madrid is not a city for birds.")

It is Bea who speaks this last sentence, words reminiscent of Fernán Caballero in *La gaviota,* as it becomes the refrain of the narrative. The narrator ends his memory of Bea with "Ahora sé porqué Madrid no es ciudad para pájaros" (Now I know why Madrid is not a city for birds) (194). The fragility and helplessness of the birds as well as their opposition (by definition) to artificiality is yet another, albeit intuitive, reference to their need for a protecting mother. Unlike the birds and by extension the narrator, Bea returns regardless of the consequences. One senses the narrator's imaginary realization of his own return through Bea. His choice, however, is to stay with the awareness ("ahora sé") (now I know) that the city is an unnatural habitat with mother Africa always looming in the horizon.

In addition to the plethora of male exile-emigrant writers stand the few women authors of Equatorial Guinea, exiles in their own right, who offer different versions of the migration and the return to Mother Africa. Indeed, the inspiration for Raquel Ilombé's poetry, as discussed in chapter 1, is an absent mother. Yet, her situation as the daughter of a plantation owner in Equatorial Guinea and a mother from Corisco sets her apart from many of the writers I have dealt with, a woman who left Africa involuntarily and returned many years later not definitively but on occasion, a life of comings and goings as something of an assertion of her own double identity. At the same time (again as suggested in the previous chapter), the mother figure is at once present and absent in her poetry collection *Ceiba:* absent in terms of the infrequency of direct references to the poet's mother, yet ubiquitous in the sense of loss and desire for recuperation that virtually all her poetry emotes. Moreover, in Ilombé's poetic persona we see at once a daughter of a spectral mother as well as a mother in her own right. The mother figure, for example, permeates the poem "Vivir" (Live) (37–40) as the poetic voice wanders the streets and offers observations and advice in keeping with a benevolent mother. And in a poem "Distancia" (Distance) (76), while dedicated to her husband, Luis, the "distance" lamented in the poem goes well beyond the loss of her husband. As in much of her poetry, images of the lost land abound as in the following stanza in which the motherly rocking ("meza") is reminiscent of the verses of the Hispanic mother-poet par excellence, Gabriela Mistral:

> Al chocar la lluvia con las hojas,
> con el ruido monótono del agua,
> me meza en un profundo sueño
> hasta que el sol no salga. (76)
>
> (As the rain beats on the leaves,
> with the monotonous sound of the water,
> rocks me into a deep sleep
> until the sun does not rise.)

Similarly, yet far more directly, little-known writer María Caridad Riolha, who left for Spain after the Macías dictatorship and returned to Malabo to become a teacher, deals with a forced departure in the story "Exilio" (Ndongo and Ngom 400–402). In this story, the mother figure is equally ubiquitous yet not nearly as hazy or abstract. The first-person narrator's mother is a concrete person: "Hacía unos tres años que había recibido la carta en la que mi hermano me comunicaba el estado de gravedad de mi madre. . . . ¡Pobrecilla!, ¡está tan lejos de los suyos!" (It had been four years when I received a letter in which my brother informed me of the grave illness of my mother. . . . Poor thing! she is so far away from her loved ones!) (400). As in the Ilombé poem "Distance," the separation and a longed-for return are what fuels the writing, and in the case of Riolha, that desire turns into anguish, nightmares filled with repeated images of funerals and death. The narrator-protagonist's return is at once dreaded since she is terrified of the impending death of her mother. In her recurring dream, on the top of the stairs descending from the plane that has just landed on Guinean ground, she sees the funeral cortege. Yet, the dramatic end of the story belies the dream. The mother is not missing among the many family members who come to greet her upon her (real) return home. At once, feelings of jubilation and pathos terminate the story. As the celebration of the long-awaited arrival of the departed family member begins, the last line reads, "No he podido desgranar las horas del reloj" (I haven't been able to pluck away the hours on the clock) (402). Indeed, she has been and continues to be a slave to time. That her mother is among the living is a relief, yet it provides no cure to her anguish, especially now that the character has been away. Departure, loss, deprivation, and fragmentation are the mainstays of the exilic life, even after the return to mother.

Returning to the Mother in María Nsue's *Ekomo*

Arguably, the most extensive contribution to Spanish by women of Guinean letters is by María Nsue Angüe (b. 1945, Ebebeyín) in her novel *Ekomo* (1985, two years prior to Ndongo's *Tinieblas*). Nsue, like Ndongo, is a Fang from Río Muni and, also like the author of *El metro,* emigrated to Spain at an early age but returned with independence. Her father, José Nsue, had stayed in his country to work for self-determination, yet he became a dissident during the Macías regime and suffered execution as a result. María Nsue would return occasionally but received virtually all her education in Madrid as she completed a degree in journalism from the Escuela de Periodismo. Although she returned to Equatorial Guinea to work in the Ministry of Education and Culture, she maintained contact with Europe throughout her life. The constant to-and-fro travel from Africa to Europe and back allows her the distance characteristic of the African migrant intellectual observing both cultures as an insider and outsider at once (double consciousness). Yet, in Nsue's case, as a woman, she is especially aware of the ambivalences between the woman figure as an icon of maternity and as a human being (multiple consciousness). Thus, the archetypal return, as we shall see, is rendered with particular acumen in her work.

Acquaintance with Spain's intelligentsia, medievalist and linguist, Vicente Granados, who apparently read the work in manuscript form and recommended publication, was an asset to her literary career. Yet, more important, this relationship pinpoints the familiar tensions that shape the writing and existence of African intellectuals and cultural figures who reside or who have resided in Europe. In Granados's prologue to the work, we detect a certain colonial curiosity on the part of the learned Spanish philologist, who, like the priests before him who encouraged the "natives" to transcribe their traditions (see chapter 1), finds it interesting that the Guinean woman corrected "errors" that are common in Guinean Spanish (10). He also asserts that *Ekomo* is the first novel written by a Spanish Guinean; apparently he had no access to Evita's or Jones Mathama's texts. He goes as far as to point out that one of the novel's central motifs, the "ceiba," a common tree in Equatorial Guinea that has spiritual significance, is less common in Río Muni where the novel takes place and, thus, it might have been better to choose a more autochthonous tree. But to the critic's credit, he includes the author's laconic response to his objection: "'La ceiba es el árbol del bien'" (The ceiba is the tree of good) (12). This tension is reminiscent of George Lamming's essay "The Occasion for Speaking," which describes the colonial subject's ambivalence about seeking "approval of Headquarters" (see introduction in the current volume). Nsue's exchange with Granados is a reassertion not only of her own text but also of her self.

Indeed, self-assertion is one of the mainstays of the novel. The first-person narrative voice affirms itself from beginning to end. It tells the life of Ekomo through the eyes of Nnanga, who is his lover, partner, and wife. The story line deals with events circa 1965 in the light of a brief reference to the death of Patrice Lumumba (20), yet through flashbacks, it spans several decades in the two main characters' lives. The events are based on an overarching dilemma afflicting a community in Río Muni (the real name of which is never mentioned): a shadow is cast over the village in the shape of a "lápida" (headstone) (19) formed by clouds in an ominously grey sky. Virtually all subsequent events in the novel are offshoots of these foreboding signals, as the village chief reads the sign as an indication that two people will die, a powerful member of the tribe and a young person (18–19, 31). The narrator interrupts her story occasionally with memories of her childhood: the description of rituals; how she learns to dance; her first encounter with Ekomo; the development of her relationship with him; her dealings with brothers, and childhood friends, such as Mbo, a dwarf who plays with the children as if he were one of them. All this appears within the frame of the omen and the prognostications of its meaning. When Ekomo returns to the village with an infected foot after a stay in the city, and as the infirmity spreads, the narrator's (and reader's) speculation that his sickness is connected to the form of the headstone becomes stronger. Both characters set forth on a search for a cure to the sickness, a journey that may very well be read as an allegory of exile and immigration. Ultimately, Ekomo's illness leads not only to his death but that also of Nnanga in an extraordinary narrative happening in which a first person describes her own death.

At the same time, *Ekomo* is not precisely a novel of self-realization, that is, it is not the account of an exploited woman whose imaginative journey consists of a search for self-understanding and fulfillment in a hostile world. The story of her life is intimately tied to family, and, as such, the lines between self and family and, by extension, self and community are constantly blurred. Ironically, *Ekomo* is not as much the story of the young man, Ekomo, but of Nnanga's relationship to him as told by herself. What stands out in the novel, perhaps more than any other narrative feature, is Nnanga's life. The question of the title, then, immediately arises. According to Mbaré Ngom, in the understanding of *Ekomo,* one must bear in mind that there is a tendency in African women's writing to negate the "I" ("negar su yo") of the narrative ("Relato de una vida" 82). Yet, it is also important to consider how subjectivity manifests itself in this novel. Nnanga's rendering of her own life through that of her partner amidst rituals, family life, beliefs, and customs, as well as exploration of her innermost emotions, is not a negation of subjectivity but an affirmation. Subjectivity itself, perhaps more in this than in any other of the Guinean narratives discussed thus far, is a collective force, an affirmation of life. María Zielina, in "Ekomo: Representación," a penetrating study of the Bantu belief system that structures the novel, relies on the notion of a metaphysical connection between creator and creation to explain the novel's signification, which is theorized by the Brazilian anthropologist Katangese Menahga (94). Thus, all activity in the novel is directly attributable to a line of creation in which all is subordinate to the forces of the mother and father. The word *Ekomo* is, for Zielina, not as much a character but a place, a mythological space in which all the characters move. Thus, Nnanga takes it upon herself to transmit that space to anyone willing to listen—a daunting task.

Indeed, the writing of *Ekomo* is a frightening undertaking given the circumstances of the story. As mentioned earlier, a dark cloud is cast over the village, and as in a conventional narrative presentation of a problem that is at once individual and collective, Nsue seems to intuit that "there is something rotten" in Ekomo, the place, and, by extension, in all Africa. One of the most important effects of the celestial cause, that is, the "lápida" formed in the sky in the opening chapter of the novel, is Ekomo's (the man's) sickness. In turn, as this effect becomes itself another cause, Ekomo and Nnanga both set out on a journey to find a cure. Undeniably, the search for the cure—with the related symbols attached—purification, trial, a wrong to be corrected—becomes the mainstay of this novel, or, in many ways, *Ekomo* contains all the trappings of an epic or, more precisely, counterepic.[4] Within the context of exilic and migratory writing, the willing departure from the community in search of purification could not be more pertinent. In the episode in which the leader of the community, Ndong Akele, makes the decision for the main characters to leave—it is significant that the decision is made for them—there are several references to a borderline. The border ("frontera") (100) is not only a line that must be traversed for the cure; it appears both in the words of the narrator and the chieftain as a signifying spatial marker. Ndong Akele speaks of the borders between life and death, as he seeks to debunk the Christian view of the afterlife (99–100). In the scenes immediately following, the borderline that the protagonists must cross is a specific one: "Padre Ndong Akele ha dicho que nos preparemos para salir mañana del poblado y marcharnos al otro lado de la frontera" (Father Ndong Akele has said that we should prepare to leave the village tomorrow for the other side of the border) (101). Yet, even here, the exact location of this border is not clear; it transcends a specific place or meaning. "On the other side," continues Akele, is the dwelling of the healer, Ondo el Divino, the one who will offer (or so the characters hope) a finality to the search. Akele further points out that Ekomo's mother has had to endure the deaths of her seven sons, all of whom died young even though they were strong (101). Thus, the journey is at once outward and inward, a passage from the familiar to the unknown, in order to render that unknown territory part of the domain of Ekomo and Nnanga's tribe and ultimately restore wholeness (wellness) to the community. Yet, the haunting figure of death always looms over virtually all of the happenings along the journey:

> Cruzamos la frontera en medio de las tinieblas, bien caída ya la noche. Los pies me dolían del frío por la lluvia pasada y las tantas veces que había tenido que tropezar con algún tronco o alguna raíz de árbol. Me sentía ya más próxima a la muerte que a la vida. (105)

> (We crossed the border in the dark, night had fallen some time ago. My feet ached because of the cold that the previous rain had left, and because of all the times I had tripped over a fallen trunk or root of a tree. I felt I was closer to death than life.)

And, as we shall see, death (in Nnanga's at once unique and collective vision) will become something of a solution to the problem.

Moreover, the connections between the mother figure(s) and the journey are equally dominant, for not only is Ekomo suffering from the rapidly spreading ailment in his foot, Nnanga is enduring the possibility of misfortune as well: she believes she may be unable to bear children. The intimate association between Ekomo's malady and the possibility of Nnanga's sterility comes at a crucial point of the novel at which both arrive at the dwelling of the healer who performs a series of tests to ascertain in the former's case the cause of the affliction and in the latter whether Nnanga is barren. For Nnanga, perhaps more than for Ekomo, the possibility is not as much a personal affliction with which the character must contend psychologically as it is something that vitiates against the survival of the community and against life itself. Yet, the tests prove inconclusive: the origin of Ekomo's sickness remains unclear and in Nnanga's case, after the pumpkin seeds wrapped in banana leaves reveal the figure of a male sex organ, it is determined that she will have a male child. However, adds the healer, this will not come to pass without much suffering: "pasarán muchas cosas malas por en medio" (Many things will happen in between) (110).

Thus, the trials, the journey, the sickness, and the imbalance in the natural order for Nnanga are intimately linked to motherhood. Her relationship to her ailing mate is as much maternal as romantic. In another insightful article, "Los territorios de la identidad" by Lola Aponte Ramos, the convergence of the two maladies indicates a questioning of sexual constructions of identity. The critic submits that sickness feminizes Ekomo as he becomes dependent on his partner (105). Yet, my inclination is to interpret the sickness as a force that adds to Nnanga's role as a mother without children.[5] Again, the potentiality of children in the form of a future, the continuation of the life of the community, and, along with this, the necessity for a trying journey are all paramount. Indeed, Nnanga's energy is a love force that manifests itself not only in her maternal-romantic relationship with Ekomo but also in her dancing, as she names herself "Paloma de Fuego" (Dove of Fire) (75). Early in the novel, having been married to Ekomo for two years, she describes what seems as a primordial urge that surpasses volition. Here she prepares for a village dance:

> Siento sin saber una excitación que me domina en las venas, en la sangre, sobre la piel y . . . en el espíritu, todo mi cuerpo es puro cosquilleo inevitable, inexplicable. Una fuerza oculta me llama en las sombras. Fuera se oyen risas excitadas y gritos que no dicen nada. Como los gritos de alguna fiera en la noche. . . .

> Hasta madre, que se cuida de frotarme el cuerpo, al ir a pasarme la mano en el rostro, he sentido su palma caliente temblar al rozarme mis mejillas. . . . Y, por primera vez, intento imaginarme cómo sería aquella mujer, marchita dada al llanto, cuando tenía mis años. (33)

> (Unwittingly, I feel an excitation that dominates me through my veins, my blood, my skin and . . . in my spirit, in my whole body there is a prickling sensation, inexplicable. A hidden force calls me from the shadows. Outside there is excited laughter and cries that don't say anything. Like the yowls of beasts in the night. . . . Even Mother, who takes care of rubbing my body, as she passed her hand over my face brushing my cheeks, I feel the trembling of her warm palm. . . . And, for the first time, I try to imagine what that woman was like, all wrinkled from crying, when she was my age.)

While this passage may appear at first glance as a description of the sensations of a girl passing through puberty, it is more in keeping with the designs of the novel that Nnanga is feeling an urge for life, that is, the desire for children. Given that the character has been married for two years and that she constantly compares herself to her mother, the inexplicable urge she feels is not as much sexual as cosmic.

Perhaps most compelling among the many maternal figures that abound in the novel is that of (again) Mother Africa. *Ekomo* is indeed a novel not only about Equatorial Guinea but about Africa. As I (and other critics) have been suggesting, it is far more than a novel of customs such as Evita's *Cuando los combes luchaban* or Jones Mathama's *Una lanza* (see chapter 3), even though these prior novels may suggest a transcendence or an outdoing of that genre. María Nsue's Africa is suffering from an affliction, and the affliction has much to do with its relation to Europe. The journey out of the continent in *Ekomo* manifests itself as a movement out of wholeness and into fragmentation. The character Nfumbaha is a model: He is characterized in the opening chapter as the one who had spent time in Europe or, more precisely, had come back from Europe ("había regresado") (19). He is the immigrant whose story is told from the perspective of those who stay at home. His return, however, is anything but restorative, the damage has been done. In a noble effort to find himself, he sets out on yet another journey, but this time the destination is the bush ("la selva") (59). This final trip for Nfumbaha will turn out to have no definite destination other than his own death:

> Entonces Nfumbaha cogiendo su escopeta, se despidió de los presentes, de todos, sin mirar a nadie en especial, y todos, nadie en especial, le vieron partir hacia la selva. . Había estado mucho tiempo en Europa, y había perdido el

respeto a la tradición. Podía salvarse quizá del embrujo de la selva, porque era ya medio blanco. (59–60)

(And then Nfumbaha, grabbing his rifle, said good-bye to those present, all of them without looking at anyone in particular, and everyone, no one in particular, saw him take his exit into the bush. . . . He had been in Europe for some time, and he had lost respect for the traditions. He could save himself from the jungle's spell because he was already half white.)

Yet, Nfumbaha never returns. His fate is at once pathetic and predictable. While the men in the community organize a search party, it is fruitless. The African wilderness has proved too daunting, too elusive for him to regain. Most significant in his story, however, is its lesson, a moral offered by the mothers:

Nfumbaha, el africano de hoy, hombre del mañana, tras estar dos lluvias en Europa, dejó su tradición encerrada entre los libros. . . . y regresó a su pueblo con un disfraz del europeo sin el europeo dentro. . . . Las lágrimas de la madre son las del Africa y sus lamentos se esparcen alargados por el aire hasta los confines de la tierra por todos aquellos hijos perdidos y no hallados. ¿Quién puede escuchar el llanto de la madre de Africa sin sentir compasión por esa mujer que no hace más que echar hijos al mundo para ver como poco a poco van perdiendo su personalidad? Y sin embargo, cada vez que cae uno de sus hijos, Africa llora personificándose en cada una de las madres del Nfumbaha. Hijos prefabricados por los supermercados de la evolución histórica . . . y mueren con las chaquetas puestas seguros de haber cumplido su misión. (85)

(Nfumbaha, today's African, the man of tomorrow, after having been in Europe for two rainy seasons, left his tradition and locked himself up in books, and he came back to his village in the trappings of a European but without a European inside. . . . The mother's tears are Africa's, and her laments are spread out lavishly through the air to the ends of the earth for all those children lost and not found. Who can hear the wailing of the mother of Africa without feeling compassion for that woman who does no more than cast children all over the world, while slowly they lose their personality? However, every time one of her children falls, Africa weeps as it becomes each one of Nfumbaha's mothers. Children prefabricated by the supermarkets of historical evolution. . . . and they die with their jackets on, certain that they have accomplished their mission.)

However, despite these eloquently condemning words that encapsulate a vision of Africa akin to that of the author, and in light of both the thematic and linguistic structure of the novel as a whole, one must be careful to attribute an unquestioning or unmediated embrace of African essentialism in *Ekomo,* particularly in regard to the mother figure. Clearly, there is something terribly wrong in Ekomo and Nnanga's world, but righting the wrong by simply returning home to Mother is too easy, if even possible. Nsue's African woman incarnated in the mother is a far cry from Senghor's "femme noire." Moreover, her vision of Africa, as manifested in the themes and rhetorical devices of the novel, does not involve a cry for the return to an African essence, rather her world view asserts the human condition as a process constantly changing.

Most salient in this regard is Nsue's portrayal of death in the final scenes of the novel. With the death of Ekomo, several forces come into play. As Nnanga desperately seeks the proper ritual that would honor her lover's life, she is confronted by both modern (that is, Christian) and traditional authorities, both of whom present obstacles to her wishes. The Christians, both the Catholic priest and the Protestant pastor, do not allow a proper burial of a man they consider a heathen, and the traditional shaman cannot perform the ritual mourning since Nnanga has committed the taboo of touching the body. Thus, Nnanga takes on the labor of mourning in her own way: with her awareness, indeed participation, in the rituals of the two world views, she creates her own finality. Her death is a departure from an old state and an arrival at a new one. Significantly, it is a death within the community of women, as seen in the following passage, as much prose-poetry as prose.

> Que lloren todas las mujeres juntas. Por cualquier motivo. ¿Por qué no han de llorar las mujeres, si sus vidas no son sino muertes? . . . ¡Que lloren las madres de las hembras, porque las hembras nacen para ser madres y esposas! ¡Que llore la mujer fértil, abrazando a la otra estéril!
> Grita mi mente:
> ¡Estás muerta!
> Grita mi rebelión:
> ¡No. No estoy muerta ni viva!
> ¿Esto qué es?—me pregunta la razón—y una voz débil contesta:
> "La frontera entre la vida y la muerte."
> Abro los ojos, eso creo, y veo un sinfín de cosas, que necesitaría todo un libro para expresar mi verdad exacta.
> Abro los ojos, eso creo, y me encuentro confundida entre la gente. Mas . . . ¡qué sola! ¡Qué tremendamente sola estoy! (194)

> (Let all the women cry together. For any reason. Why shouldn't women cry if all their lives are deaths? Let all the mothers of women cry, for women are born to become mothers and wives. Let the fertile woman embrace the sterile one.

My mind cries:
You are dead!
My rebellion cries:
No! I'm neither dead nor alive.
What is this? my reason asks. And a low voice answers:
"The borderline between life and death."
I open my eyes, and I believe it. And I see endless chain of things,
I would need an entire book to express my exact truth.
I open my eyes, and I believe it. I find myself lost among the
people. But . . . how alone! How utterly alone I am!)

And so ends *Ekomo*—in a state of loneliness and despair. Juxtaposed with the analogous lamentation at the loss of Nfumbaha ("Who can hear the wailing of the mother of Africa without feeling compassion for that woman?" [85]), in this culminating passage there seems to be no recourse for the "mother of Africa." Her children are lost in the diaspora, and when or if they return, they are unrecognizable, rendering her "utterly alone." Still, if there is anything redeeming in Nnanga's death, it is that she has not died in the conventional sense or in the sense that a Christian would attach to it. She seems to have become a spirit, like the many spirits who populate African culture and literature, and Equatorial Guinea's culture and literature is no exception as we have seen: Ndongo's ancestors in the form of the old woman who appears in a vision in *Tinieblas,* Mbomío's representation of the "mibili" in which the spirit of Father Gabriel comes back to life, the "mibili" is also represented in Ávila Laurel's drama *El fracaso de las sombras* (The failure of the shadows),[6] Bolekia's Löbëla, Siale's haunting characters in his story "Todo llega con las olas del mar" who speak as if they were dead, and in other scenes in *Ekomo* such as the appearance of Nfumbaha's spirit as "miles y miles de ánimas" (thousands and thousands of souls) surround Nnanga (87–88). At the end of the novel, Nnanga defines her own new state: the "borderline between life and death." Yet, most important, as the reader searches for some sort of redemption in the outcome, is her plea: "I would need an entire book to express my truth." That book is the one the reader has in his or her hands. Nnanga has become the female griot in the form of a spirit; she has returned to roots that she herself has planted. A new Mother Africa has emerged, just as mythical as the old one. But this new mother will define herself as she tells her "exact truth."

The narrator's voice in *Ekomo* is above all a moral one; Nnanga is at once a marginal and collective figure—she speaks as the collective other. She is marginal as an African and as a woman, yet in both these constructions, she represents a collective force. Nsue's novel falls neatly into the category of African women's writing that, as Carol Boyce Davies puts it, balances "the need to liberate African peoples from neo-colonialism and other forms of race and class oppression, coupled with a respect for certain features of traditional African cultures" (1). Nsue's "respect" for traditions, however, is not part of a multicultural critique in which all competing cosmologies converge in an enlightened synthesis.[7] Her Nnanga arises as part of African culture; she cannot exist without her community. It is true that, as a woman, she feels (or is made to feel) helpless and destitute, especially at the end. Yet, the cause of her helplessness is not men nor even a masculinist society. She accepts male authority, yet only insofar as it emanates from a powerful natural order, that is, the heavens, ancestors, the powers of a shaman, Ekomo, his brothers, his and her family (which is the same family), or the women elders. Nnanga's dilemma goes beyond all this: somehow the natural order has been broken, and the journey out of the village and eventually the return home to mother will not make it right. The break in the natural order is perhaps part of the natural order itself (as in the sign in the clouds of the headstone), and even more important for exile and emigration, it is a global rupture.

Nigerian woman scholar and poet Ifi Amadiume argues for a gendered morality in African cultures that has made for the presence of "a matricentric production unit as the basic material structure of African matriarchy . . ., common to all traditional African social structures, since it generated affective relationships" (*Reinventing Africa* 29). Granted Amadiume's assertions in *Reinventing Africa* come under scrutiny by feminists, including African feminists, who question the existence of "matriarchy" in any culture. Yet, pertinent to Nsue's work and to virtually all the texts I have discussed here as manifestations of the mythical return to Mother Africa is Amadiume's less-controversial assertion that the domain of morality in African culture tends to be represented (and perhaps even controlled) by women. Nsue's weeping mothers elicit more than pathos and sadness, their tears denote a face-to-face confrontation with the other. They encompass virtually all human relationships, particularly in the light of the tone in which the author shows them to us: "Why shouldn't women cry if all their lives are deaths?" Nsue, through her creation, Nnanga, implores her readers to look into the weeping eyes of these others, and she does so with much authority. Amadiume, albeit unwittingly, utters the same plea as Nsue's "Why shouldn't women cry?" in the poem "Nok Lady in Terracotta":

Sister-tears of denial I share today;
same sap which ran through the mother stem
now runs in her off-shoots and grows on;
once ploughed, she will crop,
though she reaps not what she sows,
for the planters pick her harvest;
pitcher of water, not your water;
river-bed carrying not your water;
so mother do you carry their sons
who in turn will marry off your daughters!

(Chipasula 71)

Indeed, the return to mother will not make for redemption unless these sister-tears are the focus of our gaze, unless we shift our eyes from the "Femme noire" to the mother carrying "water, not your water."

CHAPTER NINE

Ending with a Beginning

What happens to the cultural production of a nation when that nation becomes the victim of a siege and, as a result of that siege, the country's intellectuals are expelled or leave of their own will? The problem is not a new one, and in the Hispanic world, including Equatorial Guinea, we have seen abundant cases in the twentieth and twenty-first centuries. Expulsions, whether they have been forced into exile or obligated to emigrate, have deeply affected how the citizens of a nation think about themselves. Also, considering the slippery category in which the very notion of nation-state has fallen in the last few decades, it seems that exile and other types of political-economic migrations have exacerbated the slipperiness. Borderlines become objects of contention as does national consciousness. Migration gives rise to that sense of homelessness, disconnection, cultural alienation, and ambiguity, all too familiar in the twentieth and twenty-first centuries. And at the same time, a cosmopolitan spirit, urbanity, new cultural knowledge that allows for deeper understanding of the homeland all constitute the gains that accompany the losses of exile. George Lamming, as we have seen, is distraught about having to be scrutinized by European "headquarters" as he writes, yet it is that very tension that often sets his writing into motion. Still, it is undeniable that contact with the colonizing society has made for enlightening ambiguities, the double consciousness that, as I have been arguing throughout this book, is the dominant feature of exilic-migratory writing.

Dissemination is a related issue. In the land that has expelled the writer or producer of culture, often obstacles are created to that product's dissemination if it is not prohibited altogether. In the cases of writers and artists from Equatorial Guinea, these obstacles are overwhelming in the light not only of postcolonial realities common in virtually all African cultures but also those due to the circumstances of the publishing industry in Spain, circumstances not exceptional in first-world societies in the age of globalization. Justo Bolekia is one of the few critics who has addressed the crucial issue of dissemination as part of all the conditions that lead to major difficulties in creating visibility among Equatorial Guinean writers. He speaks of the need for a "reciprocity" in dissemination in the face of the continuing domination of colonizing culture over that of the colonized. But that reciprocity has not come about; what we have seen is anything but a reciprocal exchange of ideas, images, or texts. The immediate effect of colonization and the subsequent state-sponsored terror that came with independence has been the "deterritorialization" of Guineans, that is, the creation of a status of eternal exiles among the entire nation. Yet, the situation is not merely a sorry state of affairs, a lamentable circumstance arising from historical factors whose agency is difficult to ascertain, according to the creator of *Löbëla.* There are "aggressive" players in the processes of "deterritorialization" (see "El español y la producción literaria de Guinea Ecuatorial") (Spanish and the Literary Production of Equatorial Guinea). We might add that neglect, a form of passive aggression devastating to the Equatorial Guinean writer and intellectual, is perhaps the most glaring manifestation of "deterritorialization." It is reminiscent of Franco's official postindependence policy to classify information regarding the country ("materia reservada" [classified information]). The main culprit, for Bolekia, is what he calls "afrofobia": "The effects of this aggressive conduct is still present in the consciousness not only of the victims who witness, powerlessly, the sociocultural chaos that exists in their midst, but also the aggressors, the politicians who loyally carry out the orders of the elites and the Spanish afrophobic intellectual circles" ("El español y la producción literaria").

In the same article, Bolekia goes on to assert that Spanish colonialism and postcolonialism has had the effect of slowing down cultural production on the part of autochthonous peoples of Equatorial Guinea. He points out that Guinean writers have few publishing outlets. While they must rely on Spanish publishers, few see a need or a market for the dissemination of their work. Yet, the disparity is compounded in the light of the many energetic creative writers who seek audiences both within and outside their country as well as the fear among the rulers of exposing the dirty linen of the dictatorship: lack of democracy, economic want, malfunctioning or nonfunctioning infrastructure, torture and incarceration of dissidents, and a petro-based economy that yields windfall profits for oil conglomerates and political elites and virtually nothing for the population. In thirty-six years since independence, Bolekia reminds us, there have only been two publishing companies in Equatorial Guinea, both of which are (still) controlled by Clarentian clerics (see chapter 1).

Bolekia, perhaps unwittingly, raises one of the most important questions regarding the postcolonial other. What are the responsibilities of the former colonizing societies vis-à-vis the subjects of colonization? The challenge that the face-to-face relationship with the other presents is directed to the entire global community as the postcolonial writer, in all his or her double consciousness, explores the consequences of colonialism. It seems, according to Bolekia, that the Spanish intelligentsia and the publishing industry have either not (yet) heard the challenge or they pretend not to hear it. This brings us to the age-old question about the relations between subjectivity and reality: if something happens with no record of it having happened—no text, no recorded testimony, no document referring to it—the very truth of the event is in question. The same applies to a writer or a text. Thus, since the major communications industries pay little attention to Afro-Spanish culture, it is either unimportant or does not exist.

A concrete manifestation of Spanish deaf ears is the reception of the work of Guinean philosopher Eugenio Nkogo, a philosopher who has published a number of philosophical works, mainly on existentialism, such as *El aspecto ético y social del existencialismo* (The ethical and social aspects of existentialism) and *El método filosófico en Jean Paul Sartre* (Jean Paul Sartre's philosophical method). Nkogo writes what might seem a small-minded and peevish preface to his work *Sobre las ruinas de la República de Ghana* (On the ruins of the Republic of Ghana) written after he had lived in Ghana from 1978–80. The book is a penetrating analysis of the modern history of the country whose independence movement was led by none other than Kwame Nkrumah and the disillusionment with that very movement in the postindependence period. Nkogo has the gall to complain that he did not find a financially solvent publisher for his book and that as a consequence, he had to dip into his small savings to disseminate his study:

> Once again I have taken on the burden of my own work: for the fourth time I am going to publish this book, titled *On the Ruins of the Republic of Ghana,* using my own meager means. . . . It has been six years since I wrote it and for three years I have been seeking a publisher . . ., tired of reading and listening to the same response, which is usually an unequivocal "no." . . . These efforts have been based on false hopes. . . .
>
> How can an intellectual work on a creative project, if he must work for survival? How can an intellectual complete a rigorous reflection on the diverse forms of exchange of reality if one is saturated and fatigued by a prohibitive work schedule? "Blessed are those" intellectuals who live in a society with "an

objective spirit" of intellectual promotion, "for it is they who shall inherit" the world of creativity. (9–10)

These words sound shrill, and the taste they leave in any reader interested in the history of Ghana may be bitter. Yet, for those of us living and working "in a society with 'an objective spirit' of intellectual promotion," Nkogo's preface elicits sympathy (perhaps even guilt), especially considering the author's carefully detailed explanation in the pages that follow of the effects of colonialism on the development, or lack thereof, of a viable democracy in Ghana, as the promise of independence turned into "ruins." Indeed, Eugenio Nkogo is our other, the one we turn to as we seek the "authentic African voice," who, in turn, is the one who is not allowed into our club. Bitterness notwithstanding, the preface is perhaps the most faithful manifestation of everything Nkogo traces in his book. Similarly, one wonders if Bolekia's more than understandable protestations are part of broader issues surrounding that always-problematic relationship between the so-called global north and global south, particularly in terms of the movements to and fro on the part of formerly colonized subjects—indeed, the main theme of this book.

On a related topic exploring the publishing practices in nineteenth-century Spain, Elisa Martí-López traces French influences on the Spanish novel. The Spanish novel in the mid-nineteenth century, argues Martí-López, was not only dependent on French forms of expression but also on a readership that disdained autochthonous cultural expression and celebrated the fashions coming from outside of Spain, especially from the nation that produced Victor Hugo. These were as much market forces as literary ones. In more theoretical terms, she states, "In the context of modern cultural production, it is not enough to inquire into the forms of writing; we also need to consider the conditions for the possibility of writing itself" (11). And, of course, these "conditions" have as much to do with what we think of as "taste" as with the promotion of "taste." Spanish writers expressed their displeasure at this sorry state of affairs on more than one occasion. Publishers were indifferent to the "autochthonous novel" (38), as Spanish novelists were forced to turn to small and impoverished printing outlets to make their work accessible. The more lucrative endeavor of imitation or translation of French works led to a certain bitterness not unlike that of Eugenio Nkogo. It is not until the late nineteenth century that we see Spanish writers appeal to a national readership on their own terms.

Martí-López's elucidation of the emergence of the Spanish realist novel in conjunction with the culture of dependence on France provides a precedent for the conditions of writing in Spain's ex-colony. Admittedly, "the conditions for the possibility of writing" have changed dramatically since the nineteenth century. In an age in which the very medium of print itself is in a state of crisis with the advent of cyberpublishing, video, and the CD, one wonders if the neglect of Guinean writing lamented by both Bolekia and E. Nkogo is not due simply to the vicissitudes of a world moving toward new information technologies. Yet, the Internet and all that goes with it are by no means the only difference worthy of discussion. Indeed, the conditions described by Martí-López are aggravated by both exile and postcolonialism.

I turn to another precedent from Spain as a manifestation of the difficulties of exile publishing. For the many Spanish exile intellectuals and writers who fled to Mexico after the Spanish Civil War, difficult access to publishers and readers, financial want, and neglect were major problems despite the fact that the Mexican government of the 1930s, as scholars have pointed out, carried out an official policy of assistance to those "transterrados" (exiles speaking the same language) who had suffered the onslaught of fascism.[1] We need only recall, as an example—in all its pathos—of a little-remembered work of Spanish exile, *La librería de Arana* (Arana's Library) by Simón Otaola, in which the real exile novelist, poet, and would-be publisher, José Ramón Arana, becomes a protagonist. As he establishes his walking bookstore ("librería ambulante"), quixotically entrepreneurial, he wanders from dwelling to dwelling hawking the books of his fellow exiles living in Mexico City. Most of these books are self-published—note E. Nkogo's work on Ghana—and the majority of the buyers are the writers themselves. Otaola's novel is reminiscent as well of the writing of another exile who lived in Mexico, Max Aub (albeit somewhat more successful in the marketing sense). The (French-born) Valencian writer's short story "La verdadera historia de la muerte de Francisco Franco" (The true story of the death of Francisco Franco) is about a waiter in a Mexican café who is tired of listening to all the Spanish patrons rant about having lost the war and, as a result, sets out to assassinate the dictator, not as much as a blow against tyranny as a wish to an end to the hot air of the exiles. It has been said that the politics of exile are filled with "sterile complexities."[2] And there is certainly a truth to that statement considering the at times narrow attention that modern exiles pay to the circumstances that led them out of their land, an obsession that often falls on the deaf ears of the citizens of the host country, no matter how intellectually curious or cosmopolitan they may be.

Yet, the case of African exiles living in the land of formerly colonial powers is somewhat different, not in terms of "sterile complexities"—politics of distant lands always seem arcane to those not of that land—but in the difficult relationship between the previously colonizing reader and the previously colonized writer. The former situation of economic and political dependence is often, and in my view rightly, seen as a major factor in the absence of genuinely democratic and economically viable institutions in Africa. Thus, exile and emigration are not as much matters of a "sterile" political complexity in an exotic and little-known land, as they are a direct result of the politics of the host country. In effect, the host country's history is part of the story of exile, and the result is a relationship filled with tension and conflict. While in France this relationship works itself out in visible ways as immigrants from the former colonies enter French culture, comment on it, and at times even force a face-to-face (or word-to-word) public confrontation, in Spain the situation is different. Perhaps due to the apparent insignificance of the only Spanish-speaking colony in Sub-Saharan Africa, Equatorial Guinea is not as rooted in Spanish historical consciousness as francophone African writing is.

One of the effects of the deliberate policy of classifying, that is, censoring, information on the horrific events immediately following independence ("materia reservada") has been that the Spanish information industry has ignored realities that plague the ex-colony even after the end of Franco's rule. Also important to consider is Spain's colonial legacy in Latin America as the definitive indicator of the former colonial power's relationship with its past colonies, as Spanish activity in Africa becomes eclipsed by the historical period in which Spain was a major world power. As discussed in the introduction, the forces of nationalism in the Iberian Peninsula, along with the nostalgia for power, contribute to an effort to restore that power in the form of ventures in Africa in the early and mid-twentieth century. So much so, that the Civil War, the event that shapes the history of Spain in the twentieth century and beyond, might be seen as an event that begins in Africa due to those very nationalist and imperialist ventures. These historical realities, however, are rarely taken into consideration as twentieth- and twenty-first-century Spaniards construct identities and forge a national consciousness. When the ban was lifted on information on Equatorial Guinea with the end of the Franco regime, relatively little note was taken in the Spanish press, and when Teodoro Obiang engineered the coup against his uncle Macías in 1979, the burgeoning Spanish democracy was clearly interested in other more pressing issues such as its own constitution and the political rights of the autonomies. The presence of Africans in Spanish life did not surface until the mid- to late 1980s, the period known for the beginning of the dramatic rise in immigration. Indeed, blacks in Spain are not seen as the vestiges of empire as is the case with France or Britain; rather the appearance of Africans on Spanish soil is a sign of Spanish modernity and postmodernity. And like many postmodern cultural phenomena, the black presence seems to have come out of nowhere.

The sudden appearance of the African other in Spain—however ill represented in the mainstream cultural outlets—provides insights into the changing national consciousness. The Spanish publishing industry, in the form of powerful communications conglomerates such as Grupo Prisa (which includes *El País,* the news daily as well as the publishing house), Grupo Zeta (owned by the transnational Bertelsmann Corporation), and Grupo Anaya (which includes the prestigious literary publisher Cátedra), becomes interested in Equatorial Guinean culture when it sees a connection to what it perceives as Spanish sensibilities. Much like the publishers and writers in mid-nineteenth-century Spain who insisted in following French models as a matter of popular "taste," the twentieth- and twenty-first-century counterparts seek a market that caters to expectations of the nature of African culture vis-à-vis Spain.

A case in point is a novel *El llanto de la perra* (The bitch's cry) (2005), by Guillermina Mekuy (b. 1982 in Equatorial Guinea), published by the well-known editorial company, Plaza y Janés, an imprint of Random House/ Mondadori (part of the Bertelsmann Group). I cite this novel not as much for its literary merit as for the interest it aroused in the mass-publishing industry. Mekuy writes the first-person account of a young woman, Eldaina, born in an unnamed African country (17), who looks for fulfillment and happiness in Spain, specifically Madrid, where the family moved when she was young. The story involves a variety of mishaps and sexual adventures that are at once typical of modern-day twenty-somethings living and studying in a prosperous European city and at the same time unique due to Eldaina's origin. Indeed, it is the protagonist's difference, her otherness, that makes for an alluring story. Comparable, perhaps, to Almudena Grandes's well-known narrative *Las edades de Lulú* (The ages of Lulú), the narrative follows the patterns of a tale of sexual awakening, an experience that is universal almost by definition. While the protagonist is filled with anxiety and sadness, the cause is never explained in a way that allows readers to pinpoint a specific dilemma or malady. She does not suffer from social mistreatment, poverty, abuse, or racial prejudice—class, race and ethnicity are not integral dimensions of the story. Her sadness and alienation, as the leitmotif of the cry of an abandoned dog shows, always seems to be tempered by the joy of sex—the implicit statement is that sex conquers all. While Eldaina suffers the death of her sister and her mother as well as an expected pregnancy, she withstands these experiences with the help of family, friends, and lovers. In effect, Eldaina's alienation and sadness are more akin to the youthful angst felt by countless youngsters in developed countries in the twenty-first century. Yet, while the author is an African immigrant from a Spanish-speaking country, her "africanness" is of secondary importance, these quirks are what saves the novel from a conventional story of postadolescent sexual awakening. Indeed, the source of her very sense of loss and abandonment may be found in her otherness, even though it is muted.

More significant than the story, in my view, is the marketing strategy of the novel's publishers. The front cover of *El llanto de la perra* comprises a full-page photo of the author's face: deep, dark eyes, slightly shaded, lipstick-red lips, more the lips of a white woman than an African's, free-flowing hair, wavy strands running down either side of her face, and an expression more alluring than Mona Lisa yet less sexual than that of a *Penthouse* pin-up. Her skin color tells us that, clearly, she is of African decent, while even this feature is not exaggeratedly African, since her complexion is more brown than black. On the back flap of the novel, we see the back of the author's head with her sinuous hair covering her left shoulder. On the other side of the back cover is the de-rigueur marketing description of the novel. This description, like all book-cover introductions to novels, reveals the tactics used by Plaza y Janés to find consumers of the book:

> Eldaina, una joven de la alta sociedad de un país africano, sabe desde pequeña que a la felicidad siempre le sigue la desdicha. . . . La historia de Eldaina es un viaje por la vida y la muerte impulsado por el motor del deseo, un itinerario en el que se unen los primeros amores con la pasión más arrebatada . . . una historia sin tapujos, que transporta al lector a un universo de sensaciones donde convergen la desorientación de una mujer presa del deseo, los espejismos del lujo o la permanente búsqueda de la propia identidad.

> (Eldaina, a young woman from the high society of an African country, knows from the time she is a girl that happiness is always followed by misfortune. . . . Eldaina's story is a journey through life and death driven by desire, an itinerary in which first love comes together with the most intense passion . . . a story without restraint that transports the reader to a universe of sensations where there is a mixture of aimlessness of a woman imprisoned by desire, the illusory pursuit of luxury, and the constant search for identity itself.)

While the preface to *El llanto de la perra,* "Unas palabras de presentación a Guillermina Mekuy" (A few words of introduction to Guillermina Mekuy) by Emilio Porta, continues in this vein, the reader learns something about the author—that she was born in Malabo, that her ethnicity is Fang, that she came to Madrid at a young age, that she is a law and political-science student at the Autonomous University of that city—as well as about her intentions: "'Yo quiero ser escritora'" (I want to be a writer) (9). This, according to Porta, is what the author communicated to him as she spoke about the possibility of continuing with her studies as she writes fiction. In an uncommon revelation of the communication between the author and the publisher, we also learn why the latter thought the manuscript was worthy of publication: "unquestioned literary skill, a bold book, original, a book that would surprise people because its author was so young, so different, yet so much the same as so many women of her age" (9). Reminiscent of Vicente Granados's prologue to María Nsue's *Ekomo,* Porta describes the conversation he had with the author about the novel: "There are a few things, the theme, the title. . . . I don't know if anyone will be scandalized" (10; ellipsis in original). Thus, it is difficult to ignore the Spanish publication industry's interest in the novel: it titillates. Even the suggestion that some people might be offended points to a possible market, a focus group—most likely the twenty-somethings who don't normally buy dense novels—that, in the eyes of the marketing personnel, might be enticed into Mekuy's sensuous (albeit alienating) world. At the risk of overinterpreting the words of a dust jacket, it seems that Mekuy chooses not to deal with race and ethnicity is for the editors a positive feature of the novel, an indication that Spanish youth have gone beyond these issues. If, indeed, this is the case, then it is interesting, if not contradictory, that Plaza y Janés highlights both the author's and the protagonist's race on the front and back covers.[3]

Thus, in the publishing industry, the colonial and postcolonial history of the relation between Africa and Spain is less important than the here-and-now. Yet, even as cultural and political critics deal with the present moment of the ex-colony of Spain, the most influential circles of the Spanish communications industry seem not to take notice. Another issue is the lack of visibility of the groups of Guinean exiles and their attempts to establish working relationships with Spaniards interested in Africa not only as an area in need of human rights reform but also as a political issue related to Spain and Spanish history. A counterpoint to this neglect is influential organization, ASODEGUE (Asociación para la Solidaridad Democrática con Guinea Ecuatorial) (Association of Democratic Solidarity with Equatorial Guinea), a group that continues to be active today. According to Adolfo Fernández Marugán, one of the association's founder's, ASODEGUE was formed in 1993 by Spaniards involved in left politics, predominantly the activists of the labor trade unions of the socialist (PSOE) and United Left (IU) parties who were concerned about human-rights abuses throughout the world, including Africa. After the release of Nelson Mandela from prison and the achievement of self-determination in South Africa in 1989, these Spanish leftists turned to Equatorial Guinea with one overarching goal in mind, a principle akin to the policies of the Spanish Foreign Affairs Ministry during the early years of the presidency of Felipe González: to move toward the democratization of third-world countries. The realization of this goal involved fomenting relationships with the Guinean opposition to Teodoro Obiang's dictatorship. According to Marugán, ASODEGUE's activity was (and remains) similar to that of an NGO, even though there was a loose connection with the Spanish Foreign Affairs Ministry.[4]

Yet, ASODEGUE's interests are not only political, they have been cultural as well. Mainly through its Web page (www.asodegue.org), the organization allows free access to the ideas and writing of virtually all the cultural and political figures the current study has dealt with. A link to Ndongo's anthology of Equatorial Guinean literature (1984), in its entirety, provides anyone interested in the texts of these writers, many of which have been analyzed in the current volume, at no cost other than access to the World Wide Web. Equally important is that the organization, again with its electronic site as its main vehicle of dissemination, has provided a forum in which the exiles and emigrants can not only express themselves but also find readers and other activists, people who will listen, react, and enter into a dialogue on Guinean politics and culture. The electronic medium in which this dialogue takes place is the feature that makes Guinean exile anomalous within all other previous exile cultures and experiences of the Iberian Peninsula. The possibility of a different relationship between the Spanish exile writers of the Civil War and their readers had they access to the cyberworld is open to question. As has been pointed out in a variety of other contexts, in the late twentieth and early twenty-first centuries, the Internet has taken the form of a new Gutenberg press, and as such, it allows for a greater possibility of a presence of and a dialogue with the African other.

Indeed, the floating, virtual, intangible world of the Web may be the medium of exile par excellence. Like the placelessness of exile and emigration, cyberspace engulfs us into a no man's land (and no woman's land) in which we can not only *be* in two or more places at once but we also can participate in the politics and social life of those places. Cyberspace creates a new and ambivalent location that lays bare the condition of being nowhere and everywhere at once. The "sterile complexities" of exile politics may become less sterile and more within our reach. The future of Equatorial Guinea and those who represent it, like all the writers, political figures, and intellectuals dealt with here, depends not solely on economic factors such as control and compensation for the vast reserves of petroleum within that nation's sovereign borders. It also depends on the consciousness and agency of the human beings affected by that economy, for the transition from print to electronic media may make for a change in that very consciousness.

Many of the writers whose creative works and ideas I have been exploring engage in cultural production regardless of the possibilities of reaching a wide readership, that is, without the support of the publishing industry controlled by transnational corporations. Some even write without the hope of publication. Yet, while their works are at times excruciatingly difficult for consumers to find, more so for consumers who do not have access to libraries and/or computers, their reality surfaces through other means: small publishers, the Internet, word of mouth, public presentations (in areas where their work is not censored), sponsorship on the part of sympathetic first-world agencies. In the last analysis, even though the reality of a diaspora is difficult to reckon with, it emerges at times in unexpected contexts and situations: ultimately, it never ends or disappears. The writers I have considered are exiles, emigrants, and immigrants writing from within *a* diaspora and *the* diaspora. The indefinite article refers to the experience of a collective exodus, in this case Africans leaving their land as a consequence of the arrival of European explorers, settlers, colonizers, merchants, and slavers. And the definite article refers to a specific manifestation: the departure of Equatorial Guineans from their homeland, a historical phenomenon of the twentieth and twenty-first centuries.

Diasporic cultures experience all the salient issues of this book: double consciousness, otherness, placelessness, forced departures, voluntary departures, waiting for return. For the nondiasporic community, those who stay at home, both geographically and imaginatively, these issues are difficult to fathom or even conceptualize. Perhaps this explains—at least partially—why it has been difficult for diasporic cultures to disseminate their thoughts and works. The introduction discusses Paul Tiyambe Zeleza, a writer from Zimbabwe, whose story "Waiting" manifested virtually all of the features of exile-emigration writing elucidated in the current study. As we recall, the protagonist is one not yet born. He tells his story from the "spirit world" *waiting* for his own birth. It is precisely this spirit world that encapsulates the issues I address. What sets spirits (ghosts, specters, chimeras) apart from the mortal world is not that they live in an isolated world separate from ours, it is that they inhabit two worlds at once, in effect, they are on the outside looking in. They enjoy both distance from the people and events in our atmosphere and from immersion in it. Haunting is their *jouissance,* an at-once pleasurable and painful activity, as they intrude into a world they once occupied. They make their spectral presence known in the form of ancestors, gods, goddesses, and haunting memories in the works of writers we have explored: Jones Mathama's "hypnotizer" who abuses women; Raquel Ilombé's remembrance of a mother she never knew; Ndongo's veneration of elders as well as those strange figures—women and men—who inhabit the protagonist's imagination in *Tinieblas;* Mbomio's and Ávila Laurel's use of the *mibili;* Bolekia's goddess Löbëla and her multiple identities; Zamora's lady dressed in white gauze who haunts the poet's memory, along with his many poetic evocations of other-world figures, and his haunting memory of Lucrecia Pérez; Siale's tale of novelistic characters who return to life (albeit literary); and the entire world of Nsue's *Ekomo* ("the borderline between life and death"). Life for these spirits is exile by definition: it is, as Zeleza's narrator says, "the terrifying exile of human life" (3) and at the same time the appraisal of that life from the outside.

This out-of-body-ness has its political-cultural correlative in the lives of exiles and emigrants. In many ways, they themselves are the spirits haunting others and themselves. Their absence in the world they left is felt in the form of a memory and the things and feelings they left behind, including their mythical mothers. And their presence in the new environment is equally haunting; they are others who must be reckoned with like that unsettling notion of the not-same that Levinas explores in his elucidations of alterity. As in many of the texts commented on here, the ending of Ndongo's "Dream" is a synthesizing moment. While his character awakens relieved to learn that the trying, at times horrifying journey of emigration and immigration is not true, like a dream, it comes back to haunt. It could be true and not have happened. "'I needed to be sure that I hadn't died, that it was all a dream," his character says. "It was necessary to be then and only then. I was coming back to life" (79). Yes, coming back to life with the double consciousness of a ghost.

NOTES

CHAPTER 1: EMIXILE

1. Credible statistics on this are difficult to determine. According to the Spanish Wikipedia, "After independence thousands of Equatorial Guineans left for Spain. Some one hundred thousand fled to Cameroon, Gabon, and Nigeria due to independence due to Francisco Macías's dictatorship. There are communities of Equatorial Guineans in Brazil and other Latin American countries as well as in the United States, Portugal, and France." (Después de la independencia, miles de ecuatoguineanos partieron a España. Alrededor de 100.000 ecuatoguineanos fueron a Camerún, Gabón y Nigeria a causa de la dictadura de Francisco Macías Nguema. Muchas de sus comunidades viven en Brasil, muchos países hispanoamericanos, Estados Unidos, Portugal y Francia.") "Etnografía" (my translation).

2. Silverstein 1. See also Klitgaard, *Tropical Gangsters,* and Roberts, *The Wanga Coup.* Indeed, Equatorial Guinea's oil richness underscores a tension felt throughout this book between the nation-state and its eroding sovereignty in the midst of the economics of badly needed energy sources in the so-called first world. See Joseba Gabilondo's pertinent discussion of nationalism and postnationalism in the Spanish-speaking world in "One Way Theory."

3. I deal with Gómez de la Serna's ambivalent exile-emigrant status in my previous book *Shifting Ground* (86–88). All translations are mine unless otherwise indicated.

4. Kitty Calavita's excellent study of legal, economic, and political marginalization of recent immigrants to Spain and Italy (*Immigrants at the Margins*) adds an important dimension to the discussion by fusing the ever-changing and often-deceptive empirical data on the subject with what she calls "[the literature on] the constitution of immigrant otherness and exclusion" (9), that is, the discourse that both reflects these exclusions and puts them into practice. Indeed, in the past decade, there have been many Spanish news accounts and commentaries on African immigration to Spain. Just a few of these examples are: *El País* articles: Tomás Bárbulo, "El mayo

más africano de las islas Canarias," 3 June 2006, 26; Patricia Ortega Dolz, "Senegal suspende las repatriaciones desde Canarias tras la protesta de 99 inmigrantes," 2 June 2006, 23; Peru Egurbide, "Nueve países europeos ayudarán a España a patrullar las costas de Africa occidental," 30 May 2006, 23; and Patricia Ortega Dolz, "Marruecos repatria a 433 inmigrantes de Senegal que fracasaron en su ruta canaria," 31 May 2006, 25. See also my article "'Soy tú. Soy él': African Immigration and Otherness in the Spanish Collective Conscience."

5. "España ratifica su compromiso con África en la cumbre sobre inmigración y desarrollo de Rabat" (Spain ratifies its support of Africa in the summit meeting on immigration and development in Rabat).

6. Habermas argues this in *The Inclusion of the Other.* A discussion of Habermas's views comes later in this chapter.

7. "U.S. Slave Trade: The Middle Passage."

8. *Tarifa Traffic.* See also another documentary on African emigration to Europe, *Paradise: Three Journeys in This World,* directed by Elina Hirvonen. A similarly sympathetic treatment of Spaniards trying to cope with and understand the hardships of African immigration into Spain is Lourdes Ortiz's story, "Fátima de los naufragios" (Fatima of the shipwrecked). These are compelling renderings of the reality of immigration into Spain, yet any reader or viewer with an insider information on how African immigrants are treated once they arrive (nearly dead) on Spanish soil might point out that both Demmer's and Ortiz's recreations are partial, that is, like any rendering of reality, they can only tell part of the story.

9. Luis Martul states that exile and emigration from Galicia, Catalonia, and Euskadi intensify nationalist sentiments in all those areas: "Exile has to do with a departure from the homeland or the nation not simply from a past residence." 302.

10. Contrary to many critics dealing with conceptions of the other, I choose not to use the upper case, as does Lacan, for example, when he distinguishes between other as the one who resembles the self and Other in whose gaze we acquire identity. As far as I can tell, Levinas did not make such distinctions in his French texts, and most translators of Levinas into English also choose to use the lower case *other* consistently. There is, however, an interesting distinction, I think, between Levinas's use of the other as an idea (*l'autre*) and his equally preponderant use of "the other person," or "the other man" (*l'autre homme*). I find it notable that the very same distinction could be made when we speak of exile.

11. My analysis of Azurmendi also appears in my article "'Soy tú. Soy él'" (I am you. I am he). See also Gabilondo's critique of the Basque commentator in "State Narcissism." Calavita is equally critical of Azurmendi's naive critique of "multiculturalism" in her *Immigrants at the Margins* (149–50). Calavitas book deals precisely with all or most of the issues addressed by Azurmendi. Unlike the former ETA member, however, her analysis is far more cognizant of the problematic of the other as an essential marker of human interaction.

12. In a conversation with Donato Ndongo, I was interested to learn (yet not

surprised) that Baldwin is one of the Equatorial Guinean novelist's most revered writers.

Chapter 2: Out of Equatorial Guinea

1. See also Eley, "Historicizing the Global" 158–61.

2. Following a numerical description of the slave trade in the Bight of Biafra area, Sundiata submits: "Fernando Poo stood outside these developments" (18). Similarly Bolekia submits, "The bellicose responses of the indigenous peoples to the invasion of its waters and lands . . . kept these invaders from taking real possession of the African lands" (Aproximación 29). But while the islands in question were something of an exception, Sundiata's study reveals that Equatorial Guinean slavery and forced labor are crucial to the understanding of the African Atlantic slave trade.

3. I am relying on the following secondary sources to understand the early history of Equatorial Guinea: Sundiata, Bolekia, Ndongo, Castro, Nerín. For the classical studies and theories of the slave trade, see Gilroy, David B. Davis, and Basil Davidson, along with a more nuanced depiction by Eley. For a study of a Spanish moral critique of the slave trade in the sixteenth and seventeenth centuries, see Olsen.

4. Chapter 3 discusses Ndongo's story "El sueño," along with his novel *El metro*.

5. All translations are mine unless indicated otherwise. See also Lewis's assessment of Francoist colonization (2).

6. See Margaret Olsen on Alonso de Sandoval's critique of the treatment of blacks in Cuba, comparable in the moral debate initiated by Bartolomé de Las Casas on Spanish treatment of indigenous populations.

7. *Afro-fascism* is explained in Liniger-Goumaz's book, *De la Guinée Ecuatorial* (On Equatorial Guinea) as well as in *Small Is Not Always Beautiful:* "Fascist regimes [in Europe] . . . had no spontaneously European feature . . . ; their logical explanation is rather to be found in the working of industrial societies. . . . In post-colonial Africa, the many different types of crises which have occurred, giving rise to authoritarian or 'emergency' regimes, are also not spontaneously African." (xii).

8. In addition to all these histories and descriptions of Guinean dictatorships, see Martíniez Alcázar and Soto-Trillo for first-person accounts of Spaniards who lived through these times and were sympathetic to the Guineans who have had to endure them.

9. See www.asodegue.org for more information. In the summer of 2006, I wrote an op-ed piece for the Asociación para la Solidaridad Democrática con Guinea Ecuatorial (ASODEGUE) in which I urged the Spanish government to put pressure on the Obiang regime and shut down Black Beach, which is not the only prison in Equatorial Guinea holding political prisoners. ASODEGUE is an excellent source for information on Equatorial Guinea. See also the critical response to my editorial by Jorge Salvo in which he submits that my assertion that oil has been a curse to most Guineans is paternalistic.

Chapter 3: The First Wave

1. This essay, "El marco," first appeared in and follows the introduction in Ndongo's pioneering anthology of Guinean literature, *Antología de la literatura guineana* (11–46) (1984). Page numbers in the current text refer to *Literatura de Guinea Ecuatorial,* Ndongo and Ngom's anthology.

2. See Leopold Senghor's major work on negritude, *Négritude et humanisme* (1964). For Fanon's criticism, see *The Wretched of the Earth* 206–48. For a more positive view of negritude, see Gary Wilder, *The French Imperial Nation-State (2005).* Wilder's book is by no means an attempt to resuscitate this (by now) highly criticized cultural ideology. He does, however, invite his readers to reexamine negritude as a necessary step toward self-determination. I'd like to thank my colleague Mamadou Badiane for informing me of Wilder's study.

3. A similar view is expressed by Nigerian playwright and essayist Femi Osofisan as he refers to what he calls "post-*negritude*" as a cultural vehicle out of alienation and into a more ongoing and active confrontation of social and economic problems: "All the strategies we employ . . . are attempts to confront, through our plays, our novels and poetry, the various problems of underdevelopment which our countries are facing, and of which the threat of alienation and the potential erosion of ethnic identity constitute *only one* of the outward signals" (3). See also Elisa Rizo's essay on Ávila Laurel's *El fracaso de las sombras* for a penetrating analysis of this work. For further discussion of the aftermath of *negritude,* see Francis Abiola Irele, "In Praise of Alienation." I would like to thank Rizo for pointing out Osofisan's notion of "post-*negritude.*"

4. See Jacint Creus and Gustavo Nerín's edition of stories and testimonies concerning colonial Equatorial Guinea, *Estampas y cuentos de la Guinea Española.* Many of these "estampas" (vignettes) were written by colonial subjects as well as by missionaries and Spanish governmental administrators.

5. It is a disgrace and a tragedy that so few of the principal holdings of this journal remain. *La Guinea Española,* along with others devoted to similar themes and topics (*Diario de Guinea Ecuatorial, Unidad de Guinea Ecuatorial,* and *La Libertad*), were destroyed or disappeared at the orders of Francisco Macías during his devastating rule.

6. Lewis discusses the overlapping relation between "hispanidad" and "guineidad" in his introduction (4–7) and in his chapter in the contemporary Guinean novel. Here he implies that virtually all Guinean writing is a search for mediation between the two.

7. See Sundiata (111–15) and Bolekia, *Aproximación* (86–88); the latter uses the term *Kriós.* See also the previous chapter for the discussion of the case of Joseph Emmanuel Taylor.

8. One of the students at Jones's English school was none other than Antonio Samaranch, the famed Olympic Games commissioner, later accused of misappropriation of funds.

9. *Una lanza* is an exciting and engaging novel that has been unfairly dismissed as a colonialist. Adam Lifshey, on the other hand, deems the novel worthy of thorough analysis. In his article "And So the Worm Turns," he points out Jones Mathama's "doomed" paradox: to confine a colony within the discourse of the colonizer. Thus, the colony's "discursive existence is ever deferred into difference when an imperial pen seeks to define it" (113). I might add that this paradox comes from the exilic and migratory experience. Another study yet to be written is an in-depth analysis of the convergences and discrepancies of these two "colonialist novels": *Una lanza* and *Cuando los combes luchaban.*

10. See Ndongo and Ngom 72, 215; Ndongo, *Antología* 136–37, 138.

11. The motif of the return as a desire for reunion with the mother is the topic of my chapter 8. While there are relatively few published Equatorial Guinean women writers, figures of the African mother abound.

12. Benita Sampedro discusses this poem in her article "African Poetry" (210) as does Lewis (53–54).

Chapter 4: Donato Ndongo

1. I cannot confirm the truth of the allegation that Mba threatened to kill Ndongo with any written source other than to attribute it to the man who was being threatened. Ndongo related the incident in a conversation with me on November 10, 2006, and to this day he maintains that it happened. Ken Silverstein's October 25, 2006, article, "Mba's House," in *Harper's,* provides evidence that Mba is a known torturer. The new U.S Embassy is housed in property owned by Mr. Mba, although recently confirmed ambassador to Equatorial Guinea, Donald Johnson, claims the second Bush administration is interested in curbing human rights abuses in that country. "El nuevo embajador norteamericano, Donald C. Johnson, contesta" www.asodegue.org, 2 Nov. 2006.

2. Ndongo, Donato. Personal interview.

3. Part of this chapter appeared in Ugarte, "Spain's Heart of Darkness," *Journal of Spanish Cultural Studies* 7.3 (2006): 271–87.

4. Baldwin said these words in an interview excerpted in a segment of the video version of *The Price of the Ticket,* a collection of autobiographical essays. He explains how he sees the participation of whites in African American liberation in an essay from *The Price* titled "Dark Days" (657–66). In the documentary of Baldwin's life, William Styron, a longtime friend, relates an incident from memory in which someone asks the Harlem writer, "You don't mean that black people—" And Baldwin, according to Styron, interrupts and says, "Yes, they gonna burn your house down." At which point, the image cuts to Baldwin speaking on his own: "As long as you think you're white, there is no hope for you." Much has been made of this statement; see David Roediger's provocative book, *The Wages of Whiteness,* especially the introduction. But I think the point may also be found in one of the

many messages, if not the most important one, of *The Fire Next Time*, whose title is a reference to the biblical Noah—the next flood will not be water but fire—and, Baldwin seems to tell us, if you think you are in power when the fire comes, there is no hope for you, if for anyone.

5. As discussed later, Ndongo's novel *El metro* is based on the plot of "El sueño."

6. Contrary to the assertion by Mbare Ngom ("La autobiografía como plataforma de denuncia" [Autobiography as a platform for denunciation]), these two novels are not autobiographical in the sense that the author is re-creating his own specific experiences. María Zielina Limonta may also overemphasize the autobiographical intention of *Tinieblas*. Even in the paragraph she cites from the interview she conducted with him, one detects an attempt to create a distance between character and author. "Las tinieblas" 138. See Baltasar Fra-Molinero's excellent article "La figura ambivalente," note 1, for a clarification.

7. In his essay "Los herederos del Señor Kurtz," (The heirs of Mr. Kurtz), Ndongo submits that the heirs to the throne of Joseph Conrad's memorable protagonist are the present dictators of postindependence African nations. See my essay on the presence of Conrad's classic in Ndongo's fiction and essays, "Spain's Heart of Darkness." I am not the first to point to this relationship; see Fra-Molinero, "La figura ambivalente," which also explores the thematic relationship between Ndongo's writing and that of his friend and fellow exile Joaquín Mbomío.

8. See Lewis's analysis of this scene (151–52) in which he points out that Ada's perverse act is an attempt to outdo and humiliate the sexual power of the protagonist's white wife.

Chapter 5: *El metro* (The Subway)

1. For a full discussion of Azurmendi's views on immigration as well as an overview of African immigration into Spain, see my article "'Soy tú.'" See also "State Narcissism," Joseba Gabilondo's critique of Azurmendi as a Basque intellectual. For a European overview of the immigration issue and the ways in which the new appearance of "others" becomes the center of the construction of a "threat," see Lucassen.

2. Soja understands *thirdspace* as the "real/imaginary," the ordering, structuring, and interpretation of the copies of reality (1–6).

Chapter 6: Between Life and Death

1. See Baltasar Fra-Molinero, "La figura ambivalente del personaje mesiánico en la novela de Guinea Ecuatorial," 116, and Justo Bolekia Boleká, "El español y la producción literaria de Guinea Ecuatorial."

2. Mbomío spent time in the infamous Black Beach prison camp, which was created by the Spanish colonists and used by both the Macías and Obiang regimes to incarcerate, torture, and execute political prisoners. See his piece "Vísperas." This

camp and others like it in Equatorial Guinea, have been cited by Amnesty International and Human Rights Watch as evidence of human-rights abuse. See Silverstein, "U.S. Oil Politics in the 'Kuwait of Africa'" and "Our Friend Teodoro," as well as my editorial piece "Guinea Ecuatorial y el 'Otro' español: Cerrar Black Beach."

3. There is also an awareness of shared experiences among the members of this generation who lived the immediate postindependence period as young men and women. Rope's case is somewhat exceptional, since he is one of the few of the "lost generation"—Julián Bibang is another—still living and writing in Equatorial Guinea. After leaving the country in 1975 for political reasons, he returned in 1980 to work in various export companies as he continued to write for the journals *Poto-Poto* and *Ebano,* both of which folded due to censorship. He also participated in the Centro Cultural Hispano-Guineano when Donato Ndongo was directing, but the Obiang regime made his work extremely difficult. See his poem "Cuando el viento llora" (When the wind weeps) and other poems in the Ndongo and Ngom, *Literatura* (175–80) as well as his translation of Dulu Bon Be Afrikara's account of European usurpation of territory inhabited by the Fang (*La migración fang*) (Fang migration).

4. The town of Niefang was called Seville during the colonial era.

5. For information on exile literature of Spanish Civil War, see Ugarte, *Shifting Ground.*

6. See "El asesinato de Lucrecia Pérez" (The assassination of Lucrecia Pérez), *El País* 21 Nov. 1992, and the lyrics of the Carlos Cano song "Canción para Lucrecia."

7. In another poem by Zamora, "Salvar a copito," the poet satirizes the many sympathies expressed toward the albino panda who died in the Barcelona zoo. Benita Sampedro analyzes this poem in relation to Spanish racist sensibilities in her article "Salvando a Copito de Nieve" (Saving Copito the Snowflake).

Chapter 7: Exiles Stay at Home

1. Paul Ilie's *Literature and Inner Exile* provides an analysis of the issues surrounding interior exile in Franco's Spain.

2. For information on the Macías dictatorship, see Ndongo, *Historia y tragedia* and Liniger-Goumaz, *Small Is Not Always Beautiful.* Robert E. Klitgaard in *Tropical Gangsters* shows how the Macías dictatorship led to that of Obiang. See also Justo Bolekia, *Aproximación.*

3. Elisa Rizo ("En torno") and Igor Cusack ("Hispanic and Bantu Inheritance") discuss Obiang's attempt to forge a new national identity. See also Dosinda García-Alvite's article, "Strategic Positions of Las Hijas del Sol," on the popular singer-songwriters (Paloma and Piruchi) from Equatorial Guinea as manifestations of a more progressive and critical forging of national and ethnic identities.

4. *Áwala cu sangui* is in Annobonese; Awala is a village on the island of Annobon, formerly Santa Cruz.

5. See Lewis's description of this novella (184–89).

6. See Silverstein's article on Equatorial Guinea as the new Persian Gulf, "U.S.

Oil Politics in the 'Kuwait of Africa,'" and the U.S. Senate Investigations report "Money Laundering and Foreign Corruption." See also Ávila Laurel's more recent stinging criticism of petro politics, "¿Futuro negro?" *Guinea Ecuatorial: Vísceras* (Equatorial Guinea: Entrails) (2006), essays very much in keeping with the style of *Cómo convertir.* Benita Sampedro's "Estudio introductorio" (7–20) to these essays provides an excellent explanation of Ávila Laurel's work.

7. See my contribution to *Cambridge History of Spanish Literature,* "Literature of Franco's Spain," 611–19.

8. See Adam Roberts, *Wonga Coup.*

9. The interview was conducted by Eliza Rizo ("Una Conversación," *Journal of Spanish Cultural Studies*) in the environs of Columbia, Missouri, in the United States.

10. On the *mibili,* see Elisa Rizo's article in the same issue of the *Journal of Spanish Cultural Studies,* "El Teatro guineoecuatoriano contemporáneo: el *mibili* en 'El fracaso de las sombras'" ("The failure of the shadow"). For anthropological information on witchcraft among the Fang, see Mbana.

11. See Kathleen McNerney's review of *Adjá-Adjá y otros relatos.*

12. When I was in Equatorial Guinea in July of 2006, the then-director of the Spanish Cultural Center of Malabo working for Cooperación Española (a Spanish governmental agency devoted to educational and cultural advancement in third-world countries), expressed frustration at constantly having to pay a small "fee" (in Spanish, "mordida" or bribe) to carry out the most routine tasks, such as going from one place to another and being stopped (harassed) by someone in uniform. To show an example to the people of Malabo, she refused to pay the "mordida" and threatened to complain to higher authorities. As a result, she was usually freed from having to pay. In retrospect, I believe that in her refusal to give in, she was making an effort to set an example as a representative of the Spanish government. However, her principled response may itself be seen as a transgression: a violation of accepted behavior.

13. One of the possible literary models for Nkogo's work, albeit an unwitting one, is a celebrated novel by Ghanaian writer Ayi Kwei Armah, *The Beautiful Ones Are Not Yet Born.* It takes place in the aftermath of Kwame Nkrumah's independence, which served as a model for other African countries. The novel conveys the disillusionment of the promise of African liberation in Ghana. Ghanaian society is described as institutionally corrupt, filled with a malaise that seems to have no solution, other than yet another African awakening to the pitfalls of their own rulers.

Chapter 8: Gendering Emixile

1. See Ugarte, "Interview with Donato Ndongo," *Arizona Journal of Hispanic Cultural Studies* 8 (2004): (228–29) as well as Dorsch, "Grillots, Roots, and Identity in the African Diaspora."

2. María Zielina's in "Las tinieblas de tu memoria negra" discusses this episode

intelligently as a rite of (male) passage ("pasaje a la pubertad") (152) in comparison to the character's First Communion. While, clearly, these are rites in which masculine power relations are negotiated, as she submits (152–53), the symbolic presence of the mother adds an important dimension to the ritual.

3. Among other Guinean writers who write of the return to the mother are Antimo Esono, "No encontré flores para mi madre" (I did not find flowers for my mother) (Ndongo and Ngom 297–302), and María Caridad Rihola, "Exilio" (Ndongo and Ngom 400–402).

4. Zielina asserts, quoting Eileen Julien, that African women writers tend to avoid the patriarchal machinations of traditional novel forms such as the epic and the "novel of initiation" ("Ekomo" 93).

5. Aponte Ramos's discussion is also based on a concept of exile. She reads Ekomo's infirmity as an extension of that of the entire community; thus, it is a form of "social exile" (100). This is a perceptive reading.

6. See Rizo's insightful article "Teatro guineoecuatoriano contemporáneo."

7. This respect for traditions is in keeping with Trinidad Morgades Besari's compelling short dramatic work "Antígona," in which the archetypal character's defiance of power—in this case that of the Guinean dictator—follows a natural order dictated by "el pueblo" (the people) (243). Moreover, the "Guinean Antigony" is like Nnanga (or "Paloma de Fuego") in that her energy and moral strength are manifested in her dancing. See Kathleen McNerney and Gabriel Quirós Alpera's analysis.

Chapter 9: Ending with a Beginning

1. For a thorough and penetrating analysis of the cultural work of Spanish Civil War exiles in Mexico, see Sebastian Faber, *Exile and Cultural Hegemony.*

2. The term comes from Bertolt Brecht's antifascist activities in the early 1940s when he was living in the United States. See my book about exile, *Shifting Ground* (36; also 234n2).

3. Another novel related to Equatorial Guinea, Carles Decors's *Al sur de Santa Isabel* (South of Santa Isabel), published by a major publishing house, originally appeared in Catalan. Its subject matter is more "serious" than Mekuy's novel in that it deals with historical and political issues surrounding the independence of the country coupled with psychological dilemmas. The subject position, however, is that of the colonizer coping with life in the colony as well as with members of a previous generation of Spanish political and economic elites. That this novel was chosen by Alianza is at once perplexing and revealing of the ways in which editors read the market. I have scratched the surface of this issue. A detailed study of Spanish publishing practices in the age of transnational corporations and globalization is greatly needed.

4. Marugán, electronic correspondence to author, 17 and 19 April 2007.

BIBLIOGRAPHY

Abiola Irele, Francis. "In Praise of Alienation." *The Surreptitious Speech: Presence Africaine and the Politics of Otherness 1947–1987*. Ed. Y. Mudimbe. Chicago: U of Chicago P, 1992. 210–24.

Achebe, Chinua. *Things Fall Apart*. Oxford, Eng.: Heinemann, 1958.

Agrela, Belén. "La política de inmigración en España: Reflexiones sobre la emergencia del discurso cultural." *Migraciones Internacionales* 1.2 (2002): 93–121.

———. "Spain as a Recent Country of Immigration: How Immigration Became a Symbolic, Political, and Cultural Problem in the 'New Spain.'" Working Paper 57. *Center for Comparative Immigration Studies*. Aug. 2002. June 2006 <http://ccis.ucsd.edu/PUBLICATIONS/wrkg57.PDF>.

Amadiume, Ifi. "Nok Lady in Terracotta." Chipasula and Chipasula 70–72.

———. *Reinventing Africa: Matriarchy, Religion, and Culture*. New York: St. Martin's, 1997.

Anderson, Benedict. *Imagined Communities: Reflections on the Origins and Spread of Nationalism*. New York: Verso, 1991.

Aponte Ramos, Lola. "Los territorios de la identidad: transgénero y transnacionalidad en *Ekomo* de María Nsue Angüe." Ngom, *La recuperación de la memoria* 101–14.

"El asesinato de Lucrecia Pérez." *El País* 21 Nov. 1992.

Ashcroft, Bill, Gareth Griffiths, and Helen Tiffin. *The Empire Writes Back: Theory and Practice in Post-Colonial Literatures*. New York: Routledge, 1989.

———. *Post-Colonial Studies: The Key Concepts*. New York: Routledge, 2000.

———. *Post-Colonial Studies Reader, The*. New York: Routledge, 1995.

Ávila Laurel, Juan Tomás. *Awala cu sangui* [*Awala with blood*]. Malabo, Equatorial Guinea: Ediciones Pángola, 2000.

———. *La carga*. Valencia, Spain: Palmart, 1999.

———. *Cómo convertir este país en un paraíso: Otras reflexiones sobre Guinea Ecuatorial* [How to turn this country into a paradise: Other reflections on Equatorial Guinea]. Malabo, Equatorial Guinea: Pángola, 2005.

———. *El desmayo de Judas*. Malabo, Equatorial Guinea: Ediciones Centro Cultural Hispano-Guineano, 2001.

———. *El fracaso de las sombras*. Malabo, Equatorial Guinea: Ediciones Pángola, 2004.

———. *Guinea Ecuatorial: Vísceras*. Intro. Benita Sampedro. Valencia, Spain: Novatores, 2006.

———. *Nadie tiene buena fama en este país*. Ávila, Spain: Editorial Malamba, 2002.

Azurmendi, Mikel. *Estampas de El Ejido: Un reportaje sobre la integración del inmigrante*. Madrid: Taurus, 2001.

———. "Is MultCulturalism Helping or Hindering Integration in Spain?" *Work in Progress: Migration, Integration and the European Labour Market*. London: Civitus, 2003. 1–8. Oct. 2005 <www.civitas.org.uk/pdf/workinprogress.pdf>.

———. *Todos somos nosotros*. Madrid: Taurus, 2003.

Balboa Boneke, Juan. *O'Boriba (El exiliado)*. Mataró, Spain: Agrupación Hispana de Escritores, 1982. Also Ndongo, *Antologia* 142–49.

Baldwin, James. *The Fire Next Time*. New York: Dial, 1962.

———. *Notes of a Native Son*. New York: Ballantine, 1995.

———. *Price of the Ticket, The: Collected Nonfiction 1948–1985*. New York: St. Martin's, 1985.

Bárbulo, Tomás. "El mayo más africano de las Islas Canarias." *El País* 3 June 2006: 26.

Bibang Oyee, Julián. "Cuando el viento llora." Ndongo and Ngom 173.

———, ed. and trans. Introducción. *La migración fang (según Dulu Bon Be Afrikara)*. Ávila, Spain: Malambo, 2002. 19–30.

Bokesa, Ciriaco. *Voces de Espumas*. Malabo, Equatorial Guinea: Centro Cultural Hispano-Guineano, 1987.

Bolekia Boleká, Justo. *Aproximación a la historia de Guinea Ecuatorial*. Salamanca, Spain: Amarú, 2003.

———. "El español y la producción literaria de Guinea Ecuatorial." *Panorama de la literatura en Guinea Ecuatorial*. Instituto Cervantes. 2005. 20 Mar. 2007 <http://cvc.cervantes.es/obref/anuario/anuario_05/bolekia/p05.htm>.

———. *Löbëla*. Casa de Africa. Madrid: Sial, 1999.

Calavita, Kitty. *Immigrants at the Margins: Law, Race, and Exclusion in Southern Europe*. Cambridge Studies in Law and Society. Cambridge, Eng.: Cambridge UP, 2005.

Cano, Carlos. "Canción para Lucrecia." *Música Música: La Casa de los Sueños*. 24 June 2007 <http://galeon.hispavista.com/musicasuenos/musica-CARLOSCANO.htm>.

Carballal, Ana. "Hombre gallego y emigrante: la emigración y el exilio en la obra de Alfonso Rodríguez Castelao." Diss. U of Missouri, Columbia, 2004.

———. "Theoretical Conceptualization of Immigration and Exile in Alfonso Rodríguez

Castelao." 2005 European Studies Conference Selected Proceedings University of Nebraska-Omaha. 4 Oct. 2006 <http://www.unomaha.edu/esc/2005Proceedings/TheoreticalConcept.pdf>.

Cela, Camilo José. *La familia de Pascual Duarte.* Barcelona: Plaza y Janés, 2001.

de Certeau, Michel. *Heterologies: Discourse on the Other.* Ed. Wlad Godzich. Trans. Brian Massumi. Minneapolis, Minn.: U of Minnesota P, 1986.

Chabal, Patrick. "Aspects of Angolan Literature: Luandino Viera and Agostinho Neto." *African Languages and Literatures* 8.1 (1995): 19–42.

Chema Mijero, Juan. "¡¡León de Africa!!" Ndongo and Ngom 61–63.

Chin, Rita. "Toward a 'Minor Literature'? The Case of *Ausländerliteratur* in Postwar Germany." Special issue: Forty Years of Turkish Migration to Germany. *New Perspectives on Turkey* 28–29 (2003): 61–84.

Chipasula, Frank, and Stella Chipasula, eds. *African Women's Poetry.* Portsmouth, N.H.: Heinemann, 1995.

Conrad, Joseph. *Heart of Darkness.* In John Kucich, *Fictions of Empire: Complete Texts with Introduction.* Ed. John Kucich. New Riverside Editions. New York: Houghton, 2003. 246–321.

Creus, Jacint, and Gustavo Nerín, eds. *Estampas y cuentos de la Guinea Española.* Madrid: Clan Editorial, 1999.

Cusack, Igor. "'Equatorial Guinea's National Cuisine Is Simple and Tasty': Cuisine and the Making of National Culture." *Arizona Journal of Hispanic Cultural Studies* 8 (2004): 131–48.

———. "Hispanic and Bantu Inheritance, Trauma, Dispersal, and Return: Some Contributions to a Sense of National Identity in Equatorial Guinea." *Nations and Nationalism* 5.2 (16 Apr. 2004). May 2006 <http://www3.interscience.wiley.com/journal/119086172/abstract?CRETRY=1&SRETRY=0>.

———. "'¡Que en mis pupilas se perpetúe el fulgor de las estrellas!': Literatura e identidad nacional en Guinea Ecuatorial." Ngom, *La recuperación de la memoria* 157–82.

Dallery, Arleen B., and Charles E. Scott, eds. *The Question of the Other: Essays in Contemporary Continental Philosophy.* Albany: State U of New York P, 1989.

Davidson, Basil. *Africa in Modern History: The Search for a New Society.* London: Lane, 1978.

Davies, Carole Boyce. *Black Women, Writing and Identity.* New York: Routledge, 1994.

Davies, Carole Boyce, and Anne Adams Graves, eds. *Ngambika: Studies of Women in African Literature.* Trenton, N.J.: African World, 1986.

Davies, J. M. *Abịono.* Barcelona: Ediciones Carena, 2004.

Davis, David Brion. *Inhuman Bondage: The Rise and Fall of Slavery in the New World.* New York: Oxford UP, 2006.

Decors, Carles. *Al sur de Santa Isabel.* Trans. Ramón Minguillón. Madrid: Alianza, 2002.

De Urda Anguita, Juan Antonio. "La voz híbrida de Francisco Zamora." Literatura Afrohispana. University of Missouri, Columbia. Feb. 2006 <http://afroromance.missouri.edu/docs/deurda.doc>.

Dorsch, H. "Grillots, Roots, and Identity in the African Diaspora." *Diaspora, Identity and Religion: New Directions in Theory and Research.* Ed. Waltraud Kokot, Khachig Tölölyan, and Carolin Alonso. New York: Routledge, 2004.

Du Bois, W. E. B. *The Souls of Black Folk.* Ed. Cynthia Brantley Johnson and Norman Harris. New York: Pocket, 2005.

Eagleton, Terry. *Exiles and Emigrés: Studies in Modern Literature.* New York: Schocken, 1970.

Egurbide, Peru. "Nueve países europeos ayudarán a España a patrullar las costas de Africa occidental." *El País* 30 May 2006: 23.

Eley, Geoff. "Historicizing the Global, Politicizing Capital: Giving the Present a Name." *History Workshop Journal* 63 (2007): 153–88.

Ensema, Marcelo. "Instante." Ndongo and Ngom 65.

Epps, Brad, Keja Vlens, and Bill Johnson González, eds. *Passing Lines: Sexuality and Immigration.* Cambridge, Mass.: Harvard UP, 2005.

"Equatorial Guinea." *Wikipedia.* 22 July 2006 <http://en.wikipedia.org/wiki/Equatorial_Guinea>.

Esono, Antimo. "No encontré flores para mi madre." Ndongo and Ngom 297–302.

"España ratifica su compromiso con Africa en la cumbre sobre inmigración y desarrollo de Rabat" [Spain ratifies its agreement with Africa in the summit meeting on immigration and developnment in Rabat]. *El País* 10 July 2006. 7 Sept. 2006 <http://www.elpais.com/articulo/espana/Espana/ratifica/compromiso/Africa/cumbre/inmigracion/desarrollo/Rabat/elpepuesp/20060710elpepunac_2/Tes>.

Eteo Soriso, José Francisco. *Refranero bubi.* Literatura Oral Breve, 4. Malabo, Equatorial Guinea: Ceiba, 2005.

"Etnographia." "Guinea Ecuatorial." *Wikipedia.* 1 June 2008 <http://es.wikipedia.org/wiki/Guinea_Ecuatorial#Demograf.C3.ADa>.

Evita, Leoncio. *Cuando los combes luchaban: Novela de costumbres de la antigua Guinea Española.* 1953. Madrid: Agencia Española de Cooperación Internacional, 1996.

Faber, Sebastian. *Exile and Cultural Hegemony: Spanish Intellectuals in Mexico 1939–1975.* Nashville, Tenn.: Vanderbilt UP, 2002.

Fanon, Frantz. *Black Skins, White Masks [Peau noire, masques blancs].* Trans. Charles Lam Marmann. New York: Grove, 1967.

———. *¡Escucha, blanco!* [*Listen, Whitey!*]. Trans. Angel Abad, of Fanon, *Black Skins.* Barcelona: Nova Terra, 1970.

———. *The Wretched of the Earth.* Trans. Constance Farrington. New York: Grove, 1963.

Ferguson, James. *Global Shadows: Africa in the Neoliberal World Order.* Durham: U of North Carolina P, 2006.

Fra-Molinero, Baltasar. "La educación sentimental de un exiliado africano: Las tinieblas de tu memoria negra de Donato Ndongo." *Afro-Hispanic Review* 19.1 (2000): 49–57.

———. "La figura ambivalente del personaje mesiánico en la novela de Guinea Ecuatorial." Ngom, *La recuperación de la memoria* 115–32.

Gabilondo, Joseba. "One-Way Theory: On the Hispanic-Atlantic Intersection of Postcoloniality and Postnationalism and Its Globalizing Effects." *Arachne@Rutgers: Journal of Iberian and Latin American Literary and Cultural Studies* 1 (2001). Oct. 2006. <http://arachne.rutgers.edu/vol1_1gabilondo.htm>.

———. "State Narcissism: Spanish Opposition to Multiculturalism, Racism, and Imperialism." *Border Interrogations: Crossing and Questioning Spanish Frontiers from the Middle Ages to the Present.* Ed. Benita Sampedro and Simon Doubleday. Oxford, Eng.: Berghahn, 2008. 65–89.

Gandhi, Leela. *Post-Colonial Theory: A Critical Introduction.* New York: Columbia UP, 1998.

García-Alvite, Dosinda. "Strategic Positions of Las Hijas del Sol: Equatorial Guinea in World Music." *Arizona Journal of Hispanic Cultural Studies* 8 (2004): 149–62.

García Benito, Nieves. "Cailcedrat." *Por la vía de Tarifa.* Madrid: Calambur, 2000. 14–22.

Gilroy, Paul. *The Black Atlantic: Modernity and Double Consciousness.* Cambridge, Mass.: Harvard UP, 1993.

———. "Forward: Migrancy Culture and a New Map of Europe." *Blackening Europe: The African American Presence.* Ed. Heike Raphael-Hernandez. New York: Routledge, 2004. xi–xxii.

Godzich, Wlad. Foreword. de Certeau vii–xxi.

Gómez de la Serna, Ramón. Certeau. *Automoribundia [Self-dying].* 2 vols. Madrid: Guadarrama, 1974.

González Echegaray, Carlos. "Prólogo a la Primera Edición." Evita 11–12.

———. "Prólogo a la Segunda Edición." Evita 13–18.

Goytisolo, Juan, and Sami Naïr. *El peaje de la vida: Integración o rechazo de la emigración en España* [The toll of life: Integration or rejection of emigration in Spain]. Madrid: El País, 2000.

Granados, Vicente. "*Ekomo* de María Nsue Angüe." M. Nsue 9–13.

Grandes, Almudena. *Las edades de Lulú.* Barcelona: Tusquets, 1989.

Guillén, Claudio. "On the Literature of Exile and Counter-Exile." *Books Abroad* 50 (1976): 271–80.

Gurr, Andrew. *Writers in Exile: The Identity of Home in Modern Literature.* Brighton, N.J.: Humanities, 1981.

Habermas, Jürgen. *Inclusion of the Other: Studies in Political Theory.* Cambridge, Mass.: MIT Press, 2001.

Hall, Stuart. "The Emergence of Cultural Studies and the Crisis of the Humanities." *October* 53 (1990): 11–23.

Hutchens, B. C. *Levinas: A Guide for the Perplexed*. New York: Continuum, 2004.

Ilie, Paul. *Literature and Inner Exile: Authoritarian Spain 1939–1975*. Baltimore, Md.: Johns Hopkins UP, 1980.

Ilombé, Raquel [Raquel Del Pozo Epita]. *Ceiba*. Madrid: Editorial Madrid, 1978.

Iyanga Pendi, Augusto. "Breve presentación." Evita 19–22.

Jones Mathama, Daniel. *Una lanza por el boabí*. Barcelona: Casals, 1962.

Kim, Yeon-Soo. *Family Album: Histories, Subjectivities, and Immigration in Contemporary Spanish Culture*. Lewisberg, Penn.: Bucknell UP, 2005.

Klitgaard, Robert E. *Tropical Gangsters: One Man's Experience with Development and Decadence in Deepest Africa*. New York: Basic, 1990.

Kucich, John. *Fictions of Empire: Complete Texts with Introduction, Historical Contexts, Critical Essays*. New York: Houghton, 2003.

Kwei Armah, Ayi. *The Beautiful Ones Are Not Yet Born*. Oxford: Heinemann, 1969.

Lahiri, Jhumpa. *The Namesake*. New York: Mariner, 2003.

Lamming, George. *The Pleasures of Exile*. Ann Arbor: U of Michigan P, 1992.

Le Seur, Geta. *Ten Is the Age of Darkness: The Black Bildungsroman*. Columbia: U of Missouri P, 1995.

Levinas, Emmanuel. *Alterity and Transcendence*. Trans. Michael B. Smith. New York: Columbia UP, 1999.

———. *Totality and Infinity*. Trans. Alphonsino Lingis. Pittsburgh, Penn.: Duquesne UP, 1987.

Lewis, Marvin A. *An Introduction to the Literature of Equatorial Guinea: Between Colonialism and Dictatorship*. Afro-Romance Writers Series. Columbia: U of Missouri P, 2007.

Lifshey, Adam. "And So the Worm Turns: The Impossibility of Imperial Imitation in *Una lanza por el boabí* by Daniel Jones Mathama." *Chasqui* 37.1 (May 2007): 108–20.

Liniger-Goumaz, Max. *De la Guinée Ecuatorial: Eléments pour le dossier de l'afrofascisme*. Geneva, Switzerland: Les Editions du Temps, 1983.

———. *Historical Dictionary of Equatorial Guinea*. Metuchen, N.J.: Scarecrow, 1979.

———. *Small Is Not Always Beautiful: The Story of Equatorial Guinea*. 1988. Trans. John Wood. Totowa, N.J.: Barnes and Noble, 1989.

Loboch, Maplal. "Lamento sobre Annobón, belleza y soledad." Ndongo, *Antología* 85–86.

———. "La última carta del Padre Fulgencio Abad, CMF." Ndongo and Ngom 208–11.

López Rodríguez, Marta Sofía. "Mímica, su/misión y subversión en *Las tinieblas de tu memoria negra*." Ngom, *La recuperación de la memoria* 183–93.

Loureiro, Angel G. *The Ethics of Autobiography: Replacing the Subject in Modern Spain*. Nashville, Tenn.: Vanderbilt UP, 2000.

Lucassen, Leo. *The Immigrant Threat: The Integration of Old and New Migrants in Western Europe since 1850.* Urbana: U of Illinois P, 2005.

Luka Andeka, Pedro N. *La Bahía de Corisco y la historia de los benga.* Malabo, Equatorial Guinea: La Gaceta de Guinea Ecuatorial, 2005.

Maass, Peter. "A Touch of Crude." *Mother Jones,* Jan/Feb. 2005. Apr. 2006 <www.motherjones.com/news/feature/2005/01/12_400.html>.

Maeztu, Ramiro de. *Defensa de la Hispanidad.* Madrid: Gráficas Nebrija, 1952.

Martí, José. *Versos sencillos. Simple verses.* Trans. and intro. Manuel A. Tellechea. Houston, Tex.: Arte, 1997.

Martí-López, Elisa. *Borrowed Words: Translation, Imitation, and the Making of the Nineteenth-Century Novel in Spain.* Lewisberg, Penn.: Bucknell UP, 2002.

Martínez Alcázar, Javier. *Morir en Guinea.* Málaga, Spain: Algazara, 2005.

Martin Márquez, Susan. *Disorientations: Spanish Colonialism in Africa and the Performance of Identity.* New Haven, Conn.: Yale UP, 2008.

Martul, Luis. "Las revistas del exilio gallego en México." *El exilio de las Españas de 1939 en las Américas.* Ed. José María Naharro-Calderón. Barcelona: Anthropos, 1991. 301–17.

Marzo, Jorge Luis, and Marc Roig. *El planeta Kurtz: Cien años de* El corazón de las tinieblas *de Joseph Conrad.* Barcelona: Mondadori, 2002.

Mbana, Joaquín. *Brujería fang en Guinea Ecuatorial.* Casa de Africa. Madrid: Sial, 2004.

Mbomío Bacheng, Joaquín. "En Guinea si no eres 'opositor,' 'no tienes problemas.'" *La Diáspora. Angelfire.* Jan. 2006 <http://angelfire.com/sk2/guineaecuatorial/juambom.htm>.

———. *Huellas bajo tierra.* Malabo, Equatorial Guinea: Ediciones Centro Cultural Hispano Guineano, 1998.

———. *El párroco de Niefang.* Malabo, Equatorial Guinea: Ediciones Centro Cultural Hispano Guineano, 1996.

———. "Vísperas." *Asociación de Solidaridad Democrática con Guinea Ecuatorial (ASODEGUE),* 22 Aug. 2004. 15 Mar. 2007 <www.asodegue.org>.

McNerney, Kathleen. Rev. of *Adjá-Adjá y otros relatos* by Maximiliano Nkogo. *World Literature Today* (Summer/Autumn 2001): 116–17.

McNerney, Kathleen, and Gabriel Quirós Alpera. "A Guinean Antigone." *Arizona Journal of Hispanic Cultural Studies* 8 (2004): 235–38.

Mekuy, Guillermina. *El llanto de la perra [The bitch's cry].* Barcelona: Plaza y Janés, 2005.

Melodians, The. "The Rivers of Babylon." *Reggae Exchange.* 27 June 2007 <www.reggaeexchange.com/lyrics/l/riversofbabylonbymelodians.html>.

Mengue, Clearence. "Lectura del espacio en *Los poderes de la tempestad* de Donato Ndongo." *Arizona Journal of Hispanic Cultural Studies* 8 (2004): 185–96.

Míguez, Alberto. *El pensamiento político de Castelao* [*Castelao's political thought*]. Paris: Ruedo Ibérico, 1965.

Millás, Juan José. "Cuando los españoles éramos los árabes de los alemanes." *El País* 23 Nov. 1992. *Académie de Grenoble.* 26 June 2007 <www.ac-grenoble.fr/espagnol/libreta/textos/exilio/jauja.htm>.

Miller, Kerby. *Emigrants and Exiles: Ireland and the Irish Exodus to North America.* New York: Oxford UP, 1985.

Morales Lezcano, Víctor. *Inmigración africana en Madrid: Marroquíes y guineanos (1975–1990).* Madrid: Universidad Nacional de Educación a Distancia, 1993.

Morgades Besari, Trinidad. "Antígona." *Arizona Journal of Hispanic Cultural Studies* 8 (2004): 239–45.

Murrell, Nathaniel Samuel. "Turning Hebrew Psalms to Reggae Rhythms: Rastas' Revolutionary Lamentations for Social Change." *Crosscurrents.* 27 June 2007 <www.crosscurrents.org/murrell.htm>.

Nabokov, Vladimir. *Speak, Memory: An Autobiography Revisited.* New York: Putnam, 1979.

Ndongo-Bidyogo, Donato. "1. Pensando en Franz Fanon." *Indice* 318 (1972): 11–12.

———. "2. Pensando en Franz Fanon: La colonización." *Indice* 320 (1972): 38–39.

———. "3. Pensando en Franz Fanon: Fanon y el racismo." *Indice* 321–22 (1973): 42–43.

———. "4. Pensando en Franz Fanon: La sexualidad interracial." *Indice* 323 (1973): 41–42.

———. "5. Pensando en Franz Fanon: Máscaras, la 'alienación.'" *Indice* 324 (1973): 31–32.

———. "6. Pensando en Franz Fanon: La emacipación." *Indice* 325–26 (1973): 71–72.

———, ed. *Antología de la literatura guineana.* Madrid: Editora Nacional, 1984.

———. "La crisis portuguesa: Spínola, primer acto." *Indice* 354 (1974): 24–25.

———. "The Dream." Trans. Michael Ugarte. *Iowa Review* 36.2 (Fall 2006): 75–79.

———. "Los herederos del Señor Kurtz." *El planeta Kurtz: Cien años de* El corazón de las tinieblas *de Joseph Conrad.* Ed. José Luis Marzo and Marc Roig. Barcelona: Mondadori, 2002. 123–40.

———. *Historia y tragedia de Guinea Ecuatorial.* Madrid: Cambio 16, 1977.

———. "Leoncio Evita, o el nacimiento de la literatura guineana." Evita 23–32.

———. "Literatura moderna hispanófona en Guinea Ecuatorial." *La Web Cultural de Guinea Ecuatorial.* Artículos de Interés de Guinea Ecuatorial. 26 June 2007 <www.angelfire.com/sk2/guineaecuatorial/literatura.htm>.

———. "El marco de la literatura de Guinea Ecuatorial" [The frame of Equatorial Guinean literature]. Ndongo and Ngom 31–57.

———. *El metro.* Barcelona: El Cobre, 2007.

———. *Los poderes de la tempestad.* Madrid: Morandi, 1997.

———. *Shades of Your Black Memory.* Trans. Michael Ugarte. Chicago: Swan Isle, 2007.

———. "El sueño" [The Dream]. *Papeles de Son Armadans* 211 (1973): 83–89. Rpt. in Ndongo and Ngom 204–7. Citations are to the latter source.

———. *Las tinieblas de tu memoria negra* [*Shadows of Your Black Memory*]. Trans. Michael Ugarte. 1987. Barcelona: Ediciones del Bronce, 2000.

Ndongo-Bidyogo, Donato, Mariano Castro, and José Urbano Martínez. *España en Guinea: construcción del desencuentro: 1778–1968.* Madrid: Sequitur, 1998.

Ndongo, Donato, and Mbaré Ngom. *Literatura de Guinea Ecuatorial (Antología).* Casa de Africa. Madrid: Sial, 1999.

Nerín, Gustau. *Guinea Ecuatorial: Historia en blanco y negro.* Barcelona, Spain: Península, 1998.

Ngom, Mbaré. "La autobiografía como plataforma de denuncia en *Los poderes de la tempestad*" [The powers of the tempest]. *Afro-Hispanic Review* 19.1 (2000): 66–71.

———, ed. *Guinea Ecuatorial: textos y contextos culturales e históricos.* Spec. issue of *Afro-Hispanic Review* 19.1 (2000).

———. Introducción. Ndongo and Ngom 11–29.

———, ed. *La recuperación de la memoria: creación cultural e identidad nacional en la literatura hispano-negroafricana* Madrid: Universidad de Alcalá de Henares, 2004.

———. "Relato de una vida y escritura femenina: *Ekomo* de María Nsue Angüe." *Journal of Afro-Latin American Studies and Literatures* 3 (1995): 77–91.

Nkogo Esono, Maximiliano. *Adjá-Adjá y otros relatos.* Ávila, Spain: Malamba, 2000.

———. *Nambula.* Madrid: Ediciones Cyan, 2006.

Nkogo Ondó, Eugenio. *El aspecto ético y social del existentialismo.* León, Spain: Ediciones Leonesas, 1982.

———. *El método filosófico en Jean Paul Sartre.* Oviedo, Spain: Universidad de Oviedo, 1983.

———. *Sobre las ruinas de la República de Ghana.* Madrid: N.p., 1987.

Nsue Angue, María. *Ekomo.* Ed. and intro. Vicente Granados. Madrid: UNED, 1985.

Nsue Otong, Carlos. "Estudios de los personajes en *Las tinieblas de tu memoria negra* de Donato Ndongo-Bidyogo." *Afro-Hispanic Review* 19.1 (2000): 58–65.

Obiang Nguema, Teodoro. *Guinea Ecuatorial, país joven: testimonios políticos.* Malabo, Equatorial Guinea: Ediciones Guinea, 1985.

Ocha'a Mbe, Constantino. *Guinea Ecuatorial: Polémica y realidad.* Fuenlabrada, Spain: Anzos, 1985.

———. *Semblanzas de la hispanidad.* Fuenlabrada, Spain: Anzos, 1985.

Olsen, Margaret M. *Slavery and Salvation in Colonial Cartagena de Indias.* Gainesville: U of Florida P, 2004.

Ortega Dolz, Patricia. "Marruecos repatria a 433 inmigrantes de Senegal que fracasaron en su ruta canaria." *El País* 31 May 2006: 25.

Ortiz, Lourdes. *Fátima de los naufragios*. Barcelona: Planeta, 1998.

———. "Senegal suspende las repatriaciones desde Canarias tras la protesta de 99 inmigrantes." *El País* 2 June 2006: 23.

Osofisan, Femi. "Theater and the Rites of 'Post Negritude' Remembering." *Research in African Literatures* 30.1 (1999): 1–11.

Otabela Mewolo, Joseph-Désiré. *La literatura como compromiso: la obra de Donato Ndongo-Bidyogo*. Madrid: UNED, 2008.

Otabela Mewolo, Joseph-Désiré, and Sesthène Osono-Abela. *Literatura emergente en español: Literatura de Guinea Ecuatorial*. Madrid: Ediciones del Otro, U of Minnesota P, 2004.

Papastergiadis, Nikos. *The Turbulence of Migrations: Globalization, Deterritorialization, Hybridity*. Cambridge, Eng.: Polity, 2000.

Paradise: Three Journeys in This World. Dir. Elina Hirvonen. Media Center Lume, University of Art and Design, 2007.

Porta, Emilio. "Unas palabras de presentación a Guillermina Mekuy." Meku 910.

Price, Nicole. *"Materia reservada" No More: The Post-Colonial in the Equato-Guinean Narrative*. Diss. U of Missouri, Columbia, 2005.

Price of the Ticket, The. Dir. Karen Thorsen. Prod. Karen Thorsen, William Miles, and Douglas K. Dempsey. Videocassette. Video California Newsreel, 1990.

Psalm 137. "Lament over the Destruction of Jerusalem." Hebrew Scriptures. *Hope College*. 27 June 2007 <http://faculty.hope.edu/bandstra/netbible/>.

Reverte, Javier. Prólogo. Zamora, *Memoria de laberintos* 7–8.

Ridau, José María. Book presentation. Casa de Africa, Madrid, 24 May 2007.

Rihola, María Caridad. "Exilio." Ndongo and Ngom 400–402.

Rizo, Elisa. "*La carga* de Juan Tomás Ávila Laurel: novela historiográfica postcolonial guineoecuatoriana." *Arizona Journal of Hispanic Cultural Studies* 8 (2004): 197–204.

———. "Una conversación entre guineoecuatorianos: Donato Ndongo Bidyogo y Juan Tomás Ávila Laurel." Ugarte and Vilarós 259–70.

———. "El teatro guineaecuatoriano contemporáneo: el *mibili* en 'El fracaso de las sombras.'" Ugarte and Vilarós 289–310.

———. "En torno a la obra de Juan Tomás Ávila Laurel." *Hispanic Research Journal* 6.2 (2005): 175–78.

Robbins, Jill. *Altered Reading: Levinas and Literature*. Chicago: U of Chicago P, 1999.

Roberts, Adam. *The Wanga Coup: Guns, Thugs and a Ruthless Determination to Create Mayhem in an Oil-Rich Corner of Africa*. New York: Public Affairs, 2006.

Rodríguez Castellao, Daniel. *Obras de Castelao, Castelao no destierro, na guerra, no exilio, Sempre en Galiza*. Ed. Henrique Monteagudo. Vigo, Spain: Galaxia, 2000.

Roediger, David R. *The Wages of Whiteness: Race and the Making of the American Working Class*. 2nd ed. New York: Verso, 1991.

Rope Bomaba, Jerónimo. *Album poético*. Malabo, Equatorial Guinea: Centro Cultural Hispano-Guineano, 1994.

Said, Edward W. *Beginnings: Intention and Method*. New York: Basic, 1975.

———. "Intellectual Exile: Expatriates and Marginals." *The Edward Said Reader*. Ed. Moustafo Bayoumi. New York: Random, 2000. 368–81.

Salvo, Jorge. "ASODEGUE." *Asociación de Solidaridad Democrática con Guinea Ecuatorial (ASODEGUE)*. 11 Sept. 2006. May 2007 <www.asodegue.org>.

Sampedro, Benita. "African Poetry in Spanish Exile: Seeking Refuge in the Metropolis." *Bulletin of Hispanic Studies* 81 (2004): 201–14.

———. "Estudio introductorio." Ávila Laurel, *Guinea Ecuatorial* 7–20.

———. "Salvando a Copito de Nieve: Poesía, globalización y la extraña mutación de Guinea Ecuatorial." *Revista de Crítica Literaria Latinoamericana* 29.58 (2003): 303–16.

Senghor, Léopold. *Chants d'ombre suivi de Hosties noires poèmes*. Paris: Seuil, 1945.

———. *The Collected Poetry*. Trans. Melvin Dixon. Charlottesville: U of Virginia P, 1998.

———. *Negritude et humanisme*. Paris: Seuil, 1964.

Siale, José Francisco. *Autorretrato con un infiel*. Barcelona: El Cobre, 2007.

———. *Cenizas de Kalabó y termes*. Ávila, Spain: Editorial Malamba, 2000.

———. *La revuelta de los disfraces*. Ávila, Spain: Editorial Malamba, 2003.

———. "Todo llega con las olas del mar." Siale, *La revuelta de los disfraces* 67–109.

Siedel, Michael. *Exile and the Narrative Imagination*. New Haven: Yale UP, 1986.

Silverstein, Ken. "Mba's House: Bush Administration renting embassy property from known torturer." *Harper's*. 25 Oct. 2006. May 2006 <http://www.harpers.org/archive/2006/10/sb-mbas-house-1161784135>.

———. "Our Friend Teodoro." *Harper's*. 18 Apr. 2006. May 2006 <http://www.harpers.org/archive/2006/04/sb-obiang-eg>.

———. "U.S. Oil Politics in the 'Kuwait of Africa.'" *Nation* 22 Apr. 2002: 11–20.

Soja, Edward. *Thirdspace: Journeys to Los Angeles and Other Real-and-Imagined Places*. Malden, Mass.: Blackwell, 1996.

Soto-Trillo, Eduardo. *Los olvidados: Revelaciones de un viaje a la dramática realidad de Guinea Ecuatorial*. Madrid: Foca, 2004.

Stratton, Florence. *Contemporary African Literature and the Politics of Gender*. New York: Routledge, 1994.

Sundiata, Ibrahim K. *Equatorial Guinea: Colonialism, State Terror, and the Search for Stability*. Boulder, Colo.: Westview, 1990.

Tarifa Traffic. Dir. Joakim Demmer. Dschoint Ventschr Filmproduktion, Betamcam SP, 2004.

Ugarte, Michael. "Guinea Ecuatorial y el 'Otro' español: Cerrar Black Beach." *Asociación de Solidaridad Democrática con Guinea Ecuatorial (ASODEGUE)*. 11 Sept. 2006. May 2007 <www.asodegue.org>.

———. "Interview with Donato Ndongo." *Arizona Journal of Hispanic Cultural Studies* 8 (2004): 217–34.

———. "Introduction to Postcolonial Exile." *Arizona Journal of Hispanic Cultural Studies* 8 (2004): 177–84.

———. "Literature of Franco's Spain." *Cambridge History of Spanish Literature.* Ed. David T. Geis. Cambridge, Eng.: Cambridge UP, 2004. 611–19.

———. *Shifting Ground: Spanish Civil War Exile Literature.* Durham, N.C.: Duke UP, 1989.

———. "'Soy tú, Soy él': African Immigration and Otherness in Spanish Collective Consicousness." *Studies in Twentieth and Twenty-first Century Literature* 30.1 (2006): 170–89.

———. "Spain's Heart of Darkness: Equatorial Guinea in the Narrative of Donato Ndongo." *Journal of Spanish Cultural Studies* 7.3 (2006): 271–87.

Ugarte, Michael, and Mbaré Ngom, eds. Equatorial Guinea and Spanish Letters. Spec. section of *Arizona Journal of Hispanic Cultural Studies* 8 (2004): 107–245.

Ugarte, Michael, and Teresa Vilarós, eds. *African Spain.* Spec. issue of *Journal of Spanish Cultural Studies* 7.3 (2006): 199–310.

Unamuno, Miguel de. *San Manuel Bueno, mártir.* 1931. Ed. Mario J. Valdés. Madrid: Ediciones Cátedra, 1979.

"U.S. Slave Trade: The Middle Passage." *National Great Blacks in Wax Museum.* 26 June 2007 <www.ngbiwm.com/Exhibits/middle_pass.htm>.

U.S. Congress. Senate. Committee on Homeland Security and Governmental Affairs. Permanent Subcommittee on Investigations. *Money Laundering and Foreign Corruption: Enforcement and Effectiveness of the Patriot Act. Case Study Involving Riggs Bank.* 15 July 2004. 26 June 2007 <http://hsgac.senate.gov/public/_files/ACF5F8.pdf>.

Velloso, Agustín. "Living in Oil, Living on the Breadline." Unpub. article. 2007.

Vollendorf, Lisa. "'Rostro de mujer': Human Rights and the Feminization of Immigration in Spain." Unpub. ms. June 2006.

Wa Thiong'o, Ngugi. *Decolonizing the Mind: The Politics of Language in African Culture.* Oxford: Currey, 1986.

———. "Literature and Double Consciousness: Warring Images in Afro-American Thought." Wa Thiong'o, *Writers in Politics* 37–52.

———. "Return to the Roots: Language Culture and Politics in Kenya." Wa Thiong'o, *Writers in Politics* 53–64.

———. *Writers in Politics: A Re-engagement with Issues of Literature and Society.* Portsmouth, N.H.: Heinemann, 1981.

Whyte, Hayden. *The Content of the Form: Narrative Discourse and Historical Representation.* Baltimore: Johns Hopkins UP, 1987.

Wilder, Gary. *The French Imperial Nation-State: Negritude and Colonial Humanism between the Two Cold Wars.* Chicago: U of Chicago P, 2005.

Zamora, Francisco. "Bea." Ndongo and Ngom 191–94.

———. *Cómo ser negro y no morir en Aravaca: Manual de recetas contra el racismo.* Madrid: Ediciones, 1994.

———. *Memoria de laberintos.* Casa de Africa. Madrid: Sial, 1999.

———. "Prisionero de Gran Vía." Ndongo and Ngom 161.

———. "Salvad a copito." Ndongo and Ngom 160.

Zeleza, Paul Tiyambe. *The Joys of Exile: Stories.* Concord, Ontario: Anansi, 1994.

Zielina Limonta, María. "Donato Ndongo-Bidyogo: Un escritor guineano y su obra." *Afro-Hispanic Review* 19.1 (2000): 106–16.

———. "*Ekomo*: Representación del pensamiento mítico, la magia y la psicología de un pueblo 'fang.'" *Afro-Hispanic Review* 19.1 (2000): 93–101.

———. "Las tinieblas de tu memoria negra: la emotiva exposición de un rito de pasaje en una comunidad guineana." Ngom, *La recuperación de la memoria* 133–56.

INDEX

MICHAEL UGARTE is Middlebush Professor of Romance Languages at the University of Missouri. His publications include *Madrid 1900: The Capital as Cradle of Culture* and *Shifting Ground: Spanish Civil War Exile Literature.*

STUDIES OF WORLD MIGRATIONS

The Immigrant Threat: The Integration of Old and New Migrants in Western Europe Since 1850 *Leo Lucassen*

Citizenship and Those Who Leave: The Politics of Emigration and Expatriation *Edited by Nancy L. Green and François Weil*

Migration, Class, and Transnational Identities: Croatians in Australia and America *Val Colic-Peisker*

The Yankee Yorkshireman: Migration Lived and Imagined *Mary H. Blewett*

Africans in Europe: The Culture of Exile and Emigration from Equatorial Guinea to Spain *Michael Ugarte*

The University of Illinois Press
is a founding member of the
Association of American University Presses.

University of Illinois Press
1325 South Oak Street
Champaign, IL 61820-6903
www.press.uillinois.edu